NOT THIS TIME: CANADIANS, PUBLIC POLICY, AND THE MARIJUANA QUESTION, 1961–1975

Drugs are part of every society, consumed for ritual or religious purposes, for pleasure, to enhance athletic performance, or as a means to cure ailments or relieve pain. Throughout the twentieth century, however, an arbitrary and shifting distinction was made between legal drugs that were prescribed and administered by the medical profession and illegal drugs that were subject to state control and suppression.

Illegal in Canada since 1923, marijuana is the most controversial of banned drugs. Because it lacks the same addictive and harmful qualities as other illegal substances, such as heroin and cocaine, its social impact is a matter for debate. In the 1960s, many Canadians began demanding changes to the Narcotics Control Act that would decriminalize or legalize the possession of marijuana.

In *Not This Time*, Marcel Martel explores the recreational use of marijuana in the 1960s and its emergence as a topic of social debate. He demonstrates how the media, interest groups, state institutions, bureaucrats, and politicians influenced the development and implementation of public policy on drugs. Martel illustrates how two loose coalitions made up of interest groups, addiction research organizations, and bureaucrats – one supporting existing legislation, and the other favouring liberalization of the Narcotics Control Act – dominated the debate over the legalization of marijuana. Those favouring liberalized drug laws, while influential, had difficulty presenting a unified front and had problems justifying their cause while the effects of marijuana use on health were still in question. Exploring both sides of the debate, Martel presents the history of a controversial issue that continues to reverberate in the minds of Canadians.

MARCEL MARTEL is an associate professor in the Department of History and holder of the Avie Bennett Historica Chair in Canadian History at York University.

MARCEL MARTEL

Not This Time
Canadians, Public Policy,
and the Marijuana Question,
1961–1975

UNIVERSITY OF TORONTO PRESS
Toronto Buffalo London

© University of Toronto Press Incorporated 2006
Toronto Buffalo London
Printed in Canada

ISBN-13 978-0-8020-9048-5 (cloth)
ISBN-10 0-8020-9048-6 (cloth)

ISBN-13 978-0-8020-9379-0 (paper)
ISBN-10 0-8020-9379-5 (paper)

Printed on acid-free paper

Library and Archives Canada Cataloguing in Publication

Martel, Marcel, 1965–

Not this time : Canadians, public policy, and the marijuana question,
1961–1975 / Marcel Martel.

Includes bibliographical references.
ISBN-13: 978-8020-9048-5 (bound)
ISBN-13: 978-8020-9379-0 (pbk.)
ISBN-10: 0-8020-9048-6 (bound)
ISBN-10: 0-8020-9379-5 (pbk.)

1. Marijuana – Government policy – Canada – History – 20th century.
I. Title.

HV5840.C3M37 2006   362.29'5'097109046   C2005-906189-8

Every effort has been made to obtain permisson to reproduce the material
in this book. Any omissions brought to the attention of the publisher will
be corrected in future printings.

University of Toronto Press acknowledges the financial assistance to its
publishing program of the Canada Council for the Arts and the Ontario
Arts Council.

University of Toronto Press acknowledges the financial support for its
publishing activities of the Government of Canada through the Book
Publishing Industry Development Program (BPIDP).

This book has been published with the help of a grant from the Canadian
Federation for the Humanities and Social Sciences, through the Aid to
Scholarly Publications Programme, using funds provided by the Social
Sciences and Humanities Research Council of Canada.

Contents

List of Illustrations

Acknowledgments

WARNING – THE READING OF MY BOOK IS HARMLESS BUT ...

This is not an essay on the merits or dangers of marijuana use. It is not a passionate plea for the legalization of marijuana, nor an attempt to demonize it. If these first lines disappoint you but you still persist to read it, do not be surprised if my book leaves readers unsettled about the legalization of marijuana.

This manuscript became reality because it received help from various sources. The research project got a standard research grant from the Social Science and Humanities Research Council of Canada and seed funding from York University. In January 2004, my stay at Meiji University in Tokyo helped me to finalize the draft version of the manuscript. Very skilled graduate history students at York University assisted me in various stages of my research: Marc Baldwin, Tony D'Erles, Mario Gravelle, Jennine Hurl, Julie Lalande, Alexis Lachaine, Mathieu Lapointe, Kato Perdue, Andrew Robertson, and Jon Sufrin. I would like to thank my friends who, while I was doing research at the National Archives in Ottawa, agreed to let me use one of the extra rooms: Jim Cincotta, Aida Kaouk, and André Larose. The personnel and archivists at the Access Information Section and at the National Archives of Canada (Julie Attallah, Gabrielle Blais, Alena Dufault, Lana Merrifield, Kimberley Foreman, and Elizabeth Mongrain), at the Ontario Provincial Archives, at the National Archives in Quebec (Raynald Lessard and Pierre-Louis Lapointe), at the Centre for Addiction and Mental Health (John P.M. Court), at the Canadian Medical Association head office (Deborah Scott-Douglas and Kerry Guglielmin), and at the Canadian Association of Chiefs of Police facilitated greatly the research process. Finally, I would like to thank the University of Toronto Press and in particular my editor, Len Husband, for believing in my project; Frances Mundy, for her professionalism and understanding; and John St James, the copy-editor, who did a remarkable job.

Friends and colleagues read parts of the manuscript and made useful suggestions. In particular I would like to thank Ramsay Cook, Marie Lebel, Martin Pâquet, Robert Perin, Robert Pinet, Terry Penfold, Nigel G. Spencer, Matteo Sanfilippo, and Molly Ungar and give special thanks to Randy Hesp for his support.

NOT THIS TIME: CANADIANS, PUBLIC POLICY,
AND THE MARIJUANA QUESTION, 1961–1975

Introduction

During the taping of the television program *Under Attack* in January 1970, the minister of national health and welfare, John Munro, said that the federal government would legalize marijuana. As Canadian public opinion was very divided on this issue, the minister's statement would have been regarded as either a courageous gesture or political suicide. However, Munro took pains to qualify his pronouncement, adding that it would 'be totally irresponsible if we didn't legalize it' if a 'significant minority' of Canadians smoked it.[1] In view of the fact that the Commission of Inquiry into the Non-Medical Use of Drugs, appointed by the federal government in 1969 and better known by the name of its chair, Gerald Le Dain, had estimated that about 1.5 million Canadians had tried marijuana at least once, it appeared that Munro's 'significant minority' existed. As we know, however, legalization did not come about.

Since mid-1960s, Canadians had been of two minds on the marijuana issue. In a letter sent to the Le Dain Commission, a twenty-five-year-old female film technician stated that marijuana was 'almost universally harmless.' This implied that changes to the existing law were required. But others did not share her point of view. A mother of two male adolescents, whose eldest son smoked marijuana, pleaded for help. In order to buy drugs, her son had stolen money from his parents. All attempts to reason with him had failed; moreover, the son argued that many scientific experts and politicians believed that marijuana was not dangerous. 'How do we save him?' asked the worried mother. She even wondered if she should 'chain him to his bed.'[2]

These accounts are indicative of the public debate that took place in the sixties in Canada and elsewhere in the western hemisphere. What could be done to help this anxious mother? Should the government relax its public policy on drugs, as suggested by the female film technician? Or should it actively discourage marijuana use and, by doing so, lend help to distraught parents?

This book is about the sixties, a historical period that is still embedded in myth and nostalgia, but its focus is recreational drug use. More specifically, it looks at marijuana, a psycho-active product that comes from the flowering tops of the female plant known as *Cannabis sativa*, the fibres of which have been used for centuries to make rope and paper. Marijuana has been an illegal substance in Canada since 1923. In the sixties, the Narcotic Control Act and the Food and Drugs Act were the legislative core of Canadian public policy on drugs. From 1961 marijuana was classified under the Narcotic Control Act, which, among other things, increased legal penalties for its possession, trafficking, exportation, importation, and cultivation, and removed the minimum penalties for most offences. Thereafter, anyone charged with possession of marijuana could face a maximum penalty of seven years in jail.

My study analyses the emergence of marijuana as a topic of social debate. The 1960s have been described as the era of peace and love and flower power, but it was also a period of protest, of cultural conflict and confrontation.[3] Beside political issues that left no one indifferent, such as the spectre of nuclear conflict and American involvement in Vietnam, social values and mainstream lifestyles were challenged: gambling, alcohol use, women's rights, the use of contraception, the legalization of abortion, and the constructions of sexuality and homosexuality came to dominate the public agenda. In the face of such issues, Canadians found that there was little neutral ground. The issue of drug use was no exception, and in fact was part of the larger discussion.

Pundits and observers of the political scene in the sixties pointed out that the debate over marijuana highlighted a demographic division in Canadian society. Many young Canadians advocated legalization of marijuana, or at least a significant reduction of penalties for its possession, while those over thirty opposed such changes. The conflict over marijuana revealed what sociologists and other social scientists characterized as a generation gap. The promotion of values and lifestyles in opposition to those that had until then dominated the post-1945 society became the domain of youth.

Many studies have focused on the actions of the baby boom generation, those born between 1945 and 1964 (although there is no consensus among experts on when the baby boom ended). For instance, Doug

Owram and François Ricard argue that drugs became a social issue because the baby boom generation championed recreational drug use.[4] In the sixties, studies undertaken by social scientists to assess the extent of marijuana use indicated that mainly young people used this illegal drug.

The demographic shift that altered drug consumption and practices became a focus of the debate. With 50 per cent of the population in Canada under twenty-one in 1966, baby boomers constituted a demographic force and used their demographic strength to initiate social and political change. In the sixties, Theodore Roszak used the term *counterculture* to characterize the new culture that was 'radically disaffiliated from the mainstream assumptions of ... society.' Roszak wrote that for some this counterculture took 'the alarming appearance of a barbaric intrusion.'[5] In the context of generational tensions exacerbated by the counterculture movement that shook the West, drug use was perceived either as a threat to the social order or as part of a new value system – what became known in that period as 'lifestyle.' By smoking marijuana, baby boomers challenged mainstream values and made a gesture of defiance. The opponents of drug use for non-medical purposes regarded gaining pleasure, facilitating social interaction, or embarking on mystic quests by means of drugs as a dubious, dangerous endeavour that jeopardized the work ethic.

As Ricard states, baby boomers questioned the foundations of authority and championed new values that came to be defined as the counterculture. As 'instigator[s] and recipient[s] of social change,'[6] they were confident of their ability to initiate and impose change, in particular change to cultural values and moral order. They were inspired by Timothy Leary, who argued that people should live 'for pleasure instead of living according to the punishment-reward system that an up-tight society wants to keep us all trapped in.'[7] They rejected the material comforts that derived from a period of economic growth and aspired to emulate Allen Ginsberg's example: 'I have burned all my money in a waste-basket.'[8] They challenged the Puritanism and social conservatism shaped by the Cold War context, and promoted looser attitudes towards premarital sex by advocating sexual openness and experimentation. Baby boomers questioned rigid gender roles and conservative attitudes towards marriage as the paragon of social achievement. They used clothing, hairstyle, and rock and roll as rebellious political gestures against mainstream social values. Because of the boomers' confidence and strong sense of control over their destiny, civil disobedience and sit-ins became a form of activism. Since many baby boomers attended universities, they invigorated student associations, organized demonstrations on campuses, and were credited with forcing the democratization of university governing bodies. On this last account, Rochdale College in Toronto was an attempt to reinvent higher education by allowing students to have a greater say on pedagogical and administrative issues.[9] Others joined the expanding workforce, challenged labour leadership, and contributed to an increase in labour militancy.[10] Finally, baby boomers were political by embracing, among other issues, campaigns for nuclear disarmament. Ricard describes them as an important force behind the Quiet Revolution in Quebec – the relatively non-violent, rapid political, institutional, social, and cultural changes that occurred in Quebec and led to a transformation of the provincial state's role in society, as well as the decline of the Catholic church as an agent of social control.

Nevertheless, the demographic strength associated with the baby boomers was not enough to shake the foundations of drug regulation in Canada. Put simply, baby boomers encountered resistance from the federal state but also from specific segments of the population. These forces of resistance and opposition oblige us to consider other factors to explain the marijuana debate in Canada in the context of the counterculture and why it did not lead either to the drug's legalization or decriminalization. In his synthesis of the sixties, Arthur Marwick argues that the rising influence of young people was not enough to initiate the changes that occurred in the sixties. Although there was 'a genuine liberal tolerance and willingness to accommodate' in the era that helped baby boomers in their efforts to impose change in fashion, culture, gender relations, or sexuality, other aspects of the counterculture were not successful.[11] In this regard, the marijuana debate constitutes a good case study.

In the field of drug studies, a growing body of literature has used the concept of moral panic to explain the genesis and the prevalence of repressive drug legislation in the West, and in particular in North America.[12] Throughout the twentieth century, an arbitrary and shifting distinction was made between 'legal' drugs that were prescribed and administered by the medical profession and those that were proscribed, such as cannabis, cocaine, and heroin, whose users were subject to state control and repression. In simple terms, the theory of moral panic argues that public debates about drugs have always been framed in moral terms. Proponents approve their use by arguing that drugs are part of society. They are consumed for ritual or religious purposes, for pleasure, to enhance athletic performance, or as a means to cure ailments or relieve pain. Opponents denounce drug use as undermining the traditional understanding of the acceptable way to function in society. People on drugs, opponents argue, constitute a threat to society but also to themselves by becoming emotionally unstable, by escaping daily reality, and by promoting unrealistic views about the meaning of life. Furthermore, drug users lack productivity. In the case of young people, drug use is a reprehensible act that distracts them from 'pursuing their studies and careers at a crucial phase' of their development.[13] By promoting the repression of recreational drug use, opponents of illegal drug use encourage society to adopt moral behaviour. In the morality-charged atmosphere of drug debates, moral values necessarily prevail, and states have no choice but to make drug use illegal, except for those taken under the supervision of a physician. When social actors challenged repressive drug legislation, as was the case in the sixties, they were condemned to fail because any new episode of moral panic strengthens repressive drug legislation in society.

As my book shows, there are some problems with this theory. Although the theory of moral panic embraces the role of interest groups and the attempts by some of them to target individuals and groups whom they perceived as deviant because of their behaviour, lifestyle, or values, it has some limits. It does not reflect the dynamics and complexity of the public policy process in this instance. Social actors mobilized in order to shape the issue, public opinion, and the views of those in positions of influence and power who could revise drug legislation. They could create strategic alliances to increase their chances of influencing those who were part of or close to decision-making centres. In the case of the debate on the legalization of marijuana, its symbolic place in the spectrum of public policy on drugs would not be altered. In other words, no change took place at the macro level since marijuana remained an illegal substance in Canada. Yet it is a different story when we consider how drug legislation was implemented. In order to explain this change, it is important to look at the development of public policy and the roles played by interest groups, as well as the influence of provincial organizations and various actors within the federal government.

In the developing historiography on Canadian drug law, much of the existing literature has analysed the origins of the repressive approach in dealing with drug consumption. The public policy that criminalized the use of certain drugs has its roots in the 1908 Opium Act and developed throughout the twentieth century. Moral judgments, hostility against racial minorities, especially Chinese, pressure by enforcement officials and bureaucrats, economic considerations, and a trend throughout the West, but most particularly in the United States, in favour of the criminalization of drug use were key factors in the development of Canadian public policy on drugs.[14]

However, particularly in the case of opium and marijuana, researchers have neglected what happened after the repression of certain drugs became public policy.[15] Although several studies assessing the popularity of drug use in the sixties have been published,[16] few studies have been published on drugs and Canadian public policy during this period. Those that have are often essays focusing on the weaknesses of Canada's drug policy.[17] As a topic for research, the sixties constitute a defining moment when state control and the arbitrary distinction between legal and illegal drugs were under scrutiny.

What follows will be an examination of how the media, individuals, interest groups, state institutions, bureaucrats, and politicians influenced the development and implementation of public policy on drugs.[18] I argue that these actors competed to shape the debate on the legalization of marijuana. Social control through state action became an issue for these groups and institutions. Some wanted the state to cease control of marijuana use, while others felt that any retreat by the state on the drug front would trigger the collapse of drug policy altogether. The pro-marijuana lobby, consisting of university student associations, some physicians, and other interest groups, was in fact a minority voice in the debate. It did not have the resources to sustain action over a long period of time. Rather, the debate would be dominated by two loose coalitions. The first was made up of individuals, interest groups such as the Council on Drug Abuse, provincial addiction research organizations such as the Narcotic Addiction Foundation of British Columbia, police forces and the RCMP, the Prince Edward Island government, and bureaucrats from the federal Department of Justice. They supported existing drug legislation and found themselves arrayed against those (individuals, bureaucrats, and organizations such as the Canadian Medical Association, the Office pour la prévention et le traitement de l'alcoolisme et des autres toxicomanies, the Alcoholism and Drug Addiction Research Foundation, and the Department of National Health and Welfare) who favoured a liberalization of the Narcotic Control Act in order to reduce legal penalties.

Those in favour of liberalization saw their efforts undermined by the other coalition and by their own difficulties in justifying their call for liberalization while the health benefits of marijuana use were still in question. Advocating the reduction of penalties while being aware that marijuana was not a harmless drug, proved to be a difficult balancing act. The coalition that favoured the status quo capitalized on these divisions, as well as the fact that the drug problem could not be solved without taking into consideration continental and international realities. The provinces and the federal government developed different responses in their attempt to tackle the marijuana issue. They created education strategies, put in place treatment programs, and increased control over drugs that were not already regulated. However, the federal government saw its ability to design its drug policy circumscribed by its international obligations and its relations with the American government.

This book starts with an examination of efforts to document the phenomenon of recreational drug use. The first chapter focuses on the media and the construction of recreational drug use, partly in order to gauge the extent of drug use in society. Social scientists, many of them employed by provincial state addiction research foundations, measured and reported on drug consumption in order to ease some of the fears surrounding the phenomenon of recreational drug consumption.

The second chapter looks at four interest groups. Although many groups contributed to make drugs a topic of social concern between 1961 and 1975, four in particular played a crucial role: university students; police forces (in particular the Canadian Association of Chiefs of Police); the medical community and its professional organization, the Canadian Medical Association; and the pharmaceutical industry (through the action of an institution created in 1969, the Council on Drug Abuse). Social control through state action became the central issue for these groups. However, the influence and power of these four interest groups varied in terms of skills, knowledge, strategies, financial resources, networking capabilities, and access to centres of decision-making.

Chapter 3 analyses the action of four provincial governments – those in British Columbia, Ontario, Prince Edward Island, and Quebec. My choices stem from the fact that the drug use issue cut across several jurisdictions: justice, law enforcement, health, and education. Since the last two are provincial matters, an analysis of provincial responses is necessary. British Columbia, through its own addiction research foundation, came to work with the RCMP in an attempt to undermine the pro-marijuana lobby; Ontario, through its Addiction Research Foundation, developed a very close relationship with the National Health and Welfare department; Prince Edward Island assumed leadership of the anti-drug lobby among the provinces; and Quebec was anxious to defend its jurisdictions over health and education. A comparative approach allows one to compare and contrast how cultural factors and political culture can explain, for instance, the relative tolerance of the Quebec government as opposed to the more strict approach favoured by Charlottetown.

Since the federal government had the constitutional authority to classify drugs, the last two chapters analyse its handling of the recreational drug use issue. It employed several strategies; one of them was the appointment of a Commission of Inquiry into the Non-Medical Use of Drugs, better known as the Le Dain Commission. Chapter 4 looks at the work undertaken by the Commission from 1969 to 1973. By appointing a commission of inquiry, the federal government set in motion a catalyst for the discussion of drug use. Individuals and interest groups with conflicting views on the issue took part in the public discussion and politicized the public policy process.

The last chapter analyses the drug use debate that pitted National Health and Welfare officials (who tried to promote a health-based approach as a complement to law enforcement), against Justice and RCMP officials (who were against any significant amendment of drug policy due to the symbolic power attributed to marijuana and Canada's international obligations).

1 'A Growing Problem': Reporting and Measuring the Use of Illegal Drugs

In 1968, *Chatelaine* magazine published the story of Keith, a twenty-one-year-old man from a 'good' family, who was arrested for possession of marijuana and got a six-month jail sentence. His father was outraged, since he considered Keith's action a benign offence: 'What good will it do, putting a boy like that in jail?' His mother was angry and frustrated since she could not understand a society that relied more and more on drugs to cure ailments or deal with stress and at the same time prohibited marijuana. She blamed the courts for giving harsh penalties, 'the irresponsibility' of the media 'too prone to put sensationalism ahead of information,' and scientists and physicians who 'continue to throw marijuana in a mixed bag with heroin and LSD, [and] label it a narcotic.'[1]

This chapter looks at the transformation of a new social reality, recreational drug use, into a social problem. Its focus is on the media, especially print media, and how they constructed the recreational drug use phenomenon. The print media had a dual role: they reported on the new phenomenon of recreational drug use, but at the same time their reports, and sometimes their alarmist tone, contributed to mobilize groups. Two drugs in particular inevitably dominate any discussion of drugs during the 1960s: LSD (lysergic acid diethylamide-25) and marijuana. These are the two drugs on which public curiosity and discussion centred.

At the time, however, little was really known about these substances. Essentially, the short-, medium-, and long-term health and behavioural effects were far from clear. Equally unknown was the number of people actually using recreational drugs. This chapter also examines how members of the scientific community, especially those employed by provincially funded organizations such as the Addiction Research

'Wonderful! To think at one time we couldn't even get him to mow the lawn.'
Source: *The Journal* 1:3 (August 1972), 6; © 2004 Centre for Addiction and
Mental Health

Foundation of Ontario, measured and reported the new phenomenon
of recreational drug use. Although the print media had a tendency to
adopt an almost alarmist tone, researchers attempted to counter this
with a more realistic and tempered approach.

Print Media and the Drug Issue: Diversity in Concepts of Drug Use

During the sixties, the print media published several stories about the
new phenomenon of recreational drug use, focusing on two in particu-

lar: LSD and marijuana. Their conception of these two drugs was, however, markedly different. LSD use, as opposed to marijuana consumption, constitutes an interesting case study of the relevance of the theory of moral panic. Since this theory is widely used to explain the development of drug legislation in Canada and the Western world, let's start by defining it.

Briefly, the theory of moral panic refers to the sudden rise of an issue, often out of proportion with reality, and its more or less equally rapid disappearance from the public agenda. It argues that whenever society discusses illegal drug use a climate of fear will result, often due to the efforts of the media, law-enforcement agencies, and other interest groups to justify a repressive approach. This concept helps to explain the concern that drugs generated in the sixties.

In the context of the counterculture movement of the sixties, the theory of moral panic refers to fears that widespread drug use threatened social values. The drug issue triggered judgments and strong feelings over what constituted acceptable or condemnable behaviour. It was during the sixties that the baby boom generation championed recreational drug use, and the demographic shift that altered drug consumption and practices became a focus of debate. Generational tensions exacerbated by the counterculture movement shook the West, and in this context drug use was perceived either as a threat to social values or as part of a new value system. Young people were perhaps the most visible of the proponents of these new values, but they also were made scapegoats by those who felt besieged. Gaining pleasure, facilitating social interaction, or embarking on mystic quests through drug use became morally suspect activities for those opposed to non-medical drug consumption. For opponents, these aspects of drug use were equated with passivity, loss of self-control and productivity, and the attainment of pleasure through contemptible means. Furthermore, recreational drug use constituted an attack on morality and excited 'strong feelings of righteousness.'[2] Episodes of moral panic often generate responses from authorities and policy-makers and can result in social changes.[3] According to Goode and Ben-Yehuda, any new episode of moral panic concerning illegal drug use serves to reinforce the status quo. They argue that such an episode leaves an institutional legacy that can be altered only with difficulty, since successive moral panics maintain and sometimes strengthen the status quo in order to discourage recreational drug use.[4]

The concept of moral panic is also a good starting-point for analysing the media portrayal of the phenomenon of recreational drug use. One major characteristic of an episode of moral panic is the concentration of media coverage in a brief period of time. In a study of the role of newspapers and magazines in the representation of illegal drug use prepared for the Le Dain Commission, its author reviewed the chronology of the appearance of articles on LSD and marijuana. He observed a steady increase in the number of such articles between 1966 and 1970. For instance, of the fifty-nine articles published in 1967, fifteen were concerned with marijuana, whereas seventeen concentrated on LSD. In the latter case, eight highlighted possible damage to human chromosomes. According to the study's author, if it is true that periodicals probably played a role in amplifying the impact of marijuana, the same holds true for LSD, at least in 1966 and 1967.[5]

The second indication of an episode of moral panic is the tendency to point to a 'minority group' or a 'scapegoat' whose behaviour is presented as a threat to social and moral values. In his article on the media and the perception of moral panic, Hay looks at the selectivity that guides the media and the orientation of news reports 'which portray [a minority population] in a negative light.'[6] In the sixties, the consumption of LSD and marijuana for pleasure was associated with a particular group, young middle-class people, and not with a specific ethnic group. This was in contrast to the situation at the beginning of the twentieth century, when one of the arguments supporting the criminalization of certain drugs was undeniably racially motivated: it was believed that the legal repression of opium would help discourage Chinese from both immigrating to, and working in, Canada.[7]

The last characteristic of an episode of moral panic concerns the presentation of news and a way of reporting social reality that favours a specific angle, which in this case was sensationalistic and tragic. Media representations of LSD and marijuana differed considerably in this regard.

Newspapers highlighted injuries, deaths, and suicides attributed to the ingestion of LSD, without attempting much analysis of the phenomenon. In March 1967, Toronto newspapers reported the death of a twenty-year-old music student whose suicide his father attributed to LSD. The father blamed a conference on LSD, held that February at the University of Toronto, for the tragedy that had affected his family. For this parent, there was 'not the slightest doubt that disciples of LSD contributed to his death, his murder ... So does every publication that in any way glorifies this drug as a magic gift that can broaden and enlighten anyone.'[8] Both the *Toronto Telegram* and *Toronto Daily Star* mentioned that the young student had attended the University of Toronto psychedelic festival and was interested in psychedelic drugs. In March 1967, this tragic and sensational piece of news influenced the tone of the discussion and the perception of this phenomenon by the members of the Ontario Legislative Assembly during their debates on the issue of illegal drug use. This was also the case in April 1967, when Canadian senators debated the bill on the criminalization of LSD possession, as will be seen in chapter 5.[9]

At other times, the media privileged disturbing stories of unusual behaviour attributed to LSD. On 16 October 1968, for instance, The *Toronto Telegram* ran a front-page story with the headline 'LSD Trip Father Terrorizes Hospital.' In her article, Sheila Gormely reported the story of a twenty-two-year-old father who terrorized the emergency room of a suburban hospital for three hours. Few details about the incident were provided. Two years later, the story of a Toronto musician who tried to tear out his eyes received significant news coverage. On 3 February 1970, both the *Globe and Mail* and the *Toronto Telegram* ran the same headline on their front pages: 'Musician gouges own eyes during LSD trip.' According to the *Globe* story, by Peter Whelan, a musician found 'on a street corner ... with a finger shoved deeply into each eye socket' had already lost one eye 'and probably will lose the sight of the other.' The *Toronto Daily Star* was somewhat less dramatic when it ran the headline 'Musician on LSD May Lose Sight after Jabbing Fingers into Eyes.' The newspaper reported that a young saxophone player who 'tried LSD because he no longer got "kicks" from marijuana may have partially blinded himself ... by sticking his fingers in his eyes.'[10] The incident was mentioned in other newspapers, notably the *Calgary Herald* and *La Presse*. However, a study for the Le Dain Commission noted that the media treatment of the story changed in the following weeks, when the facts revealed themselves to be less dramatic. 'The story was retracted, shrunk in size and moved to the inside pages because it turned out he had not ripped one eye so that it was dangling out, which is the way it was first reported. He had tried to damage his eyes, but had succeeded in doing real damage to neither.'[11] Nevertheless, this event caught the attention of groups opposed to the liberalization of the Narcotic Control Act. In its brief to the Le Dain Commission submitted in February 1970, the government of Prince Edward Island referred to this story as evidence that LSD was a dangerous drug.[12]

This particular view of LSD targeting a particular group – young people – and a specific angle of approach – sensationalism and tragedy – was not lost on contemporary observers. Some even asserted that media reactions to this new social phenomenon were out of proportion to the threat. When reporting suspected deaths from LSD, headlines leaned toward sensation rather than analysis. Journalist Sheila Gormely worked for the *Toronto Telegram* in the sixties and wrote several stories on LSD use. One of them captured the attention of many, including members of the Ontario Legislative Assembly, in March 1967. Gormely wrote about Michelle, an LSD user, under the headline 'A Girl Who Survived 40 Acid Trips.' In her 1970 book on the drug scene, Gormely reflected on that particular episode. 'By using "survived" as the operative word,' wrote Gormely, the headline 'implied that she was lucky to be alive.'[13] Gormely questioned her own newspaper's selective policy, as well as that of other newspapers, in reporting stories related to LSD, as opposed to socially acceptable drugs such as alcohol. 'Why ... didn't newspapers run this kind of headline: Alcohol-crazed Adult Staggers into Traffic, or Girl Survives 40 Drinking Bouts?'[14] The incident led her to conclude that 'newspapers don't print stories about "good trips," consequently readers are left with an impression, reinforced by their own biases, that terror usually occurs in the use of LSD.'[15] Concerning the issue of bad versus good trips, the Le Dain interim report stated that in a study of street drug users, University of Toronto psychiatrist Dr Solursh found that bad trips occurred 'in 24 of 601 "acid trips."'[16] In his 1968 book *The Smug Minority*, Pierre Berton supported Gormely's comments. Indeed, he went so far as to use the expression 'national hysteria' in order to describe the discussion about LSD that took place. His comments were based on an assessment made by Dr Abraham Hoffer, director of Psychiatric Research at the University Hospital in Saskatoon and well known for his research on LSD in the treatment of alcoholics, when describing the debate that took place in Parliament from 1967 on.[17] For his part, Reginald Whitaker wrote that the LSD scare 'peaked' in 1967.[18]

Coverage of recreational marijuana use in the print media differed from that of LSD and did not completely conform to the model of moral panic. Certainly, marijuana use was clearly associated with a specific group: young people. However, the media coverage in this case was spread over a longer period of time. At first, the media simply investigated and reported their findings. However, with the appointment of the Le Dain Commission in 1969, they began to cover drug use in general, but more particularly that of marijuana. Consequently, newspapers assigned more resources and tried to answer questions, such as, Why did people smoke marijuana? What were the effects? Were there other means than the legal approach to deter use and make young people more responsible about consumption? As the number of social actors taking part in the debate on the legalization of marijuana increased, partially because of the Le Dain Commission, newspapers could not ignore the debate about the strengths and weaknesses of a repressive approach that sought to criminalize marijuana. Thus, young people were portrayed by some daily newspapers such as the *Globe and Mail*, the *Toronto Star*, and the *Montreal Gazette* as victims of an unfair law. Legal repression handicapped young people's futures by imposing criminal records, and sometimes even jail terms, for possession. In short, the punishment was considered too severe for the crime. A similar trend can be observed in American newspapers over the same period.[19] The level of hostility towards marijuana users was not as high as it was towards users of LSD.

The Le Dain Commission was preoccupied by the part the media played in the perception of illegal drugs. Forty-six print media, excluding ethnic and weekly newspapers, answered a questionnaire sent by the Le Dain Commission to identify their role and position toward drugs, and in particular marijuana. The conclusion of the study offers stark contrasts in the role played by the written media.

The first element considered was editorial policy. Conservative newspapers, compared with liberal ones, preferred medical over judicial coverage of the marijuana issue. Furthermore, there was no common position even among daily newspapers owned by the same publishing conglomerate, such as Southam, Free Press, or Thomson. Finally, daily newspapers were forced to diversify their sources of information because of the significance of the phenomenon, as well as the durability of its impression on the public mind. The drug issue, which some people had considered temporary, remained a reality at the beginning of the seventies. At first, daily newspapers relied on the courts and police as sources of information. Later, they referred, without ignoring the latter, to studies on drug use by provincially funded drug and alcohol research institutions and by the medical profession.[20] In 1971, according to a survey of newspapers and magazines conducted for the Commission by Claude Héndult, '45.9 per cent of Canadian newspapers use[d] general reporters as their primary source of articles on non-medical drug use. This compares with only 18.9 per cent for police reporters and 5.4 per cent for court reporters.'[21] Not only did the survey's author note a variety of opinions among daily newspapers that took part in the study, but he also warned against using editorials to identify the sympathies of daily newspapers.

> Editorially, Canadian newspapers have not even begun to approach a consensus on the issue of non-medical drug use ... On the issue of cannabis, survey results show that newspapers are more liberal, or non-repressive, than they let on editorially ... In other words, editorials could be as liberal as their writers, if some solid authority issued a liberal statement on cannabis, which [the editorialist could use].[22]

In spite of inherent limitations, the study examined editorials published by six daily newspapers from 1964 to 1971 in order to identify their depiction of drug use and more particularly of marijuana.[23] Certainly this media survey has its limits: in particular, French-language daily newspapers were not well covered. In spite of these constraints and the difficulty associated with the task of systematically analysing the contents of the main dailies of every province, I refer to this study because it reveals the variety of opinions in English-language newspapers.

The *Vancouver Province*, a British Columbia daily, is a useful starting point. During the 1962–71 period, this newspaper showed a deep interest in the drug issue, an interest that can be explained, according to the author of the study, by the long association between drugs and Vancouver. He wrote that 'because of the city's phobia about its sizable-seeming oriental community, and the linking of this community with opiate narcotics, the issue of use of opiate narcotics has been kept a hot one in the newspaper's columns, including the editorial columns.' During this period, the *Province* adopted an all-embracing definition of drugs, including those prescribed by the medical profession; those classified as illegal by legislation, such as heroin and marijuana; as well as legal social drugs, such as tobacco and alcohol. Nevertheless, it did not question the merits, and less so the logic, of the repressive approach to illegal drugs as classified by legislation. In fact, the *Province* was against adding other drugs, such as barbiturates, tranquillizers and amphetamines to the list of those legally proscribed. Yet it did not encourage politicians to liberalize the status of drugs already classified as illegal. It was in the application of the law, of which young people were victims, that the *Province* questioned the merits of punishment, especially in cases of possession for personal use.[24]

Since marijuana use for non-medical reasons was not a passing phe-nomenon, the *Province* pleaded in its editorial of 15 November 1967 for an investigation into the effects of this drug. The newspaper noted that carrying out studies on marijuana was complicated by the drug's legal status, and cited this as a reason to justify further investigation. The editorial recounted the experience of a University of Victoria psychol-ogist who asked the Department of National Health and Welfare to conduct a study on marijuana and its effects on rats. The university professor was told 'there would appear to be no value whatsoever in experimental work that is either designed to condemn marijuana, which is already condemned, or to attempt to cast it out of the position that has already been taken internationally.' Consequently, the *Province* urged scientific research on this drug and, depending on the results, a subsequent amendment to the Narcotic Control Act.[25]

When enforcement of the Narcotic Control Act meant that young people were arrested, convicted for possession, and then jailed, the newspaper questioned the legislation, especially compared with the treatment of users of socially accepted drugs such as alcohol. The 17 May 1968 editorial 'Which Crime Fits the Punishment?' questioned the wisdom of a law that condemned a nineteen-year-old found guilty of simple marijuana possession to a 'nine months definite and six months indefinite' sentence, as opposed to the fine of $200 imposed on another nineteen-year-old 'who, while under the influence of alcohol, and driving without a licence, crashed his car into a guardrail, killing two passengers.'[26]

The implications of the Narcotic Control Act for young people forced the *Province* to question the law as a deterrent to marijuana use. Its 11 January 1969 editorial, entitled 'Drug Education: First, the Facts ...,' contemplated the dangers attributed to marijuana. It asked whether marijuana was 'sufficiently dangerous to the user or to society to justify the harsh penalties that presently try to discourage its use.' In an attempt to answer its own question, the newspaper reminded its readers that 'nobody knows.' Why? Because 'there hasn't been enough research to provide unequivocal answers. Most of the research and expert opinion, however, indicates marijuana is perhaps, at worst, no more harmful than alcohol.'[27]

In the case of Alberta, two newspapers published in Calgary were included in the Le Dain Commission's study on the role of media. In informing its readers about the drug phenomenon, the *Calgary Herald* did not disguise its support of repression as the legislative means to fight drug abuse among young people. However, repression, the newspaper specified, 'should be aimed at the "pusher" of cannabis products, while the youthful first offender who merely possesses or uses the drug is seen as deserving of some degree of legal clemency.' The newspaper had a tendency to use non-scientific evidence, such as the story of the Toronto musician who tried to blind himself, in order to sustain its position on illegal drug use.[28]

A different, but minority, point of view was expressed by the *Albertan*, distributed in Calgary. In its description of the drug phenomenon, the newspaper reminded its readers that the discussion involved the use of drugs for both medical and non-medical purposes. Because of this, it would be absurd to make a distinction between good drugs – those consumed on the advice of a physician – and those that were illegal because of a decision made by the state. Consequently, the medical profession, rather than the justice system, should treat abusers of legal and illegal drugs alike. The *Albertan* favoured the legalization of marijuana so that the drug would be treated in the same manner as alcohol. It justified its stand by citing medical research instead of relying on current opinions and judgments on recreational drug use.[29]

In Saskatchewan, the study looked at the *Star Phoenix*, published in Saskatoon. In terms of drug abuse, the newspaper's main focus was alcoholism. Indeed, regarding marijuana, the newspaper's stand was ambiguous. According to the Le Dain study, it was 'a mixture of mild opposition to present practices and uncertainty about what else to do.' In terms of solutions, the newspaper preferred medical treatment to legal repression, but its proposals were short on details.[30]

In Ontario, the researcher examined the *Globe and Mail* and the *Toronto Daily Star*. Between 1961 and 1971, the *Globe* adopted a progressive position, in that it favoured the legalization of marijuana. Its definition of the drug phenomenon was liberal, since it focused on the use and the abuse of all drugs, including those prescribed by members of the medical profession. However, the newspaper put one drug in particular front and centre: marijuana. Why? According to the author of the study, this was because of the newspaper's 'impatience with the slowness of coming of legal modifications which would at least place [marijuana] under the Food and Drugs Act.'[31] This position expresses clear disagreement with the repressive approach to marijuana use chosen by the federal government. It is also evident that the *Globe and Mail* was concerned about drug use among young people. Its proposed solutions were education and law reform. To summarize the comments of the study, in terms of marijuana, '[E]ditorials express the view that "the law is an ass" because of its treatment of marijuana in the same manner as heroin.' Until changes were implemented, the Toronto daily reminded its readers, the federal government had no choice but to enforce the Narcotic Control Act as it stood.[32]

The *Toronto Daily Star* adopted a similarly progressive position. Between 1964 and 1971, it supported the role of the state as an instrument of social control.' However, on the marijuana issue, the newspaper had to reconcile its confidence in the state with the fact that the Narcotic Control Act did not work. It was evident that a more effective approach was required.[33]

Magazines were another source of information considered in the study for the Le Dain Commission. This part of the study is disappointing because few Canadian magazines participated. The importance of American magazines, which at the time dominated the Canadian market, allows us to appreciate the American influence on the Canadian vision of the recreational drug use issue. American influence in the debate on drug use took diverse shapes. Canadians had access to American opinion through multiple channels, such as magazines, interest groups related to American ones, and cross-border relations between state and non-state bodies. I will return to this question in the last chapter. For the moment, however, I wish to emphasize the importance of American magazines as a source of information.

In his study for the Le Dain Commission, the author pointed out the determining influence of American magazines. He based his observation on two factors. First, Canadians preferred American periodicals to Canadian ones. Second, U.S. magazines published more news about drugs than did Canadian ones. The case of Quebec represented, however, an important exception. The author noted that 'the language barrier,' despite the existence of a translated version of *Reader's Digest* (*Sélection du Reader's Digest*), 'is still far from completely bridged.'[34]

What conclusion should we reach about print media coverage and drug use? Despite the limits of my analysis, a range of opinions was expressed by daily newspapers and magazines. There was also a gradual change in the approach daily newspapers took to the drug issue. Newspapers 'did not begin to reflect an interest in youth's use of non-medical drugs until the phenomenon was well under way in Canada and began to be reflected in arrest statistics.' Initially, they relied on the courts and police as sources of data. Starting in 1969, they referred to scientific and medical reports in their description of the drug phenomenon.[35]

Besides a change in sources of information, there was also a shift in editorial position. the *Vancouver Province* is a case in point. The newspaper questioned the punishments imposed on young recreational drug users and expressed doubts as to the dangers inherent in marijuana. Probably it did so with a view to urging legislators to soften the law, because it suggested that marijuana might not be as dangerous as some people had maintained. The author of the media study for the Le Dain Commission formulated the hypothesis of 'nice young experimenters' to explain the appeal of softening the law. As long as law enforcement meant the condemnation of marginal and criminal groups for marijuana possession, the *Province* supported the repressive approach, but when repression meant the arrest and conviction of 'nice young experimenters' (who could, after all, be anybody's children), it disagreed with the approach. To protect these now-vulnerable, 'nice young experimenters,' the newspaper found itself 'forced to argue against the application of the law,' unless marijuana was 'dangerous' or viewed as such. The *Province* consequently decided 'that marijuana is not dangerous,' and was able to 'proceed with its argument against enforcement of the law.'[36]

In the early 1970s, the federal government informed its Crown attorneys that they should liberalize their approach by asking for absolute or conditional discharges for cases of simple possession of cannabis in which there was no criminal record and no previous conviction. the *Province* at this time modified its editorial position. Since such a shift in the administration of the Narcotic Control Act meant that 'nice young experimenters' would no longer be subject to punishment disproportionate to the crime, many newspapers, like the *Province*, returned to the 'belief that marijuana is [or may be] harmful.'[37]

Was there a mood of panic in the media scrutinized? First, it is important to remember that the media scene in the 1960s was not limited to newspapers and magazines, since radio and television were also important sources of information and disseminators of public opinion. For lack of a systematic analysis of these media, it is impossible to answer the question definitively. In any case, media interest changed over time, as noted above in the section on daily newspapers. In the beginning, marijuana was subject to the same sensationalist emphasis as LSD, before a shift occurred that gave more attention to the sometimes contradictory medical reports on it.[38]

Daily newspapers were only one set of participants in the debate on illegal drugs. Radio and television were also important sources of information and disseminators of public opinion. Numerous social actors drew their information from the media, but would often denounce them if newspapers' comments contradicted their own viewpoints. As Gormely notes, those who supported the legalization of marijuana, or its decriminalization, tended to denounce news articles opposed to their stand. A similar behaviour can be observed among those who denounced the drug phenomenon as a whole. They claimed that journalists were stirring up public opinion and interest groups.

The media also managed to get the attention of decision makers, notably politicians who depended on the media to validate their positions. During a debate in the Senate about LSD, some senators blamed the media, and in particular the Canadian Broadcasting Corporation (CBC), for encouraging young people to consume LSD. For his part, Senator A. Hamilton McDonald argued that 'television programs would have done a much better service to the people of Canada if, rather than glorifying a drug such as LSD in the minds of our people, they had presented a program to be reviewed by the Canadian people, indicating the dangers associated with the use of this drug.'[39]

While senators pointed an accusing finger at the media, they also received support from outside Parliament. For instance, an indefatigable opponent of marijuana legalization, G.K. Cowan, an adviser to the Prince Edward Island (PEI) government and an active member of the PEI Drug Education Committee, reprimanded the CBC for its coverage of the drug issue, which he considered far too favourable. In particular, Cowan took issue with inviting individuals such as Timothy Leary or Allan Ginsberg to appear on TV shows such as *This Hour Has Seven Days*. Other media outlets, such as the National Film Board and the *Globe and Mail*, were, according to Cowan, equally culpable.[40] OPTAT (the Office for the Prevention and Treatment of Alcoholism and Other Toxicomanias), the body created by the government of Quebec in 1966, also denounced the media. In his brief to the Le Dain Commission, OPTAT's director, André Boudreau, attributed many of the worst aspects of the drug phenomenon to biased media coverage:

One saw on the front pages of all our newspapers the photo of a hippy who had appeared in the American Senate smoking a marijuana cigarette. In a period of controversy, the media will easily obtain interviews with leading agitators, and will be content if their subjects provoke even greater debate. The media are simply giving these people a forum to promulgate their views. Further still, the information media, in relating a piece of news, exaggerate certain aspects, to the point of caricature if it will make the story more unusual.[41]

A study for the Special Senate Committee on Mass Media, chaired by Senator Keith Davey, demonstrated that these were not merely voices crying in the wilderness, but rather reflections of Canadian public opinion. In-depth interviews with 2254 Canadians revealed that 61 per cent blamed television for an 'increase in drug addiction.' Nor did newspapers escape negative public opinion, since 51 per cent of those interviewed blamed them too. Although there were no important regional variations, differences did emerge when cultural background and age group were taken into consideration. For example, 54 per cent of French-speaking people who were interviewed in Quebec criticized television and newspapers equally. Of people under the age of twenty-five, 55 per cent blamed television, though in the case of newspapers, there was no significant age-related difference.[42] Of those interviewed, 54 per cent believed television devoted too much coverage to drug use, and 45 per cent were of the same opinion about newspapers. As in the preceding case, while there were no significant regional differences regarding television, the case was different for newspapers. Regional differences were significant, because only 30 per cent of those from Saskatchewan blamed newspapers, as opposed to 46 per cent of British Columbians and 47 per cent of Albertans. French Canadians, by contrast, faulted newspapers to a much greater degree (60%) than television (49%). Finally, the age factor was significant only for television, as 43 per cent of those under the age of twenty-five blamed this medium.[43]

This public criticism of the media was also expressed unofficially. During the 1968 Interprovincial Health Ministers' Conference, the Ontario minister denounced the CBC and its efforts, which in his opinion incited young people to consume illegal drugs. The CBC offered a form of 'free advertisement' that minimized the dangerous effects and 'piqued students' interests, often by leading them to believe that the consumption of hallucinogens has no grave consequences, that a significant number of students uses them, and that they are easy to obtain.'[44]

This public debate can be attributed to a fear of social change and especially to a dismay with the questioning of social values by young people. Young people, as a social group, and recreational drug use as a particular behaviour, were targeted. The media approach to this social reality was characterized by concern and sensationalism. This is especially true of the debate surrounding LSD, which, according to *Time* magazine in 1967, was an international phenomenon associated with the generation gap. There was a fear, created and maintained in the media, that young people might want to reject the post-war social and moral values in areas such as relations between men and women, gender constructions that confined women to motherhood and men to breadwinning, sexuality and its definition within the framework of marriage, and the meaning of marriage as a key social achievement for both sexes, and – when it came to drugs in particular – want to flout the laws that regulated their use.[45] In short, the issue of recreational drug use is one angle by which to approach the baby boom generation and its challenge to a society that it defined as conservative, authoritarian, defensive, and apprehensive of change. Nevertheless, the challenge did not go unanswered. There was a real fear that institutions would be incapable of responding to new attacks against social and moral values.

The print media reported the new phenomenon of drug use and offered their solution. For many, the softening of the penalties for possession of marijuana was appropriate in order to reduce the social cost of repression for young people. At the same time, however, daily· newspapers had difficulties assessing the popularity of soft drug use among young people, a task that was undertaken by social scientists.

Scientists and the Optics of the Drug Issue

In December 1966 H. David Archibald, head of the Alcoholism and Drug Addiction Research Foundation of Ontario (ARF), which advised the Ontario government on drug and alcohol dependence and treatment issues, shared his concerns with the Ontario minister of health. 'As you know,' he wrote, 'the question of usage among the younger population of Toronto has been troublesome. We have been asked numerous questions about the problem of marijuana but have not been in a position to speak from first-hand knowledge because of the lack of opportunity to study the users of marijuana within any organized framework.'[46] It was vital that a study of recreational marijuana use quickly be undertaken, as this was a frequent topic of discussion in the media, and politicians were raising the issue during question period at Queen's Park.

Once scientists began to take an interest in examining drug behaviour, a distinct user profile began to emerge. In a survey of twenty-two studies of drug consumption in Canada conducted between 1968 and 1970, it was found that almost the only behaviour targeted was that of high school students (17 surveys out of 22). In short, very little was known about other socio-professional categories of drug users. Furthermore, the data gathered on drug users focused especially on urban centres in Ontario. By 1970, there was still no pan-Canadian survey on drug use, a responsibility finally assumed by the Le Dain Commission. Outside Ontario, few studies had been completed, except in Quebec, Halifax, and Vancouver.[47] This state of affairs can be explained by the activities of the ARF.

Although the Ontario government did not have primary responsibility for revising the federal narcotics law, it was not immune to the social controversy surrounding recreational drug use. For this reason, precise data needed to be collected on the use of drugs among Ontarians. A lack of concern would be seen as negligent, since the government had to help school boards develop drug education programs as well as to encourage health organizations to develop action plans in the field of treatment. As a result, the government sought the help of the ARF.

Starting in 1968, several studies were undertaken by the ARF to better understand drug use among young people, something that had never been done before.[48] The interest in youth was partially a direct result of media attention. All of the research undertaken on drug use relied upon the method of anonymous self-reporting, and for the studies conducted in Toronto, the young person had to have his or her parents sign a consent form.

Published in 1969 and 1970, the studies revealed that there was a problem with drugs, but not with those who were the focus of so much media attention. First, the typical drug user was a young individual between the ages of twelve and twenty. Within this age group, studies demonstrated that drug use increased with age. Second, the typical drug user was more interested in cigarettes and alcohol than in any of the ten other drugs listed on the questionnaire (among them LSD, solvents, marijuana, and speed). Indeed, it was found that alcohol was the drug of choice of 46 per cent and 60 per cent of the Toronto high school students taking part in the 1968 and 1970 studies, respectively.[49] With the exception of marijuana, more than 92 per cent of the respondents had never experimented with any of the other drugs listed. Marijuana had been

'Well, at least you two finally have something in common ... a hangover ...'
Source: *The Journal* 2:2 (February 1973), 6; ©2004 Centre for Addiction and
Mental Health

consumed by 6.7 per cent of the study group in the six months preceding
the 1968 study, a figure that had reached 18.3 per cent by 1970.[50]

No significant regional differences were found when studies,
inspired by that of 1968, were conducted in other parts of Ontario, in
Montreal, and in Halifax.[51] For instance, in 1969, of the 4509 Montreal
Island students surveyed in thirty-two high schools and four colleges,
48 per cent indicated that they consumed alcohol at least once a month,

and 8.6 per cent reported using marijuana at least once over a six-month period. Only 3 per cent of young people reported consuming LSD. When the same survey was repeated two years later, this time with thirty-five high schools and six CEGEPs, the percentages were 55.4 for alcohol, 23 for marijuana, and 8.1 for LSD. In surveys undertaken in Toronto, Halifax, and London in 1968 and 1969, the percentages for LSD use were 2.5, 2.37, and 1.24, respectively.[52] However, in the 1969 Montreal survey, there were some significant differences. For instance, 12 per cent of those attending Anglo-Protestant schools, 8.7 per cent of those attending Anglo-Catholic schools, and 7.7 per cent of those attending Franco-Catholic schools reported smoking marijuana at least once in the previous six-month period. For LSD, the percentages were 2.8, 3.5, and 2.9, respectively. Two years later, consumption rates for marijuana were 27.3, 18, and 18.9. For LSD, they were 11.7 for Anglo-Protestant schools and 7.1 for Anglo-Catholic and French Catholic schools.[53] In the case of Halifax, 6.63 per cent of the 1606 students surveyed in 1969 and 17.3 per cent of 1081 students in 1970 reported using marijuana in the previous six months.[54] The authors of these studies highlighted the fact that, except for LSD, consumption rates observed in Montreal and Halifax were similar to those reported in other major urban centres. Consequently, experimentation and illegal drug use among adolescents in these cities could be seen as part of a broader North American phenomenon.

In Vancouver, the Narcotic Addiction Foundation of British Columbia (NAFBC) conducted an initial survey that involved seventy-two marijuana users in 1966. The survey did not, however, assess the number of users in the city. Nevertheless, the author of the survey wrote that 'psychedelic drug use is far more widespread among the general population than was originally believed.'[55] Three other studies were carried out documenting the specific characteristics of the drug scene in British Columbia. The first was completed in six school districts, but did not include Vancouver. Although alcohol and tobacco, as in Halifax, Montreal, and Toronto, were the preferred drugs, the incidence of marijuana use was 19.7 per cent, glue 12.4 per cent, tranquilizers 27.3 per cent, and LSD 6.6 per cent. Heroin was clearly not a drug of choice, since the incidence of its use was only 1.4 per cent. The high consumption rates for the other drugs could be explained by the wording of the question. As opposed to the Halifax, Montreal, and Toronto surveys, where students were asked if they had used drugs during the last six months, in British Columbia they were asked if they had ever used any drugs.[56] Two other studies would, however, demonstrate a higher incidence of drug use in British Columbia. In 1970 and again in 1974, the NAFBC surveyed eighteen high schools in Vancouver. Although the conclusions echoed previous studies done in Halifax, Montreal, and Toronto (namely, that alcohol and cigarettes were high school students' preferred substances), a different trend emerged concerning marijuana. In 1970, 38.9 per cent of students reported cannabis use, whereas four years later, 41.5 per cent said that they had used it during the six months before the survey, a consumption rate much higher than anywhere else in the country.[57]

A gender gap was identified in Toronto, Montreal, and Vancouver, as the results revealed that, compared to males, a lower number of urban young women had experimented with drugs. For example, in 1968, 40 per cent of female respondents in Toronto and Montreal had consumed alcohol in the six months preceding the survey, but more than 94 per cent had never tried marijuana. In Vancouver in 1970, the percentage of women who had never tried marijuana was lower than in Toronto and Montreal, but at 64 per cent was higher than the rate for men, which was 55.7 per cent.[58]

This gender gap also manifested itself in terms of substances. It was found that tranquillizers were clearly the drugs of choice for young women. In 1968, 10.4 per cent of 3097 Toronto teenage girls and, in 1969, 9.5 per cent of their 4509 Montreal counterparts surveyed had used tranquillizers on at least one occasion in the previous six months. With the exception of alcohol and tobacco, young women were not interested in experimenting with other substances, such as LSD or glue.[59] The story in Vancouver, however, was different, tranquillizer use among women being lower than that of marijuana and LSD, which in 1970 and 1974 were less popular than alcohol and tobacco. However, it should be noted that the reference to tranquillizer use was more restricted, since it included only prescription tranquillizers.[60]

Finally, the gender gap was also evident in terms of frequency of consumption. Female students in Toronto reported experimenting once or twice, whereas boys were more habitual users of drugs such as marijuana. It should be noted, however, that the overall percentage of users was low.[61] A 1970 study of teenagers conducted in the semi-rural Niagara Region duplicated the results obtained in Toronto: only 2.4 per cent of females and 5.7 per cent of males had consumed marijuana more than seven times during the previous six months.[62]

The authors of the 1970 study attributed the rise in illegal drug use after 1968 to an increase in the number of young Toronto women who had experimented at least once; a similar study done in 1971, which involved 7419 Montreal high school students, recorded a similar trend.[63] This growth underlies the note of pessimism in the authors' conclusion. 'At the present rate of increase it would take only four years until marijuana is used by more students than is alcohol, and less than six years until everyone is using marijuana.'[64]

Not everyone shared this pessimism, however. In his study of drug use among Halifax high school students, Paul C. Whitehead reached a different conclusion. While not denying that the rate of increase was troublesome, he nevertheless remained cautious: 'The projections mentioned above are conveniently based on the assumption that the pattern of increases will be a linear one. However, it is far more likely that the pattern would be curvilinear, reach a peak, and level off well before experimentation with it became universal.'[65]

In 1974, the authors of a new study on Toronto students noted that drug use had stabilized as the gender gap had closed.[66] They wrote that 'in 1968 drug use appeared to be primarily a male dominated activity but gradually over the past six years sex differences have been diminishing.'[67]

Differences did, however, persist in the types of drug consumed. Toronto adolescent males were more likely to consume alcohol, marijuana, and LSD, whereas young women were choosing tobacco, barbiturates, and tranquillizers.[68] The authors of the Toronto study offered no explanation for the progressive disappearance of the gender gap, even though the study did not take into account frequency of consumption, which could have challenged the contention that the gender gap was, in fact, disappearing. They did, however, suggest that teenage girls were likely to exhibit the same behaviour as teenage boys as a result of the 'recent concern given to sexual equality in many areas of life.'[69]

One difference reappears consistently whenever female and male consumption patterns were compared. Teenage girls constituted the majority of users of tranquillizers and mood-modifying drugs. This gender difference had piqued the curiosity of scientists, and led Ruth Cooperstock, who was associated with the ARF, to write on the subject. Whereas many researchers had blamed social norms for the preference of alcohol by men and of tranquillizers by women, Cooperstock attributed the difference to the construction of gender. According to her theory, the social construction of femininity rested on the assumption that women, unlike men, found it easy to express their emotions in public; it was also assumed that women were better able to share their feelings with their doctors. In turn, the medical professional 'as a member and representative of the society that sanctions these feelings, expects female patients to be more emotionally expressive than male patients.'[70] Cooperstock's analysis thus used power relationships in society and discourses of control to explain male and female gender roles in drug consumption.

Another gap became evident when scientists considered the language spoken at home. In 1971, the Quebec study revealed that 32.8 per cent of English-speaking students had used marijuana at least once over the last six months. The rates were 21.1 per cent for French speakers, 23.3 per cent for German- and Yiddish-speaking students, and 23.1 per cent for those who spoke an Eastern European language at home. However, no explanations were offered for these differences. Other anomalies, such as consumption patterns for other drugs, were also highlighted by the study.[71]

All of these studies examined the associations that could be made between certain factors and adolescent drug experimentation, especially with illegal drugs, and regular drug use. First, they looked at a possible correlation between class and drug use. More Toronto students from middle- and upper-middle-class families tended to experiment with drugs, as opposed to those from families headed by skilled, semi-skilled, and clerical workers, and farmers.[72] This trend nevertheless disappeared in subsequent studies, which revealed more non-middle-class adolescents trying illegal drugs. Quebec and British Columbia studies indicated that the class factor was not significant: marijuana users came from every social background, with the exception of the agricultural, a point the 1970 Russell study revealed.[73]

If the class factor did not offer a convincing explanation, what could explain consumption patterns for legal and illegal drugs? Some researchers looked at religious background. The 1969 study of Montreal Island high school and college students demonstrated that students from Catholic and Protestant backgrounds were less likely to experiment with marijuana than Jews and those with no professed religious affiliation (7.8, 10.9, 15.6, and 22.8% respectively).[74] A similar trend was again evident in 1971 (20.9, 30.6, 43.2, and 47.5% respectively).[75] However, little explanation was offered for the causes of these differences. In studies done among BC students, religious background was not considered.[76]

Other researchers looked at parental behaviour. It was found that if high school students tried alcohol, cigarettes, and other drugs such as tranquillizers, it was due to the fact that they came from families where these drugs were already consumed.[77] In the 1971 Quebec study, similar conclusions were reached, except that the drugs used by the parents were barbiturates, tranquillizers, or stimulants.[78] In British Columbia, although parental drug use was not taken into consideration, researchers did take into account relations between youth and parents, and observed that those who had 'some' or 'considerable friction' with their parents had a higher incidence of marijuana use than those who reported good relations with them.[79] In Quebec, the parental factor was also considered among youth living at home. Those who no longer did so tended to use marijuana in greater percentages than those who lived with their parents. Another factor considered was whether or not parents were living together. In this instance, 21.9 per cent of adolescents living with both parents reported marijuana consumption, as opposed to 29.6 per cent of those whose parents were separated, and 30.6 per cent with one or both parents deceased.[80]

Finally, in British Columbia and in Quebec, studies looked at the relationship between incidence of drug use and motivation at school. Results showed that students who performed 'below average' or poorly were more likely to experiment with marijuana than those who did well academically.[81]

What about the assumption that marijuana was the stepping-stone to hard drugs? Although surveys proved that young people practised multiple-drug use, it was difficult to make a link between marijuana and heroin consumption, an argument often used by opponents to the legalization of marijuana. Studies done for the NAFBC, ARF, and OPTAT demonstrated that such a link was very insignificant, as opposed to that between marijuana and LSD use.[82]

Aware that society at large expressed concern, and sometimes panic, about the use of illegal drugs, the authors of these studies adopted a reassuring tone, especially to politicians who were being pressured by interest groups to respond to calls for more anti-drug legislation. Researchers pointed to the fact that the consumption of illegal drugs was generally not very high, and educational programs were seen as the key to curbing illegal drug use.[83] Yet studies in British Columbia and in Quebec deflated hopes that education could have a positive impact on drug consumption. Russell's studies demonstrated that schools were not the primary source of information about drugs for high school students who experimented with them. In fact, friends and personal curiosity played much greater roles. Moreover, in schools with drug education programs, these did not appear to have an impact on a student's decision to use marijuana. This prompted the authors of the 1974 study to write that 'drug education programs presented in Vancouver secondary schools in the 1973/74 school year did not contribute to a decrease in student drug use.'[84]

What about university students? Studies conducted from 1968 to 1970 focused on high school students, which partially contributed to the media's portrayal of the drug issue. Since the term 'youth' refers to both high school and university students, it is curious that so few studies were conducted to determine the extent of drug use among post-secondary students.

In 1969, a survey conducted during the previous summer among 8518 Quebec high school, CEGEP, and university students revealed that 7.5 per cent had used marijuana once in their life, and 0.38 per cent had consumed LSD. However, 87.74 per cent of these made no mention of marijuana, LSD consumption, or glue-sniffing. Those who indicated that they had sniffed glue, or had taken LSD or marijuana, cited curiosity as their main motivation.[85] However, this survey did not distinguish between high school students and university students. Six other surveys were conducted among post-secondary students. For instance, at Bishop's University, 19.55 per cent of full-time students in 1968, and 27.26 per cent in 1969, reported marijuana consumption. At Loyola College in 1968, 700 freshmen were interviewed; 15 per cent of males and 7 per cent of females reported that they had used marijuana. In Ontario, a 1967 survey among students in an introductory psychology class at the University of Toronto revealed that 5 per cent had used marijuana. At the University of Western Ontario in 1970, 23.2 per cent of students interviewed indicated that they had consumed marijuana. In 1970, the Quebec Department of Education released the results of a survey conducted in 1968 in three CEGEPs in Montreal, Quebec, and Lac St-Jean, an English-speaking college, a school of fine arts, and five universities. Of these, 7.5 per cent in one of the French-speaking CEGEPs, and 6.5 per cent in one of the French-speaking universities reported having consumed marijuana. In English-speaking institutions, the percentages were 14 for CEGEPs and 18.5 for universities. In terms of LSD use, the percentages were 1.6 for French-speaking CEGEPs and 1.3 for French-speaking universities. Among English-speaking institutions, the percentages were 2.1 and 3 respectively at

CEGEPs and universities.[86] As Smart and Fejer noted, studies conducted among university students did not shed much light on drug use. In fact, a great deal was still unknown about this demographic group, since there were too few studies, and it was thus impossible to formulate any definitive conclusions.[87]

Conclusion

Media, as the survey carried out by the Special Senate Committee on Mass Media stated, had an influence on the debate concerning drug use. Newspapers and television were blamed for influencing the public and for being overzealous in their reporting of drugs. During the 1960s, newspapers devoted much column space to drug stories. These articles seemed to follow a certain pattern, which typically featured lurid effects attributed to LSD. When reports dealt with drug users in major cities such as Toronto, they engendered a sense of panic or, at the very least, one of strong concern. Still, the variety of opinions and solutions expressed in newspapers demonstrates that the views on recreational drug use were more complex than one might initially believe. For certain media, the consumption of any illegal drug was bound to be dangerous, hence their alarmist tone. Others supported the liberalization of narcotics laws that, they argued, meted out punishment disproportionate to the crime. However, it can be said that all media contributed to a greater awareness of the social reality of drug use. Much remained unknown about drug consumption, especially in areas such as long-term effects, the mechanisms triggering recreational drug use, the causes and factors behind experimentation, possible links between soft and hard drugs, and the grey zone between experimenters and addicts.

When considering research into patterns of consumption, the ARF, NAFBC, and OPTAT were not immune to the concerns expressed by many observers and media, since their studies focused on young drug users. However, they tried to put them into context. They reminded legislators and other social actors that drug use and abuse were not as prevalent as alcohol consumption, and thereby tried to shape the public debate on drug use and counteract media influence. Nevertheless, it did not take long for the inherent weaknesses of drug consumption surveys to be revealed, since the factors considered did not always offer satisfactory explanations. Despite their limits, these studies had an impact on governments, since alcohol consumption came to be defined as a priority by the mid-1970s.

The theory of moral panic is not wholly adequate in explaining the drug issue and how the state responded to it. The role of social actors, bureaucrats and politicians, for example, must be considered. During the sixties, social actors in agreement with, or in opposition to, media and social scientists, mobilized and tried, as much as they could, to influence the debate and rally public opinion and legislators behind their cause. At this point, an examination must be undertaken of some of the social actors who influenced the debate.

2 'We Can't Afford to Take a Neutral Position': Interest Groups and Marijuana Use

Speaking before the Empire Club in 1969, James P. Mackey, chief of the Metropolitan Toronto Police Department, declared that he could not 'afford to take a neutral position' on the drug issue, and even less so could his public.[1] These words accurately distil the motivations of certain interest groups in the media-fuelled debate on drug use.

Interest groups wish to shape public opinion, of course, but they are still more interested in reaching the ears of politicians, because, after all, they are the ones to implement or amend public policies. As Kingdon and especially Lemieux note, the study of public policy is not only about the development of new policies to address particular issues but also about the absence of such policies or the government's refusal to proceed.[2] The choice of doing something or nothing is a complex process because of internal and external constraints on the state as well as of interventions by social actors.[3] In his work on the development and implementation of public policies, Lemieux demonstrates that their inherent complexity is due to the intervention of different social actors in the process. Outside governmental circles, there are those that Lemieux refers to as 'interested parties' – organized groups such as professional, scientific, and cultural associations, and so on, and 'private individuals' – the population in general. This chapter focuses on interested parties or interest groups. Each of these has had the capacity to mobilize, access, and influence centres of decision-making that have varied according to its available human and financial resources, its symbolic capital, and its ability to sustain action, organized or not, over a period of time. A final important factor about interest groups in general is their capacity to create strategic or incidental alliances with other social actors, resulting in the creation of coalitions based on a common interest. To summarize Hunt's expression, any social issue has a probable 'umbrella effect' because it sets the stage for the creation of alliances between interested parties that sometimes have divergent ideological interests but nevertheless join with one another on specific issues.[4] This certainly characterizes the drug debate in the 1960s and early 1970s in Canada.

The capacity for interest groups to convey their views and exert influence on public opinion, on other social actors, and on officials (elected or not) varies, because their actions are limited. For example, the interest groups who supported a change of status for marijuana in the Narcotic Control Act, even to the point of legalization, proposed an alternative social construction of the drug phenomenon: illegal drug use was not a vice, nor a sign of delinquency or deviance, and even less a criminal act. Following the example set by reformers at the beginning of twentieth century, they pressured the state to re-evaluate what seemed to them intolerable, illogical, and inadequate prohibitions. Quickly, however, they noticed that they were testing the limits of social tolerance and were encountering resistance and opposition from other interest groups. Their opponents' arguments – that recreational drug use undermined the work ethic, provided an escape from social reality, and risked making antisocial behaviour fashionable – were often similar to those that had successfully led to the criminalization of opium and marijuana at the beginning of the twentieth century. The main challenge for all these interest groups, whatever their particular views, was to transform their agenda into public policy. To achieve this goal, they aimed to influence politicians (the legislators who would ultimately determine the status of different drugs) on the drug issue.

Interest groups do not have unlimited reach. To summarize Foucault's thoughts on the concept of power, an interest group's reach is evident and can be measured in the context of interactions and interrelations with other powers or micro-powers.[5] As Valverde demonstrates in her analysis of social regulation movements in Canada at the end of the nineteenth century, 'the state has no monopoly on moral regulation, and private organizations – notably, the medical and legal professions and the philanthropic groups – have exercised crucial leadership in the regulatory field.'[6] In the context of the 1960s and the counterculture movement, four groups came to play a role in the drug debate, arguing that they were claim-makers since they had something to gain or lose. They were the players who influenced the debate and pressed the state to liberalize or preserve the status quo on drug legislation.

Young people formed the first of these interest groups. This is evidently a very broad category, and so I have decided to highlight students – in particular university student associations – since they would be the most vocal in questioning the factors that led to the inclusion of marijuana in the Narcotic Control Act. They were also significant because their voice was heard before and during the Le Dain Commission in the form of letters to politicians, and briefs submitted, and in the organization of a pan-Canadian referendum on the marijuana issue. Finally, students are noteworthy because they often defined themselves as the voice of their generation. Either by making statements or by smoking marijuana, young people provoked reactions from other groups, such as police forces and educational institutions.

Law-enforcement officers constituted the second significant group. They had to enforce the anti-drug legislation included in the Food and Drugs Act and the Narcotic Control Act. In an environment where the moral values behind the criminalization of certain drugs were being challenged, law-enforcement officers would take the position that society was under siege.

The last two interest groups were in the health domain. First, I will examine what may be called the medical establishment, principally the Canadian Medical Association (CMA). The CMA became a privileged group with the federal government and, naturally, with the Le Dain Commission. However, on the marijuana issue, it had difficulties reaching an internal consensus. The last group was the pharmaceutical industry, which intervened in the debate by creating the Council on Drug Abuse (CODA). Not only did this initiative reflect the desire to enlist the corporate world in a campaign against illegal drug use, but it also testified to a strong impulse to safeguard the control that the pharmaceutical industry enjoyed over manufactured drugs. CODA also attempted to confer scientific legitimacy on those who defined recreational drug use as a social and health danger, and thus it became an entity that challenged the expertise of the CMA.

On Behalf of the Youth Generation: University Students

In the 1960s recreational drug use was dropped into the ferment of other social issues. Media reports noticed the emergence of a new social and cultural phenomenon: the consumption of marijuana, other hallucinogens, and psychotropic drugs for recreational purposes. In addition, the media focused on one particular group: young people.

The drug scene had changed, since recreational drugs were no longer linked to specific subcultures and groups such as artists and writers, or certain ethnic groups such as blacks and Mexicans. Gradually, society woke up to the phenomenon of marijuana use, which eventually became a social practice to which political meaning had been attached. To summarize Burnham's observations, the bourgeoisification of drug taking – the fact that young people from the middle class took drugs – aroused both discussion and fear.[7] By smoking marijuana in public places and denouncing its criminalization, its proponents, including many young people, challenged social values. They furthermore succeeded in forcing a public debate on drug legislation, especially in questioning the reasons which had first led the state to class marijuana as illegal. In this role, young people were perceived as the spokespeople of the baby boom generation. They even received official public recognition with their choice as 'Man of the Year' by *Time* magazine in 1967. This vague social category, without neither gender, ethnic, or class difference, aroused curiosity and provoked harsh criticism.

Gastown in Vancouver, the carré Saint-Louis in Montreal, or Yorkville in Toronto were places where young people (in particular those who became proponents of the counterculture movement) gathered. These neighbourhoods became epicentres of the public debate on recreational drug use. In fact, many observers formed their understanding of recreational drug use and the new generation by visiting such places. Toronto is an illuminating starting point, since it has been better documented.

The Yorkville district attracted young people, but exactly why did they go there? In the 1950s, the City of Toronto re-zoned Yorkville (the area comprising Cumberland and Yorkville Streets between Bay Street and Avenue Road) for commercial use. This meant that upscale boutiques and restaurants would come to be established in the neighbourhood's renovated old houses. At the same time, artists and musicians started to move to Yorkville because of newly opened coffee-houses, and crowds flocked to hear their favourite singers and musicians. Over time, Yorkville thus became the visible manifestation of the counterculture movement, since it was the place to go in Toronto if one wanted to drop out of society. The area provided a gathering place whence hippies, university students, and other supporters of the countercultural movement could challenge the established values, such as social conservatism and materialism, embodied by the political and economic elites. It was also a place where one could defy those in power as well as those who enforced the law, in this case, mainly the Toronto police force. In short, Yorkville was where youth, university students, hippies, and artists clashed with the 'establishment.'[8]

Relations between business owners and young people, hippies and counterculture proponents, soured over the years. Merchants complained to Toronto city officials that counterculture supporters discouraged customers from frequenting the neighbourhood, and would consequently affect their commercial activities. Although the media and municipal politicians focused exclusively on hippies due to their high visibility (through their particular clothing and behaviour), in fact a variety of groups frequented the neighbourhood. This was revealed in a 1968 study based on a sociological observation of Yorkville over a period of six months. Its authors identified four distinct groups. Other than hippies (who were, in fact, a minority in the area), there were members of motorcycle clubs, as well as 'greasers' and 'weekenders.' These groups constituted the disparate population of this Toronto neighbourhood.[9]

From 1966 to 1968, municipal politicians and the media targeted Yorkville. For instance, in 1968 there was a hepatitis scare, and hippies were singled out as the cause. Newspapers, notably the *Toronto Telegram*, encouraged the fear of many restaurant owners that customers would avoid their area because of the health risk. A year before, the newspaper described Yorkville as a 'cancer that is spreading through Metro as more teenagers crowd in from around the nation.'[10] Allan Lamport, a city councillor who had been Toronto's mayor from 1952 to 1954, had no sympathy for hippies and their values. He convinced city council to chase the hippies away because, he argued, their presence would inhibit commercial activity. According to him, hippies constituted a threat to law and order, simply because many citizens went to Yorkville to look at these people whose habits and customs contrasted with the social norm. As part of the campaign to displace hippies, rooming houses and coffee-houses were inspected and police forces became visible in the area. In August 1967 there were numerous clashes between the police and hippies.[11]

Besides youth gatherings, young people expressed themselves by other means in the public domain. Students, especially those attending universities, defined themselves as the spokespeople of youth, and advocated change that would hopefully lead to a socio-cultural revolution. Their voice was expressed in multiple ways, one of which was the student university press. For instance, on 30 January 1969 the York

University student newspaper *Excalibur* pleaded for the legalization of marijuana. With its title 'End Hypocrisy: Legalize Marijuana,' the editorial denounced what it called the social hypocrisy surrounding the debate on recreational drug use. It dismissed the arguments advanced by opponents of legalized marijuana by reminding its readers that, 'since the use of marijuana is not more dangerous for the individual or for society than the use of cigarettes, alcohol, or sex, we cannot reach any other conclusion but to legalize its use and consequently its distribution.' On the other hand, it argued, controls were required for other drugs, such as hallucinogens.

Students organized meetings, conferences, and other activities to provoke debate on recreational drug use, such as the Loyola Conference on Student Use and Abuse of Drugs, held by the Canadian Student Affairs Association in November 1968, and the Fifth Annual Social Science Conference, which dealt with drugs and was sponsored by the University of Winnipeg Students' Association in February 1969. In February 1967 one of these events caught the media's attention when University of Toronto students organized Perception '67, a psychedelic symposium. They invited well-known American icons of the counterculture movement, such as poet Allen Ginsberg, Richard Alpert, and Timothy Leary, the former Harvard University professor who had become the 'high priest of LSD.' Leary's presence was assured by financial support from the University College Literary and Athletic Society and the CTV television network. These efforts were in vain: Leary was unable to attend the two-day symposium because the Department of Immigration refused to allow him to enter Canada, citing his conviction for trafficking in marijuana. The fact that Leary was barred from attending the symposium by no means saddened former Toronto mayor Philip Givens and certain Toronto media. The *Toronto Daily Star* applauded the decision of the Department of Immigration. Its editorial asserted that Leary could not come to Canada because there was 'the possibility of real harm, and even tragedy, if Dr. Leary induces some of his hearers to experiment with LSD.' 'His proposed visit,' stated the editorial, 'carries a genuine element of danger to the community.' Freedom of expression was thus subordinated to the perceived social risk that Leary represented.[12] Moreover, the University College principal had informed the organizers of the symposium that, because of his favourable views on LSD, Leary would be prevented from speaking. However, Leary made an appearance on tape and repeated his famous expression: 'Drop out, turn on, tune in.'[13] Besides concerts (including a performance by the rock group The Fugs), lectures, and seminars on LSD use and the legalization of marijuana, organizers of Perception '67 proposed a psychedelic journey or a 'mind excursion' by Toronto artist Michael Hayden, intended to 'simulat[e] psychedelic experiences.' This 'mind excursion' was created by 'electronic music, strobe lights, suggestive aromas and specially-produced films.' Thus, 'feelings of disorientation, fear, calm and sensuality [were created] in those who [took] the excursion.'[14] This experience earned the praises of *Toronto Daily Star* journalist Robert Fulford.[15] In the wake of the success of Perception '67, further conferences on drugs were organized at the University of Toronto in subsequent years.

University students also used more formal means to publicize their demands. On one occasion, 5500 students and professors from the University of Toronto and York University signed a petition urging the legalization of marijuana.[16] Student associations, such as the General Congress of the Canadian Union of Students and the Council of York Student Federation, adopted resolutions for the legalization of marijuana in 1968 and in November 1969, respectively.[17] Others communicated their positions directly to politicians. The Student Council of the University of Western Ontario supported the decriminalization of marijuana and denounced those who claimed the consumption of marijuana created dependence and pulled the user inevitably toward hard drugs. The Council also argued against the arbitrary repression of drug users, noting that 'enforcement is often unequal in big cities, professional men being more exempt.'[18] For its part, the student council of Humberside Collegiate favoured education as the best approach to make young people exercise judgment with drug use. It even suggested that Ontario Premier John Robarts consider entrusting the sale of marijuana to a provincial body, on the example of the sale of alcohol.[19] Finally, a pan-Canadian referendum was organized in Canadian universities in October 1970. Out of a possible forty-three, the sixteen university campuses that participated approved the legalization of marijuana (with the exception of Mount St Vincent University). No French-language university participated, and in Ontario only Carleton University and Waterloo Luthern University took part in the referendum.[20]

This student activism demonstrated significant efforts to offer a different construction of recreational drug use. The presence of students in Gastown, carré Saint-Louis, or Yorkville, or the efforts deployed by student associations in sending letters and organizing conferences, were aimed at excluding marijuana consumption from the definition of drug abuse. In this way, smoking marijuana became a challenge to the

> ## Over 2500 people have signed the Petition to Legalize Marijuana. If you haven't signed yet, don't wait! -There are only two days left!!! You can sign it at the tables in Sidney Smith Hall, The Buttery (Trinity), the Coop (SMC) and the Refectory (UC) anytime from 11 am to 2 pm. There are tables at both Erindale and Scarborough Colleges.

Source: *The Varsity*, 15 October 1969, 14

medical establishment. Young people disputed medical opinion by systematically attacking the arguments put forward by some physicians that were used to justify repression. These young people questioned the dire health effects of marijuana on its users. In fact, they declared quite the opposite, arguing that marijuana had no dangerous health impact at all. And even if it had any effects, these were no more dangerous than those of alcohol or cigarettes, drugs accepted by a large segment of society, as Carleton University students reminded the National Health and Welfare minister, John Munro, in 1970.[21] Students also questioned the addictive nature of marijuana and rejected the assertion that its consumption inevitably caused experimentation with other substances, notably hard drugs such as heroin.

Smoking marijuana also constituted an act of political defiance. Students challenged the state's punitive legislative approach to deter people from using drugs without proper medical supervision, an approach that also reduced the availability (by limiting the supply) of illegal drugs. The fear of being arrested and sent to jail was certainly a disincentive, but in the context of the 1960s and of the counterculture movement, state policy had become ineffective. In short, young people questioned the rationale that led to the classification of marijuana as an illegal drug, and argued for its legalization, since the law had lost its deterrent effect.

Marijuana use was also a rebellious gesture. Some students smoked pot as a symbolic rejection of mainstream values that defined what proper social behaviour was. They did it to shock their parents and anyone in position of authority, since adolescents gained satisfaction from doing the opposite of what was expected from them. They also denounced attempts by adults to educate youth about illegal drug use. They criticized the moralizing tone of this education and its lack of credibility, especially concerning the apparently devastating consequences on users' health.

In their arguments, young people identified numerous positive aspects of marijuana consumption. According to them, marijuana use induced positive feelings, since it helped its users to explore their subconscious minds and become better individuals, more loving and less aggressive. It also facilitated the socialization process because it was often consumed in the company of friends. Since it was a social activity, it helped to form bonds between people. It also had a ritualistic aspect. As mentioned by Owram in his study on baby boomers, the first experiences of marijuana use sometimes took place in closed, secure environments: 'The door was locked, and a towel might be stuffed under it in the vain attempt to prevent the smells from escaping. Incense was often burned, both to mask smells and as part of the ritual.'[22]

In any case, it should be noted that the voice of students in the debate varied. There was in fact no unanimity, contrary to the perception that the university student lobby wished to create. For example, in Oshawa, Ontario, the Durham College of Applied Arts and Technology student newspaper was hostile to a softening of the federal drug legislation on marijuana. As the editor wrote: 'I don't see how our society could function if about one-tenth of it were constantly high, and then three-quarters of our population spent a certain percentage of their day in the same condition. Add to this the number of hippies, tramps, and alcoholics that already are liabilities to our country, and our problems would skyrocket.'[23] The authors of a 1968 study on drug consumption in Quebec schools demonstrated that 76 per cent of students were of the opinion that marijuana and LSD use, or glue sniffing, were not dangerous. Despite this, they still wanted the legal repression of these drugs to remain in effect. In fact, 72 per cent of the study's 8518 students judged that drug laws were not severe enough. Unfortunately, the study did not clarify what 'severe enough' meant.[24]

For their part, parents, school board trustees, and sometimes teachers and school principals pressed school authorities to implement appropriate policies in order to deal with recreational drug use. In 1970, Elizabeth White, on behalf of the North Toronto Committee Concerned About Youth, informed the Toronto Board of Education that Toronto high school students 'can put [their] order in at nine [a.m.] and get [their] drugs at four [p.m.] in any collegiate.'[25] To those who were already anxious about the drug phenomenon, White's comments offered no reassurance. Such social actors demanded action, but also recognized that their means were limited, since only the federal government could liberalize the status of marijuana, maintain the status quo, or increase the repressive effects of law enforcement. How did schools, school boards, and provincial education authorities react? Let us concentrate on the cases of Ontario and Quebec.

Starting in 1966, the Ontario Department of Education issued curriculum guidelines, developed in collaboration with ARF, that required teachers from grade 10 to 12 to address alcohol and other drugs within the health education program. The basic philosophy was 'to outline to the student the value of certain chemicals when used properly, and to outline the nature of dependency that might arise when they are used improperly.' In 1971 the department justified its philosophy in terms of teaching young people to become responsible for their physical development and the choices made to that end. In short, it was necessary to educate students so they could make informed, responsible decisions about drug use.[26]

However, school boards were free to choose their own implementation strategies for drug education programs. As well, the objectives of school boards themselves varied. Some, like the Waterloo County Roman Catholic Separate School Board, wished 'to assist youngsters in developing attitudes and gaining knowledge which will help them make informed decisions, hopefully leading to abstinence from any form of drug abuse.' Others, such as the Stormont, Dundas and Glengarry County Board of Education, tried to furnish 'reliable information' about drug use and abuse to help students acquire 'a healthy understanding of human development.'[27] Although boards were free to adapt the department's guidelines according to their values and needs, few of them rushed to create a drug education program. By 1971, provincial education officials still did not know the number of school boards that had created alcohol and drug education programs.[28]

In Quebec, the Department of Education was initially taken by surprise by the drug phenomenon. It eventually invited school boards to formulate internal regulations and develop education programs about illegal drug use, although any such initiatives required the department's approval.[29] For instance, beginning in 1970 the Commission scolaire des écoles catholiques de Montréal (CECM – the Montreal Catholic School Board) set up an educational program on drug use. This was done in collaboration with the Office for the Prevention and Treatment of Alcoholism and Other Toxicomanias (OPTAT), the Quebec state institution created in 1966. The drug prevention program led to the publication of a document, *Trouver le Joint* (Find the Joint), which was distributed to its teaching personnel in 1973. According to school board officials, 'This document is inspired by a preventive educational philosophy and by a sensitization of adults [teachers and parents] rather than direct intervention with students.'[30] The objective of the document was to reject repression as an approach, even if a board by-law prohibited the possession of illegal drugs in schools, and it invited principals to take 'all measures which are imperative, while respecting individual rights, and taking into account the gravity of situations.'[31] It was necessary that the educators explain, without making moral judgments, the dangers to 'the physical and mental health of children and teenagers' of any 'licit or illegal' drug not supervised by a physician. Educators were also encouraged to suggest that drug abuse was 'the indication or the symptom of a social or individual illness.' It was necessary to teach 'the necessity of, and respect for, the law' in bringing the young person 'to make an enlightened personal decision ... on drugs.'[32]

The CECM initiative was badly received by the Department of Education. Invited to evaluate the document, a provincial government official denounced its moralizing tone, its lack of scientific information, as well as the lack of effort to understand the realities of young people and the counterculture. He criticized the definition of drug abuse that was restricted to drugs used with no medical supervision. The authors of the CECM document forgot, according to this civil servant, that other drugs, such as alcohol, cigarettes, and those prescribed by a physician, could also lead to abuse and dependence. Among other statements, the government official found the following advice inappropriate: '[D]rugs will only ever be crutches. Some can be useful for handicapped persons. But a man who knows how to walk does not need a crutch.'[33]

The CECM document also drew a negative reaction from members of the Interministerial Committee on Drug Addiction, formed by the

Quebec government in 1972. During a discussion, described in the minutes as 'vigorous,' the members criticized the overly 'moralizing and paternalistic' tone of the document. They noted that the document displayed an ignorance of the youth milieu, its values, motivations, and aspirations.[34]

When CECM officials attended a meeting of the Interministerial Committee in February 1974, they mentioned that certain schools in their school board had hired security personnel to combat drug use. However, they also conceded that the number of these guards had decreased.[35] The presence of security personnel represented a problem, according to the members of the Interministerial Committee, because it ran counter to the education department's goal of diffusing 'objective' information. This entailed not alarming or threatening students, but rather creating activities to stimulate a dialogue on the drug issue, and properly training teachers and other school personnel, while also including disciplinary measures. The question of how to enforce disciplinary measures remained. At the time, no answers were offered, but the hiring of security officers was roundly criticized. As the committee chair observed, security officers in schools would 'cause the atmosphere to deteriorate more and could even produce results contrary to those which we are trying to obtain.'[36] In the end, the department left the responsibility of determining appropriate drug-related penalties to individual school boards.

The question of disciplinary measures led to the submission of an action plan to the Interministerial Committee in 1975. This plan reflected the intentions of the federal government to transfer marijuana from the Narcotic Control Act to the Food and Drugs Act, an issue that will be discussed in the last chapter. The action plan urged school boards to avoid resorting to police forces as a means of repression. At the same time, it encouraged the police to adapt their intervention techniques on school premises when their presence was required. The plan recommended avoiding sending young people to prison for simple possession of marijuana, for the reason that 'as long as there is no victim, there should be no police intervention.'[37] Consequently, the police would proceed to make arrests in school only if they obtained the permission of school officials. In the case of young people in possession of marijuana or small pushers 'who distribute[d] without receiving money,' these young people were not to be targeted. The authors of the action plan considered the educational approach preferable to repression in these specific cases. Legal repression was, however, acceptable in the case of dealers who operated in schools and were associated with organized crime. The following attitude underlay these recommendations: 'To the degree that a student who consumes drugs is aware of the dangers he may encounter and when this decision involves only himself, judicial intervention is not necessary.'[38]

Elsewhere in Quebec, school boards mobilized school personnel, psychotherapists, and resources provided by OPTAT in the fight against drugs by means of consciousness-raising and prevention campaigns.[39] For its part, the Committee on Drug Abuse of the Montreal Protestant School Board developed an educational program for youth based on a 'non-moralizing' and fact-based approach. At the same time, it was necessary to increase extracurricular resources, notably counselling services. Finally, disseminating information was a task shared by teachers, parents, and students.[40]

What were these initiatives able to achieve? The CECM officials offered a cautious answer: 'There is still some ignorance, anxiety and panic.' According to them, the program would not 'produce miracles.' In fact, 'several years will be needed before attitudes will change.'[41] By 1974, CECM officials recognized that recreational drug use was no longer the most important issue. Instead, alcohol consumption and behavioural problems in schools had become priorities.[42] On the one hand, this observation was similar to opinions expressed by other specialists, for many noted that marijuana and other illegal drug use had disappeared from the radar screens of the media and the politicians. On the other hand, it also reflected the fact that parents were reassured by the implementation of a drug education program and they could now move on to deal with other issues.

Post-secondary institutions did not rush to adopt regulations on illegal drug use on their premises. The Université de Montréal, for instance, had no particular regulations. Conversely, according to the University of Toronto student paper *The Varsity*, students who used illegal drugs were expelled.[43] York University had no regulations: every case was individually studied, which not surprisingly, led to certain inconsistencies. Initially, at least according to its president, the York University administration adopted a hard line. During the 1967–8 academic year, four students were expelled from the university for possession of illegal drugs. During the fall of 1968, the administration changed tactics, partially because society, according to York president Murray Ross, was more lenient toward marijuana users. In the fall semester, three students were found smoking marijuana. Each of them had to pay a $25 fine and was 'placed on probation for the remainder of the year.' The next winter, eleven students were arrested for possession of drugs other than marijuana, and the administration gave them a choice: follow a treatment program or be expelled.[44]

York University's situation was not unique in Ontario, as M.B. Dymond, Ontario Minister of Health, acknowledged when questioned by Premier John Robarts. Dymond indicated that marijuana use on university campuses was a reality, although it was difficult to quantify due to a lack of specific studies, as mentioned in the previous chapter. He also noted that most universities had not adopted regulations on drug use. In the absence of specific policies, university administrators had opted for a case-by-case approach. In the health minister's opinion, this way of dealing with the drug phenomenon did nothing to improve relations between university administrations and students. Because students denounced the absence of truly democratic structures within which they could present their demands, the approach taken by administrators to deal with illegal drug use created the appearance of arbitrary power, feeding the image of anti-democratic institutions that were not interested in including students in their administration. The minister wondered who 'within the institution ... shall formulate policies and rules? Who shall deal with infractions of its policies and rules? Is it legitimate for university rules to be made by administration and faculty without consent of the governed – the students?'[45]

In Quebec, some CEGEPs adopted guidelines, but these remained without 'regulatory force' as 'they were not produced by resolution of the Board of Directors.'[46] Besides, administrators at several CEGEPs preferred to help students arrested for possession of an illegal drug rather than to punish them. In association with OPTAT, a number of CEGEPs distributed educational material, and in other cases OPTAT personnel participated in increasing teachers' awareness of the drug phenomenon. Gradually, as in the high schools, illegal drug use by CEGEP students became less of a concern; by 1974, binge drinking was the focus of administrators' efforts. As the Interministerial Committee was informed: 'Certain beer manufacturers gave trophies or supplied sports equipment. In return, CEGEP organizations offered a "big party" identified with a beer brand.'[47]

Recreational drug use put students in the spotlight. On the one hand, some played a proactive, leadership role in the construction of this phenomenon by insisting that the state legalize marijuana and review its classification of other drugs. On the other hand, the fact that drug use was associated with young people obliged educational institutions to react, often under pressure from interest groups. These interest groups, however, were rejected by young people as challenging their construction of the drug issue. Among the groups denounced were police forces.

Police and Illegal Drug Use: 'The Floodgates Should Never Be Let Open'[48]

The consumption of illegal drugs by the population in general – and by young people in particular – was bound to involve police forces, because some of them had the responsibility of enforcing drug legislation. However, newspapers occasionally reported comments by municipal police chiefs that revealed a lack of consensus. For example, in reaction to a 1968 statement concerning reduced penalties for marijuana possession by National Health and Welfare Minister John Munro to members of the Canadian Pharmaceutical Association, Vancouver Police Chief Ralph Booth observed that he would be able to adapt to the change proposed by the minister 'in certain situations.' Winnipeg's police chief believed that marijuana should be removed from the Narcotic Control Act. James P. Mackey, Metropolitan Toronto Police Chief and head of the Canadian Association of Chiefs of Police for 1965–6, was at the opposite end of the spectrum, as he categorically rejected this suggestion.[49] Mackey had an opportunity to explain his position to the members of the Empire Club of Toronto in 1969. He strongly opposed the legalization of marijuana and pleaded for caution as to whether the state should opt for its decriminalization, as studies on the health consequences were incomplete and sometimes contradictory. At the Empire Club, Chief Mackey depicted a worrisome situation. He argued that marijuana was a problem affecting young people, and in particular schools, which had been overrun by drug use. Furthermore, young people were badly informed. According to Mackey, 'the youth of this country, and some adults, are being *misled* in the use of drugs, and we should do everything in our power to prevent their indiscriminate use.' Faced with this reality, it was necessary to take a position. Naturally, he invited his audience to adopt his views, because marijuana was dangerous for the health of its users, led to the use of hard drugs, and constituted a 'disruption of family ties.' In short, marijuana had no practical use except when prescribed by physicians.[50] In 1971, his successor,

Chief Harold Adamson, expressed his own opposition to the legalization of marijuana.[51] A year later, Adamson successfully convinced the members of the Ontario Association of Chiefs of Police to support a resolution opposing any liberalization of marijuana laws.[52]

These reactions by police chiefs contrast with the actions of their national organization, the Canadian Association of Chiefs of Police (CACP).[53] Judging by the resolution passed at its annual meetings between 1965 and 1975, as well as articles published in its bulletin, recreational drug use and the legalization of marijuana were not issues that preoccupied the CACP. The 1968 annual meeting did, however, unanimously adopt a resolution opposed to the removal of cannabis from the Narcotic Control Act, a resolution repeated in 1970, and again in 1972. Among the reasons given was the absence of a clear social consensus on legalization. There was also the argument that marijuana use led to stronger, hard drugs. Finally, marijuana consumption had a demoralizing effect 'on the individual's cleanliness and morals.'[54] In 1973, the CACP displayed a certain flexibility in the case of individuals 'addicted to non-medical use of drugs,' in that it recognized the limits of the repressive approach in dealing with them. Instead of a police-enforced punitive approach, the federal government should be responsible for the 'compulsory medical-social institutionalization of such persons.'[55] It should be noted that the CACP did not present a brief to the Le Dain Commission.

The safety of police officers, juvenile delinquency, and capital punishment were the issues that preoccupied CACP members when they gathered at their annual meetings. These priorities are also evident from the annual reports of the Commissioner of the Ontario Provincial Police, the OPP bulletin distributed to police officers, and *La Police*, the magazine of the Montreal police force. The non-medical use of drugs had a comparatively low priority for these organizations.

This situation seems surprising, because police officers, especially in the three large metropolitan centres, were continually confronted with hippies and drug users. How does one explain this lack of activism? A collective lack of expertise in the field of drug enforcement among the CACP, OPP, and the Sûreté du Québec is the most likely explanation. It should be noted that few provincial and municipal forces had narcotics squads in the sixties. It was only in 1972 that the Montreal police, and a year later the OPP (with thirty-four officers), formed anti-drug units.[56] In the case of the OPP, a squad was created because the Royal Canadian Mounted Police (RCMP) had abandoned this task in Ontario. In fact, this was part of a larger downloading policy of RCMP responsibilities to the OPP that had begun, in 1961, with the policing of small craft on rivers and lakes, followed by enforcement of anti-counterfeiting laws, and then enforcement of drug legislation.[57] In other Canadian cities, such as Vancouver and Toronto, municipal narcotic squads worked with the RCMP. In fact, until the beginning of the 1970s, the RCMP was responsible for enforcing the prohibitions against the possession, trafficking, importation, and cultivation of illegal drugs as defined in the Food and Drugs Act and the Narcotic Control Act. In fact, police forces were content to allow the RCMP to speak for them in the drug debate.[58]

Even if recreational drug use occupied a relatively modest place in the concerns of the CACP, the organization felt it had an important voice in the public life of the country. This conviction was based both on its belief that it served an essential role in society, and on its range of influence. After all, to cite Max Weber, the state has a monopoly over the legitimate use of physical force, and police forces exercise part of this monopoly. As enforcers of the monopoly over the legitimate use of physical force, police chiefs were of the opinion that this role in turn conferred authority on their interventions with municipal, provincial, and federal decision-makers. For example, annual meetings with federal mandarins, the minister of justice, and the solicitor general were a source of pride to the CACP. To fail to consider the organization's advice and positions was seen as an insult, as the minutes from the 1974 meeting between CACP officials and bureaucrats from the solicitor general's department reveal. CACP officials emphasized that 'the Police are acting in the interest of society and that the Police [force] is actually the only one that has the "eye to eye contact with the public."'[59] The CACP believed that its briefs and letters carried more weight than anything submitted by other interest groups, because it alone knew what happened on the streets and the challenges associated with law enforcement.

This authoritative argument, based on the idea that knowledge resulting from the 'cold hard facts of life' was superior to 'hard scientific evidence,' underpinned the 1972 CACP document on illegal drugs.[60] Entitled 'CACP Position Paper on Soft Drugs,' the document dismantled the arguments put forward by marijuana proponents. First, it argued that any drug consumed for non-medical purposes constituted an abuse. The document then emphasized the dangers of marijuana and criticized those who believed that the effects of marijuana were similar to those of socially accepted drugs such as tobacco and alcohol. The document reminded its readers that marijuana affected the brain. It referred to the British medical journal *The Lancet*, specifically its affirmation that 'heavy users of cannabis show evidence of cerebral atrophy which is a wasting away of portions of the brain.'[61] The CACP paper mentioned that marijuana use impaired activity, as opposed to tobacco, whose users could 'go about other activities with minimal danger to others.' Furthermore, marijuana use affected 'the emotional and mental responses to the point of producing feelings of omnipotence.'[62] In addition, unlike alcohol and tobacco, marijuana led to other chemical or hard drugs, as well as to violence and dealings with the criminal underworld. Tobacco and alcohol, by contrast, typically 'involve[d] petty crime and leave the individual relatively unmarked.'[63] Similarly to the RCMP, the CACP believed in the usefulness of law enforcement. Taking the view that police forces were besieged and that society had become permissive due to the action of the pro-marijuana lobby (which, concluded the CACP, reflected the views of a minority and not those of society as a whole), the CACP opposed any legislative change. The organization feared that any legislative amendment would open a breach that would trigger the total collapse of a legal edifice set up over the years to regulate drugs. 'As there will always be the bootlegger, there will always be clandestine dope, but the floodgates should never be let open.'[64] The CACP particularly feared that a legislative change would trigger a process that would nullify the enforcement work done by police officers.[65]

CACP's influence had certain limits, as revealed by the issue of glue-sniffing. Worried about this practice among young people, the 1969 CACP annual meeting adopted a resolution asking the federal government to make the act an offence under the Food and Drugs Act and the Juvenile Delinquents Act. In letters sent in December 1969, the national health and welfare minister and the solicitor general rejected the CACP's resolution. They wrote that the solution proposed was inadequate. Education of children and their parents, wrote the solicitor general, was a preferable solution to the arrest and jailing of young people. Another option was to encourage glue producers to include a chemical substance in their product to discourage sniffing.[66]

In spite of CACP's limited number of interventions on the drug question per se, the drug phenomenon highlighted one particular issue that preoccupied police forces. Many in the police community believed that society had become too lenient toward drug use and that police interventions aroused criticism and sometimes even condemnation, especially by youth. In 1969, the deputy solicitor general revealed that 77 per cent of those convicted for marijuana offences in 1967 were under twenty-four years of age.[67] In Toronto, young people insisted that they were being specifically targeted. Toronto Police Chief Harold Adamson, whose comments were reproduced in the *Globe and Mail*, confirmed as much to a city resident. He was 'not concerned with the middle-aged man who in the privacy of his own home smokes pot.'[68] Rather, he admitted, he was more worried by young people. 'Our experience indicates that the majority of young persons who use marijuana also experiment with other drugs, resulting in serious consequences. Likewise our experience indicates that the more mature persons using marijuana do not go on to taking other drugs.' In short, Toronto police did target young people. Adamson stated further: 'Middle-aged people, in my mind, are those over 40 years of age, and I might add that we are as interested in prosecuting violations of the drug laws in this age group as in any other, but our concern is not as great with them as it is for the inexperienced and impressionable youth.'[69] Specifically, youth-profiling guided police action at rock concerts, and it prompted young people to renew their complaints of being unfairly targeted. Rock concerts were 'the definitive gatherings of the countercultural faithful' by providing 'dope, nudity, sex, rock, [and] community.'[70] Further, listening to music under marijuana's influence made a difference 'to the type of music and the words,' said Ringo Starr.[71] Police forces targeted these concerts and attempted to block them, but defended themselves from any wrongdoing by arguing that they were only enforcing the Narcotic Control Act.

OPP officers demonstrated the validity of these complaints in their explanation of law enforcement at rock festivals. In anticipation of the 1970 rock festival at Dunmark Park in Ancaster Township, RCMP officers trained OPP agents. During their training session, the RCMP described young drug users as 'dirty and unkempt with long hair.' To enforce the Narcotic Control Act, OPP officers should look for such individuals but look also for other signs of drug use. 'A secretion from their nostrils might indicate they were on drugs. Watery eyes and the wearing of sun glasses unnecessarily, is another indication of drug use.' Although 'not all persons in these categories would be drug users,' the RCMP believed that 'they are accurate indicators.'[72]

Police officers noticed that they were operating in a world that had become critical of their enforcement work, especially when officers intervened among young people. A 1969 study on policing done with 967 Torontonians aged eighteen and over revealed the existence of a generational gap when respondents were asked to judge the police force. According to the study, 'younger members ... were more willing to attribute abuses of authority to the police' than older respondents.[73] One year later, about twenty young people found guilty of marijuana possession in Vancouver were interviewed for a study on their perception of police work and the judicial system. They criticized the work by police and declared that drug law-enforcement officers unfairly targeted people in their age group.[74]

Police officers duly noted the need to improve their image with the population in general, and in particular with young people. The discussions at the meeting of l'Association des chefs de police et pompiers de la province de Québec summarized the police chiefs' state of mind. The changing social context had brought new challenges to police forces, accompanied by a fear of change. It was therefore necessary to develop new strategies in order to improve the police's image, and in Quebec, these new strategies were built around the experiment of 'police educators' (Policier-éducateur). These officers worked with various youth organizations, social clubs, and specialists in drug addiction. The approach was not original; in fact, it already existed in the United States (Los Angeles Juvenile Officer), in the United Kingdom (Liverpool Juvenile Liaison Officer), and in France.[75]

The aim of the project was to change young people's perception of law enforcement officers. At the 1969 conference organized by the Association des chefs de police et pompiers de la province de Québec, participants were told that it was 'important that the image that young people have of police officers not be that of police quick to use their truncheons during a demonstration.'[76] In short, policemen had a duty to inform and educate young people and the public about the nature of their work: 'It is necessary that the young person [and the public] perceive the police officer as an understanding but firm guide.'[77] The success of this approach was predicated on the assumption that it would allow people to better understand the difficulties inherent in police work and make them aware 'of often contradictory requirements [of the public] towards the police.' Furthermore, '[t]hese contacts will prevent a gulf from developing between the police and society.'[78]

From January 1966, police-educator members of the Montreal police force visited elementary and secondary schools, established links with organizations that dealt with young people, and were deployed in certain neighbourhoods to get a better understanding of young people's reality. According to Claude Labelle of the Montreal Police Department, this police action aimed to modify the police's image 'as a figure of authority, invested with a particular power whose role is to help and to protect the rights of all.'[79] This initiative within the framework of the fight against juvenile delinquency included educational efforts on illegal drug use. However, this educational work was not free of a certain bias, as police officers were instructed to describe drugs, in Labelle's words, as 'a terrible habit and a vice that reduces teenagers to slavery.' Police officers would end their presentations by explaining drug legislation and the penalties associated with these 'terrible' habits.[80]

In 1969, the Montreal police force had more than 118 members who intervened with young people, mostly in the Montreal Catholic School Board. This experiment came to exist under slightly different guises in more than fifty cities in Quebec. For example, in Laval, a city on the north shore of Montreal Island, and in Sainte-Foy, a suburb of Quebec City, these police-educators were called youth officers.[81]

The strategy of police-educators did not, however, bring about the success that was hoped for. In 1974, Sûreté du Québec representatives voiced their doubts about the efficacy of this strategy before the Quebec Interministerial Committee on Drug Addiction and pointed out that former drug users were better educators than police-educators. The lack of success encountered by police-educators might explain the decision by the Sûreté du Québec not to intervene in any more schools and to allow them to deal with drug use internally. School representatives asserted, for their part, that the failures of the police-educators strategy were due to a deficiency in training. One school principal pointed out that a police-educator, in his work in elementary schools, should possess 'adequate training and the appropriate personality.'[82] Others indicated that police-educators, by appearing as authority figures in schools, immediately gave a negative impression, because they could not win the confidence of young people. 'All figures of authority,' said Montreal Catholic School Board officials, 'tend to be badly accepted by young people at present.'[83] Department of Education representatives therefore agreed that police officers 'should not go to schools.'[84]

In English-speaking provinces, police forces, inspired by similar experiences in Western Europe and in the United States, developed community-policing programs. This was the situation in Vancouver.[85] In Toronto, the Youth Bureau of the Metropolitan Toronto Police, formed in 1959, used police officers to work in communities, notably in places where young people gathered.[86] In 1967, policemen were assigned to communities, particularly the Yorkville area, and in 1971, this special force was reorganized as the Community Services Bureau. As in Quebec, these initiatives aimed to improve relations between police and the community, as well as improve the image of police in general. The initiative also had the advantage of selecting and training certain police officers to deal with youth and specific communities, such as those in housing projects. The mandate of these officers was to bring youth and housing community projects closer to the police. How was this to be done? According to Staff Sergeant George Shaw of the Community Services Bureau, police officers in the program 'set up sports activities ... and organized other youth-oriented programs, opening up a communication with the whole of their divisional communities.'[87]

Police officers were aware of their influence as representatives of law and order, but worried about their image in a changing world. They tried to improve their image by penetrating the youth milieu, but as far as drugs were concerned, the police were content to let the RCMP speak to politicians on their behalf. Police forces preferred to ally themselves with other groups opposed to the legalization of marijuana.

Although individual officers might have expressed a liberal point of view, as a group, police forces opposed the legalization of marijuana because of the medical unknowns, the belief that marijuana would lead to experimentation with other drugs, and the perception that society was too permissive and the time had come to draw the line. If the case of Quebec is a guide, the image-improving experiment was not successful. During this period of change and uncertainty, though, the CACP would find supporters among groups who shared similar fears about the changes that might be triggered by the decriminalization or legalization of marijuana.

Strong Statements in the Public Interest:
The Canadian Medical Association

Created in 1867, the Canadian Medical Association (CMA) was a federation of provincial associations. Occasionally, its interventions benefited from the support of its affiliates, such as the Canadian Psychiatric Association, and other health professional associations, such as the Canadian Pharmaceutical Association. The CMA was a leading interlocutor on the drug issue and had relatively easy access to federal health and welfare mandarins and ministers. For instance, in 1970, there was a joint committee on methadone and the treatment of narcotic addicts. However, its interventions took place in a context of heightened tensions, and sometimes even opposition to the provinces and particularly to the federal government.

During the 1960s the federal government developed new social programs, among them Medicare. The medical profession, whether it was through the provincial associations or the CMA, reacted negatively to a proposal that aimed to limit their control over the practice and delivery of health care services. In fact, the CMA made little effort to disguise its opposition to the issue, but clearly encountered the limits of its political influence, despite the fact that 'its primary means of obtaining policy concessions from either the provincial or [federal] governments [was] its monopoly of the skills required to operate any programme of health insurance.'[88] Nevertheless, the CMA found itself in competition with other social actors with different social and political agendas, as some of them defined access to health care services as a right, and not a privilege based on an individual's capacity to pay.[89] The CMA eventually had to reconcile itself to the fact that the Liberal government was resolved to forge ahead with its Medicare project.

Besides the Medicare controversy, the medical profession intervened on other social issues. One of them was inseparable from the sexual revolution: that of the decriminalization of abortion. The CMA supported the measure because it wished to protect its members from possible lawsuits, which were a danger so long as abortion remained a criminal offence. The CMA, however, also wished to maintain control over such medical procedures.[90]

The medical profession was also involved with another issue, that of cigarette smoking. As a result of studies in the 1970s that revealed the harmful effects of smoking, the CMA suggested to its members that in the interest of setting an example as health professionals, physicians should limit their cigarette consumption.[91] This concern about smoking became part of the marijuana debate among CMA members.

It was in this changed environment that the CMA intervened on the drug issue in general, and more particularly, voiced its opinion concerning drugs used for non-medical purposes. The CMA charged its Council on Community Health Care to prepare a report by taking into account the medical, social, and legal stakes involved with illegal drugs in order to formulate the CMA's position. This council, together with several others, replaced about forty committees set up over the years to assist the CMA in its evaluation of various medical and health questions.[92]

In 1969, the Sub-committee on the Misuse of Drugs of the Council on Community Health Care was chaired by Dr Lionel Solursh, a psychiatrist at Toronto Western Hospital and a professor of psychiatry at the University of Toronto. Thanks to his research on LSD, he was a recognized authority on drug use and abuse. The Sub-committee had a specific agenda. It elaborated a conceptual revolution, since it proposed a redefinition of the concept of drug abuse. As a starting point, it was necessary to use the expression 'misuse' instead of 'abuse' because the former was much more inclusive. 'The term "abuse,"' wrote Dr Unwin, a member of the Sub-committee, 'implies value judgments which at the present time are contentious, especially if "abuse" is held to mean any drug use without medical supervision.'[93] The proposed definition of misuse was 'the use of a substance beyond the generally accepted limits of medical therapy or the limitations imposed by current laws.'[94] By adopting this term, the Sub-committee could present the increased reliance on drugs to cure medical ills as a public health problem. This review came at a time when many believed that 'there is a pill for every ill.'[95] Consequently, it was necessary to promote in the public debate the idea that all drugs, regardless of their legal classification, had the potential to be misused, sometimes even with the complicity of the medical profession. As soon as the new definition of what constituted drug abuse was agreed upon, it would then be easier to revise the classification of drugs, and, in the case of drugs that would remain illegal, ensure that the punishment fit the crime.

By promoting a new definition of drug abuse, the Sub-committee tried to enlarge the domain under the control of physicians. By doing that, it meant to interfere with the pharmaceutical industry, which was not a new interest. At the beginning of the twentieth century, representatives from the pharmaceutical industry disagreed with physicians over state control of drug production. For the pharmaceutical industry, state intervention would limit its ability to manufacture and sell drugs, and physicians were not totally opposed to this. In the sixties, physicians, at least those on the Sub-committee, wanted to increase their control over drug use and promoted a greater awareness of the potential of drug abuse, which did not suit well with the pharmaceutical industry.[96]

Besides an appeal for a reclassification of drugs, the Sub-committee insisted upon the need to combat the simplistic vision of drug use presented by certain media and interest groups. Because of increased drug use in society, it was necessary to bring individuals to question their own reasons for consuming drugs and to encourage them to recognize that all drugs had a potential for misuse. Drug misuse was thus symptomatic of difficulties in managing one's personal situation, whether in family life or in society. Also, the Sub-committee felt that greater drug use could not be dissociated from the more prominent drug-marketing role played by the media.[97]

The Council on Community Health Care's report was submitted, along with the CMA interim brief, to the Le Dain Commission in 1969. What is striking is the reluctance of the CMA's board of directors to adopt some of the Council's proposals, notably the definition of what constituted drug abuse. In its interim brief to the Le Dain Commission, the CMA adopted a restrictive definition of drug abuse, since it referred essentially to those used for non-medical purposes, although it did include some references to alcohol and cigarette consumption. Regarding possible abuse of drugs prescribed by physicians and other health professionals, the interim brief stated that health professionals were the best ones to police themselves. It agreed with the Council's report, stressing the importance of pursuing research and educating young people – as well as the general public and health professionals – about the hazards of non-medical drug misuse. The brief went on to argue that the work done by police forces was necessary, because the state relied on a legal approach in order to regulate the use of certain drugs. In addition, the report argued that law enforcement should be allied with the medical profession, because in the case of chronic users, treatment, rather than judicial measures, might be more appropriate.[98]

Since the 'conceptual revolution' proposed by the Council on Community Health Care to CMA officials failed, as revealed by the content of the interim brief, the Council faced a tougher challenge when it dealt with the marijuana issue, which came to dominate the public debate on drug use. In fact, the marijuana issue exposed the divisions that plagued the CMA.

As early as 1969, the Council on Community Health Care document stated that there were still many unknowns surrounding the health consequences of marijuana. It warned that researchers were 'diametrically opposed and [offered] mutually contradictory interpretations of available information.'[99] Furthermore, research done until then contained numerous gaps, most significantly the fact that little research had been conducted on human beings. The document noted that the few experiments done involved 'prisoners, ex-opiate users, or long-term heavy cannabis [usually marijuana] users.'[100] It drew attention to the fact that the health effects of marijuana varied according to the dose, the frequency, and the user's characteristics.

Faced with so many unknowns and disagreements, the Council nevertheless submitted its views. The 1969 report referred to the conclusions of the 1968 report of the British Advisory Committee on Drug Dependence (the Wooton report) to the effect that marijuana, used moderately, did not entail fatal health consequences. 'In terms of physical harmfulness ..., cannabis is ... no more dangerous than alcohol.'[101] Nevertheless, caution was required, as the author of the 1969 Council report mentioned, not because of the health aspect, but because of the consequences for the public image and reputation of the CMA. Here the Council's report ceased to be scientific and became political: strategic considerations regarding this divisive issue began to take precedence. Because 'society ha[d] projected its anxieties, desires, or indignations' onto marijuana, the issue had taken on social, medical, legal, and symbolic implications.[102] Consequently, 'if one makes such a statement in public or even to many physicians, he will be accused of advocating the legalization of marijuana or of encouraging young people to indulge freely in this drug!'[103] The 1969 Council report came down firmly on the side of those opposed to legalization.

The report pleaded, nevertheless, for a softening of the penalties associated with marijuana; in its opinion, the punishment, at least in the case of possession for personal use, exceeded the crime. If the argument that the punishment should fit the crime failed to rally every CMA member, the report went on to state that in any case marijuana was not a narcotic. Regardless of any mild or serious health dangers associated with marijuana use, a legislative change was required. The Council report argued for the transfer of marijuana from the Narcotic Control Act to the Food and Drugs Act. The CMA adopted the recommendation of the 1969 Council report, and its official position did not change until 1974.[104]

The issue of the dangers marijuana posed to the health of its users appealed directly to the CMA's professional sense of responsibility. Could the CMA advocate marijuana use knowing that much was still unknown and that research was still incomplete? In its attempt to come to terms with the issue, the CMA openly revealed its divisions. This only served to undermine the organization's clout with governments and other interest groups intervening in the debate and limited the influence of its medical expertise in general.

These internal divisions first became visible within the CMA structures. At the 1971 General Assembly, the Council on Community Health Care submitted its recommendations to members. The first proposal, which argued that 'simple possession of any psychoactive drug should not be punishable by [a] jail sentence,' was supported by the delegates. The second, however, met with a different fate. This proposal reflected the efforts of the Council to widen the definition of drug abuse and especially educate the medical profession about the increasing use of drugs. It invited members to denounce drug advertisements in the media, notably those for alcohol and cigarettes. Here the members opted to postpone discussions. The very definition of drug misuse divided the CMA. On the one hand, members approved a resolution to the effect that 'the non-medical use of drugs is a serious and increasing threat,' adding that 'drug misuse even with the so-called softer drugs involves serious social and psychological dangers.' On the other hand, they adopted a resolution urging that use of any drug, 'botanical or chemical agent' whose effects were unknown should not be condoned by physicians, except for research purposes.[105]

During the 1972 General Assembly, the Sub-Committee on the Non-Medical Use of Drugs of the Council on Community Health Care submitted its resolution on recreational marijuana use. It recommended the liberalization of the repressive approach. CMA members, however, decided otherwise.

The Sub-committee took great care to demonstrate that its resolution was inspired by the conclusions of a report that examined the legal status of marijuana in the United States, and by the work of the Le Dain Commission. Based on the credibility of these studies, it hoped to receive the members' support. The Sub-committee pleaded for a cautious approach, which should not, however, be used to justify the status quo. It rejected the legalization of marijuana because of the numerous unknowns that still prevailed, most notably the long-term health effects. It would be necessary, however, as recommended by a majority of the Le Dain Commission members, to transfer this drug from the Narcotic Drug Act to the Food and Drugs Act. The Sub-committee justified its recommendation by the fact that, in the preceding few years, marijuana had acquired a symbolic status that carried multiple meanings, and the medical profession, regardless of members' personal views, needed to take this into account.[106]

The members preferred the resolution presented by psychiatrist Conrad J. Schwarz, chairman of the British Columbia Medical Association's Committee on Non-Medical Use of Drugs, and since 1968 a board member of the Narcotic Addiction Foundation of British Columbia. This resolution was a reminder for the medical profession that it had the obligation to discourage marijuana use because of the dangers it represented to the Canadian population. According to the resolution, these were the dangers:

> The probably harmful effects of cannabis on the maturing process in adolescents; the implications for safe driving arising from impairment of cognitive functions and psycho-motor abilities, from the additive interaction of cannabis and alcohol, and from the difficulties of recognizing or detecting cannabis intoxication; the possibility suggested by reports in other countries and clinical observations on this continent, that the long-term, heavy use of cannabis may result in a significant amount of mental deterioration and disorder; development and spread of multi-drug use by stimulating a desire for drug experiences and lowering inhibitions about drug experimentation.[107]

Consequently, members agreed:

1. Our collective medical opinion is that the adolescent and adult public should now be clearly advised against the informal use of cannabis, either in the form of marijuana or hashish.
2. Those who disagree with this advice are urged to take the following steps:
   a. Familiarize themselves with the cautionary medical reports on cannabis contained in the Canadian, British and American Commission reports of recent years;
   b. Refrain from encouraging others to use cannabis and specifically avoid introducing new individuals to it;
   c. Users should undertake, if necessary with the help of a physician, an objective review of their own mental and physical functioning with respect to their use of cannabis.[108]

The adoption of this resolution marked a setback for the Council and its Sub-committee chairman Dr Lionel Solursh. Not only did the assembly prefer the resolution presented by Schwarz, it also rejected an amendment, presented by Solursh, that would have referred the resolution to be studied by the Council on Community Health Care. The 1972 General Assembly became another episode in the struggle that set Solursh against Schwarz, two specialists who represented the opposing poles of Canadian medical opinion and who had already publicly disagreed during the work undertaken by the Le Dain Commission.

Still, the Council did not lose the war. CMA members approved a resolution, although diluted compared to that of 1971, which suggested the CMA oppose the advertisement of alcohol, tobacco, and 'over-the-counter' drugs. However, the resolution denounced ads, not because of any danger these products represented to society in general, but because of their impact on children.[109]

The rift opened in the 1972 General Assembly did catch the media's attention, notably that of the *Globe and Mail* and the *Montreal Gazette*.[110] In explaining his motives for undermining the action of the Sub-committee, Schwartz said that it had been necessary to act in order to discourage cannabis use, and that under the circumstances, 'a strong statement by the medical profession' was required in the present context.[111]

Solursh's views and the action of Sub-committee on the Non-Medical Use of Drugs did not, however, fade into the horizon. During the 1973 General Assembly, the Sub-committee returned to its 1972 resolutions, hoping to correct the record. It reminded CMA members that the resolutions adopted the year before contradicted the CMA's own position on drugs. By targeting one drug in particular – marijuana – the last General Assembly had deviated, according to the Sub-committee, from the new framework that the CMA ought to promote for the debate on drugs. This included adopting a broad definition of drug misuse referring to all legal, illegal, and socially accepted substances.

The Sub-committee introduced four resolutions intended to rectify what it saw as the CMA's inconsistent position of the previous year. According to the first resolution, the simple possession of cannabis for personal use should no longer be a criminal act. When it came to a vote, the members sent it to the board of directors for further study. Members approved a second resolution inviting all health professionals to 'clearly and firmly discourage the misuse of all psycho-active substances, which include alcohol,' as well as a third resolution urging doctors to inform 'their patients and the public at large of the danger involved in operating motor vehicles ... while under the influence of psychoactive substances – especially alcohol.' However, the last resolution urging the CMA to support the legalization of marijuana was rejected.[112] Instead, the members concluded that

> recent and ongoing studies of the long-term effects of cannabis support the persistently cautionary clinical opinions of physicians over the years and reinforce the conclusions of the recent national commission studies in Canada, Britain and the United States that the use of cannabis should be discouraged on grounds of individual and public health concerns.

> Be it resolved that the C.M.A. reaffirms its 1972 Annual Meeting resolution and clearly advises the Canadian public against the non-medical use of cannabis[113]

At the 1974 General Assembly, members once again debated the marijuana issue. They agreed that marijuana should continue to 'be regarded as an unlawful act but that it not be classified as a criminal offence in the normal usage of that term.'[114]

CMA divisions reflected similar debates within provincial medical associations. In 1967, a committee of the British Columbia Medical Association tabled what for many members was an audacious proposal. It recommended that 'cannabis be distributed in Canada in much the same way as alcohol.' The committee wrote that it doubted the utility of the repressive legislative approach and that marijuana was 'no more harmful than alcohol to the user.' The Association's general assembly rejected the committee's report, but not before lengthy debate.[115] In 1969, the Alberta Medical Association stated that marijuana use carried risks for its users. It believed that 'marijuana, along with other "mind-altering drugs" causes injurious mental or physical effects.' Having stated this, the secretary of the organization underlined the fact that the state could nevertheless soften penalties related to marijuana use.[116]

These divisions also illustrate tensions elsewhere in the world. In 1968, the British Advisory Committee on Drug Dependence stated that 'long-term consumption of cannabis' in moderation had 'no harmful effects.' These conclusions were similar to those reached by the Indian Hemp Drugs Commission at the end of the nineteenth century and New York Mayor Fiorello H. LaGuardia's Committee on Marijuana in 1944.[117] In 1972 a group of experts assembled by the World Health Organization challenged the stepping-stone theory by asserting that 'the great majority of cannabis users never proceed to the use of morphine-type drugs'; even though they did try other drugs. Also, these experts insisted that any evaluation of the consequences of marijuana use on people and society 'must take into account the manner, frequency, amount, and duration of use and the relative numbers of persons conforming to various usage patterns.'[118]

Debates and the publication of studies to challenge existing scientific knowledge have always provided milestones in the development of medical science. However, these debates and quarrels among scientists rarely surface in public. In the case of marijuana, however, they received media coverage and were closely followed by interest groups. Indeed, the disagreement among researchers about the health consequences of marijuana use, its addictive effects, and possible initiation to other drugs, as well as the concomitant absence of unanimity in the medical community, all created anxiety among those who saw medicine as a science that spoke with one voice. Nonetheless, these divisions reassured the pro-marijuana groups, because they undermined the non-partisan image of medical science. Regardless of their views on the marijuana issue, it was clear to the public, and especially to interest groups, that scientific research could be tinged by the ideological commitments of researchers or those who financed research. In addition, the difficulties of the CMA in reaching a consensus on the drug issue, particularly on marijuana, strengthened the position of interest groups who sought legitimacy for their position. This is further discussed in the chapter on the Le Dain Commission.

'A National Association of Concerned Citizens': The Council on Drug Abuse (CODA)

Founded in 1969, the Council on Drug Abuse presented itself as a 'voluntary, non-profit, national association of concerned citizens ... joined together to aid in fighting the pressing problem of drug abuse in Canada.'[119] This group of 'concerned citizens' included representatives of drug manufacturers, distributors, and others from the private sector. Their concern was the protection of pharmaceutical-industry interests within the context of greater state intervention in this particular sector. As Burnham and McAllister note, the 1960s saw the intervention of drug manufacturers in the debate. American and international drug manufacturers wanted to protect their control over production and distribution, but they were reluctant to plead for state intervention that would legally bar the production and use of a greater range of drugs.

State control would have to be negotiated in a manner favourable to the interests of drug manufacturers, since their overall objective was to keep enforcement to a minimum. This was the case, for instance, with LSD. As McAllister notes, '[T]he profit potential of psychotropics caused the pharmaceutical industry to oppose narcotics-style regulation with great vigor.'[120] The industry agreed to limits on hallucinogens, but opposed new restrictions on barbiturates and anti-depressants, since companies were determined to protect their lucrative market.

CODA considered recreational drug use as a social evil. However, drugs prescribed by a physician and sold by pharmacists did not constitute a problem as long as there was no abuse. Medical supervision should prevent this outcome, while thereby protecting the profits of the industry. Health professionals had a duty to participate in prevention campaigns against the abuse of prescribed drugs. Worried by what it called the lack of information surrounding this 'social evil,' CODA defined its interventions as 'an answer to the urgent need for accurate information on the dangers of drug abuse.' CODA's message was simple: recreational use of illegal drugs was unhealthy. Furthermore, young people, being at the centre of public debate, should be urged not to experiment; hence CODA's unofficial motto, 'Stop them before they start.'[121]

CODA disputed the control that state organizations such as ARF or OPTAT had over drug-education strategies and programs. The Council's own strategies targeted numerous groups: young people in elementary and secondary schools, university students, parents, and the population in general. To reach them, CODA promoted teaching material that often came from the United States and proved quite creative in its dissemination methods. CODA encouraged schools and private organizations to use the Lockheed Drug Decision Program, teaching material on illegal drug use prepared by Lockheed Missiles and Space Co. of California.[122] Moreover, Nicholas Leluk, executive secretary of CODA until becoming a Progressive Conservative member of the Ontario Legislative Assembly, reassured those who worried about CODA's efforts in promoting Lockheed's school program by insisting that the Council 'was not sponsoring' it, but acted 'as an agent and would only import the programme from' the United States if there was a demand.[123] Invited to evaluate this particular educational program, ARF rejected it categorically: 'This program has been evaluated and rejected by professional educators in Canada and the United States.

The principals of CODA have been informed of this rejection. [Nevertheless, CODA continues] to promote the program.'[124]

In principle, CODA needed to obtain approval from provincial education authorities before promoting its pedagogical material in schools. In the case of Quebec, it was a 'Jacobin state' approach, which meant that the education department had to approve any and all programs.[125] However, provincial approval and CODA's plans for expansion in Quebec were not achieved during the period under discussion. In Ontario, the Department of Education accorded a margin of autonomy to school boards in their design of the anti-drug programs. Thus, the battle for influence over the minds of young Ontarians was decentralized by government policy.[126] CODA convinced some Ontario school boards to welcome its youth consultant, Norman Panzica, to educate young people on the dangers of illegal drug use and hopefully persuade them to oppose the legalization of marijuana. During a session of the annual meeting of the Canadian Pharmaceutical Association in 1970, Panzica declared: '[W]hether a man gets stoned on beer or "grass," he is equally a damn fool,' but 'booze and grass are not the same thing.' To those who argued that marijuana was harmless, Panzica suggested the reply: 'Are you talking about hash or syphilis?'[127]

CODA's educational work included universities, another place where young people could be initiated into illegal drug use. In 1970, for example, CODA, in association with the University of Toronto Faculties of Medicine and Pharmacy, organized a 'Drug Information Seminar ... conducted by pharmacy students' and an 'International Teach-In on Psychotropic drugs and their use and abuse ... organized by the medical students.'[128] By entrusting an educational role to these students, CODA hoped to reach out to other students in its fight against illegal drug use. However, CODA's welcome to the campus was less than effusive. The University of Toronto Medical Society, which organized a week of events on drug use known as Vertigo '70 – aimed at Health Science students – refused CODA's financial support. According to them, CODA's approach was inappropriate and badly conceived. 'All CODA will do is help cement unreasoning and distrustful attitudes towards drug users among parents and the public at large.'[129]

CODA's work in schools and universities constituted one aspect of its larger educational strategies for the whole population. Norman Panzica, as youth consultant, participated in workshops and other educational activities on illegal drug use, including events sponsored by organizations such as Kiwanis Clubs, Rotary Clubs, the Boy Scouts,

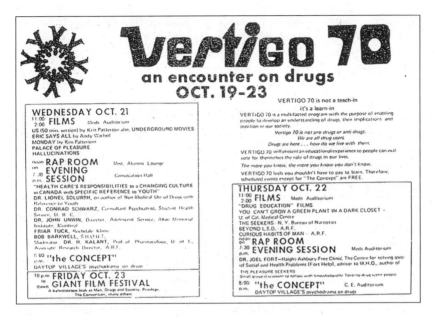

Source: *The Varsity*, 21 October 1970, 6

or church institutions – such as the Timothy Eaton Church and the Anglican Church Women of St James Church in Stratford. CODA personnel were also invited to meet the Ontario Police Association and the Youth Bureau of Municipal Police Departments. Speaking to the Empire Club in 1969, the Toronto chief of police expressed his enthusiastic support for CODA's work.[130]

CODA was also preoccupied with recruiting allies to its cause and was quite imaginative in this respect. For instance, CODA distributed information pamphlets about illegal drug abuse through Ontario drugstores. In its brief to the Le Dain Commission in 1969, the Council indicated that it intended to enlist all drugstores in the country as Drug Information Centres. It believed that pharmacists, because of their training and knowledge, had a crucial role to play in educating the population on drug use: 'As primary custodians of drugs ... pharmacists have the opportunity and responsibility to promote drug use control in their own communities.'[131] Through this initiative, CODA wanted to reassure a concerned public that the industry had the resources to discipline itself and to educate the population on the dangers of abusing either legal or illegal drugs. In 1974, CODA informed

the Department of National Health and Welfare that its Drug Information Centres were accessible in fast-food restaurants such as
McDonald's and Burger King. In order to foster its relationship with
pharmacists, CODA participated regularly in the annual meetings of
the Canadian Pharmaceutical Association, where it presented its work
and publications.

For the general public, CODA organized the International Symposium on Drug Abuse in August 1970, and the same year opened
a pavilion, entitled 'Man and His Drugs,' at Toronto's Canadian
National Exhibition (CNE). This pavilion, dedicated to the education
of parents and their children on illegal drug use, provided 'a choice ...
between established structures in society and forces of change, and the
visitor's decision in each case will determine the direction he will
move through the maze.'[132] CODA's work at the CNE was effective,
according to the ARF, but not everyone shared this assessment.[133] The
testimonies of existing visitors interviewed by the *Globe and Mail* and
the *Toronto Daily Star* revealed that some found it interesting, but
would not change their opinions on drugs. Others found the pavilion
to be confusing or a waste of money. Still others reported that they had
wanted to leave as soon as they entered.[134] CODA's other efforts to
reach the general public involved advertising in the media and the distribution of a movie.

In 1970, in order to help finance its various activities, CODA offered
$25 memberships to the public, but this effort fell short, as the Council
failed to reach its overall fundraising goal of $1.5 million. It then
enlisted the support of the private sector through its own board of
directors, a veritable 'Who's Who' of Canadian business. The board
consisted of representatives of the pharmaceutical industry, the retail
sector (among them Fred Eaton and the president of Canadian Tire
Corporation), the food industry, and news sectors (with individuals
such as John F. Bassett, vice-president of the Telegram Publishing Co.,
and Michael Harrison, vice-president of Southam News). Board members readily used their influence and relationships with federal and
provincial politicians in order to secure state financing, mainly from
the federal and the Ontario governments. Nicholas G. Leluk, executive
secretary of CODA until 1971, was a key player in linking CODA with
influential Canadians.[135]

On the marijuana issue, CODA opposed the legalization of marijuana but was favourable to its transfer, 'with respect to possession,'
from the Narcotic Control Act to the Food and Drugs Act. In its brief

submitted to the Le Dain Commission in 1969, CODA presented the following reasons for its opposition to marijuana's legalization: 'the unavailability of empirical clinical evidence as to the long term adverse effects of this drug on the human system, possible psychological dependency and possible damage to the vital body organs.'[136] It also insisted on the importance of education. Because the strategy of fighting illegal drug abuse relied on education, CODA pressed the federal government to develop a national education strategy on illegal drug abuse. However, if the federal government was unable or reluctant to do so, it should support organizations such as CODA, because they had the resources and the expertise to implement such a program.[137]

CODA's efforts attracted strong criticism, as in the case of University of Toronto students in 1970. Although CODA benefited from the support of the pharmaceutical sector, businesses, chiefs of police, social clubs, religious institutions, and the Canadian Pharmaceutical Association (which reprinted favourable articles about CODA in its magazine), groups and institutions that worked in the field of drug prevention, education, and treatment were all very critical of CODA and its activities. Its officials heard from critics when invited to meet those in charge of Project 70, an initiative intended to coordinate the work of Toronto organizations such as the ARF with Toronto young people, and notably drug users. Project 70 officials criticized CODA for its style and approach, which it qualified as 'aggressive and corporation oriented, which was quite alien to the drug subculture and those who work with kids at the street level.' Frank Buckley justified CODA's work by underlining that it used methods 'best known to them as businessmen ... [besides which], they were quite sincere in their desire to help both youth [and] parents, who were involved with drug misuse in any way.'[138]

Provincial governmental organizations were especially vocal in their criticism of CODA. In 1970, the ARF expressed strong reservations about CODA to the Ontario health minister, Thomas Wells. ARF criticized CODA for what it saw as paternalism. In addition, it considered the organization's strategies inappropriate for reaching out to young people, who were especially critical of the information coming from organizations close to what they called 'the establishment.' ARF also pointed to CODA's links to the pharmaceutical industry. The problem of drug use and abuse, the ARF noted, included legal as well as illegal substances. 'It must also be recognized that an important part of the overall drug problem is the advertising, promotion and energetic distribution of the drug industry's own psycho-active products. This is one part of the "drug problem."' These links undermined the credibility of CODA: its 'current relationship ... to the drug industry has resulted in a considerable amount of scepticism on the part of many [particularly the young] working in the drug field.'[139]

ARF's hostility can be partly explained by the fact that CODA was visible in the area of public education. CODA's Drug Information Centres operating in pharmacies competed with ARF literature produced in conjunction with the Ontario Association of Pharmacists, which was also offered to Ontario pharmacists. Beyond this desire to protect its territory, ARF also sought to answer a larger question: it asked the Ontario government to identify clearly who had the responsibility for drug education. Referring to the interim report of the Le Dain Commission released in 1970, ARF reminded the health minister and the entire Robarts cabinet that education should be the responsibility of state-supported organizations rather than of private groups, because the former, most notably ARF, were exempt from pressure by business groups.[140]

Civil servants in charge of the Non-Medical Drug Use Programs of the national health and welfare department also had some difficulty working with CODA. They considered CODA's approach reactionary and paternalistic.[141] These civil servants, in agreement with the student organizers of Vertigo '70, were of the opinion that CODA's posters, featuring slogans such as 'Drugs Are for the Sick,' 'Clean Up Mind Pollution,' 'Sniff, Smoke, Pop, Shoot, Die,' or 'You Can Hide Drugs from Everyone But Yourself,' were simplistic.[142]

Sometimes, CODA replied to its critics. When former executive secretary Nick Leluk became an elected member of the Ontario Legislature at the beginning of 1970s, he attacked ARF in the Legislative Assembly. He denounced what he called 'the permissive attitude and the casual approach' ARF took toward drug abuse. He also questioned how ARF allocated its funds, of which 65 per cent was spent on alcoholism, when 'we have now moved into an era of chemical drug abuse and we have many other drugs today to worry about.' Without mentioning CODA directly, he was critical of the fact that ARF barred private-sector organizations from involvement in drug education. Finally, he requested an inquiry into the activities of the ARF 'for the safety and welfare of Ontario residents.' These criticisms forced the Liberal Opposition to ask the health minister to either support Leluk's comments, or reaffirm the government's confidence in ARF, which the minister promptly did.[143]

Nevertheless, CODA had captured the attention of politicians, at least when the time came to obtain grants. At the federal level CODA managed to secure promises of financial support from health minister John Munro, while on other occasions Ontario Liberal Members of Parliament supported CODA's financial requests. This was the case with John Munro's former parliamentary secretary, Stanley Haidasz.[144] Federal mandarins took note of these pressures and recommended, not without hesitation, financial support for CODA. Thereby, they thought, it would be possible to change the organization's overall approach to the drug phenomenon.[145]

At the provincial level, CODA was very close to the ministerial team of John Robarts and that of his successor, William Davis. In 1970, ARF examined CODA's requests for financial support for its educational activities and its pavilion 'Man and His Drugs.' Aware of Robarts's enthusiasm for CODA, it did recommend provincial grants, although less than what CODA had requested. At other times, ARF indicated to the Ministry of Health that it would judge every application on a case-by-case basis. Thus, CODA received $10,000 for its pavilion and its international symposium, instead of the $65,000 asked for, and $75,000 instead of $230,000 for its overall activities. Eager to harmonize relations between ARF and CODA, the health minister informed Premier Robarts that a representative of CODA had been appointed to the ARF board. In return, CODA later invited an ARF representative to join its board.[146] In 1971, the health minister invited a CODA official to be a member of a new ministry-created committee to study grant applications for projects in rehabilitation and treatment.[147]

CODA did not, however, become a Canada-wide organization. In spite of a growth plan proposing the distribution of pamphlets in drugstores across Canada, CODA's limited financial resources handicapped its activities. Thus, during the period under study, plans for expansion into Quebec were put on hold, while British Columbia became the second base of operations after Ontario. CODA simply did not have the means to fulfil its ambitions on a national scale. However, its well-maintained links with police organizations and the Canadian Pharmaceutical Association increased its influence, if not on the state, at least on the Canadian population.

Conclusion

The four interest groups analysed here had unequal access to centres of decision-making, and their influence in the debate varied. For instance, university students had difficulty sustaining action over the long term, because their resources were limited and their leadership was renewed on a regular basis. However, they were able to highlight the contradiction in the classification of drugs and challenge medical expertise. They also forced educational institutions to deal with recreational drug use. These efforts took time and resulted in a variety of programs. By 1974, however, parents and school officials felt that this issue did not require as much attention as it had in the past.

Although police forces did not often intervene in the debate, their presence was felt. As law-enforcement officers and agents of social control, they represented the legitimate use of violence by the state. Yet the sixties were difficult years for them. Their enforcement activities were challenged, and their public image was tarnished by their repression of youth and hippies. However, police forces were able to sustain initiatives over a long period of time and enjoyed a legitimacy conferred by the fact that they enforced the law. Thus, their opposition to the legalization of marijuana, based on the argument that there were still too many unknowns about its health effects, remained potent. Furthermore they believed, as a result of their interaction with drug users, that marijuana led to experimentation with hard drugs. They did, however, encounter opposition, and found that their influence in the public arena was limited by groups who challenged their views.

The medical community figured prominently among interest groups who agreed with police officers that drugs represented a problem, but that the current solution, legal repression, was not always appropriate. The CMA espoused the treatment approach as a method – upheld by some as the most effective – for dealing with illegal drug use. But when it came to taking a stand on marijuana, the organization was divided. Divisions within the CMA reflected the diversity of opinion in the ranks of the medical profession, not only in Canada, but also abroad. Faced with questions such as what constituted drug abuse, how could penalties be softened without favouring legalization, and, not least, what were the many unknowns about health effects, physicians preferred caution, as the 1972 CMA General Assembly illustrated. During the period studied, the CMA had difficulty in maintaining a common front, thereby strengthening the message of other groups, such as university students, who disputed the health dangers of marijuana use.

The pharmaceutical industry, although a potential ally of the medical profession, decided to challenge the CMA. By setting up the Council on Drug Abuse, the industry opted to protect its own interests. CODA conveyed a specific message in reaching out to private-sector groups that could support its appeal and strengthen its influence. The Council's message was a simple rejection of all illegal drugs. In opposing any attempt to increase state control over the pharmaceutical industry, it invoked the sacrosanct principle of private entrepreneurship. In fact, CODA tried to convey the idea that the pharmaceutical industry had the resources to discipline itself by encouraging pharmacists to educate the public to the dangers of legal and illegal drug use. CODA enjoyed fairly easy access to politicians; but its lobbying was circumscribed by ARF and the national health and welfare department who had their own agendas and access to centres of decision-making as well.

3 The Scientific Experts and Provincial Governments: Ontario, Quebec, British Columbia, and Prince Edward Island

'I'm opposed to the legalization of [marijuana], period, double period, triple period.'[1] With these words, British Columbia premier W.A.C. Bennett made his position on marijuana clear. As well as being a media issue and a preoccupation of interest groups, the consumption of legal, and particularly illegal, drugs was sometimes a source of tension between the provinces and the federal government. As national health deputy minister J.N. Crawford underlined in July 1968, any federal action had to take into account the constitutional powers of the provinces, as the drug issue involved health and education, both of which fell under their jurisdiction.[2]

This discussion illustrated one of the realities of public policy and the Canadian political system: state power is constrained by the federal nature of the political regime. Whereas certain provinces, such as Quebec, were preoccupied with defending their jurisdictions in health and education, other provinces had different priorities. British Columbia, for instance, attempted to counter what it saw as Ottawa's inactivity on the drug front. For its part, Prince Edward Island pressed Ottawa to assume a leadership role, since the drug phenomenon was, after all, a national problem. Finally, Ontario favoured federal-provincial cooperation, but still hoped to be in charge unofficially of any anti-drug educational strategy the federal government might launch.

This chapter analyses the responses of provincial governments to the phenomenon of recreational drug use. It looks at those elected to positions of responsibility (mainly cabinet ministers and premiers) for developing and implementing public policies, but pays special attention to actors within governmental circles, such as the 'agents' (bureaucrats, governmental agencies), especially those within provincial institutions involved with the research and treatment of alcoholism and drug use.[3] Concerning the role of bureaucrats in the development of American drug policy Meier writes that their institutional position gave them 'the resources and time to exert policy influence.'[4] Any analysis of the marijuana debate should look at the role of bureaucrats as advisers and pay attention to their abilities to shape the debate.

Four provinces were chosen: Ontario, Quebec, British Columbia (BC), and Prince Edward Island (PEI). Why these particular provinces? The first three had state institutions that played a role in advising their respective provincial governments on the phenomenon of recreational drug use. In the case of Ontario, the Addiction Research Foundation (ARF) played a role that extended far beyond provincial borders; other provinces, the federal government, and even the international community solicited its expertise. In fact, ARF was very close to the national health and welfare department. Quebec has been chosen to measure how the cultural factor shaped state response to the drug issue. An examination of the Narcotic Addiction Foundation of British Columbia offers an opportunity to compare and contrast the response of this province with others to the drug issue, since BC had had a long history of dealing with recreational drug use. These three provincial organizations, active in the field of prevention and treatment of drug addiction, were nevertheless divided, as the CMA was, on the issue of recreational drug use. Finally, the PEI government took a leadership role among provincial opponents to the legalization of marijuana. In fact, PEI politicians suspected that Ottawa would become so 'soft' on marijuana that the social order of the country might come under threat. Consequently, in their anti-legalization campaign, they enlisted physicians willing to provide medical evidence of the damaging effects of marijuana.

Concern at Queen's Park: Ontario Politicians and Drug Use

Between 1966 and 1973, references to the non-medical use of drugs were by no means numerous in the Ontario Legislative Assembly. With the exception of 1967, the five debates on the subject do not reveal much concern for the matter. Apart from a few Members of the Provincial Parliament (MPPs), there was very little trace of panic, with one notable exception.

Nick Leluk, the former CODA executive director who became a Progressive Conservative MPP, instigated one of these five debates.

Another such discussion in March 1970 centred on amphetamine use. Following the publication of articles in the *London Free Press* on amphetamine consumption, the Liberal Opposition questioned the government on this issue.[5] It was, however, the 1967 debate that revealed contemporary perceptions and, most of all, the fears of certain MPPs.

The March 1967 debate took place shortly after the suicide of a twenty-year-old Toronto man whose death his father attributed to LSD. The father blamed those who vaunted this drug's merits, notably those speaking at the Perception '67 Symposium held at the University of Toronto. Emotions ran high during the debate. Due to the influence of the media, some MPPs believed, illegal drugs were easily accessible. The provincial New Democrat leader, Donald MacDonald, quoted the TV program *Viewpoint*, in which a McGill professor asserted that young people had easy access to LSD without ever having to frequent Yorkville.[6] Others used pithy comments to condemn those who promoted LSD use. In his denunciation of the 'devils' that 'invaded' Yorkville, Liberal MPP George Ben ridiculed the ideas of 'some bright eyed columnists and writers like Pierre Berton and commentator Larry Solway' for saying that there was 'nothing wrong with LSD.'[7]

Members of the Ontario cabinet were not to be left behind in offering condemnations of their own. In a commentary on his ministry's initiatives regarding LSD, health minister Matthew B. Dymond unequivocally condemned the drug and explained that he was trying to 'acquaint teenagers with the dangers.' Furthermore, the former-doctor-turned-politician would not lend a sympathetic ear to those who supported LSD use. 'I feel moved ... to condemn with all the vigour at my disposal those prophets or apostles or demons who advocate the use of this or encourage our young people to experience the thrill of a trip. I do not think that responsible people have given adequate consideration to the dangers inherent in their advocacy of the chemical.' The minister attributed his virulent condemnation of LSD and its promoters to the drug's pernicious effects. In his view, these supporters 'are putting in the hands of our young people a weapon of such potential hazard that we do not yet know just exactly what we can do.'[8]

One MPP was especially vocal on this issue. Liberal MPP George Ben, who had carried out an investigation of his own into the youth congregating in Yorkville, mentioned that these young people 'find themselves being preyed upon by the older people there, because they have money.' They became their slaves, but entered into a consensual slavery because 'they look[ed] up to them as something special, with their beards and their dirty old dungarees.' This dependent relationship led the elected member to bristle with irony: '[T]hey think they are free yet they are more slaves than ever, because they are now completely dependent on somebody.'[9]

In Ben's view, access to LSD and marijuana was apparently unrestricted. Ben stated that 'the increase in the use [of marijuana] is appalling.' He based this assessment on the number of arrests for possession since 1965.[10] Wanting to put a human face on the problem of drug dependence, Ben referred to Sheila Gormely's article about a seventeen-year-old-girl who had been 'on her fortieth trip as they call it, that is 40 times she has been under the influence of LSD at the age of 17.'[11]

Social realities like these led George Ben to describe the Yorkville area to his colleagues in the Legislative Assembly as 'the den of sin.' The neighbourhood deserved this dubious distinction because the young people who frequented it were invariably from a 'good family.' 'The children from poor families,' Ben argued, 'do not bother going because they see enough squalor right in their own neighbourhood.'[12] The incidence of venereal diseases, which were 'very prevalent among the youngsters,' testified to the abundance of sexual relationships, further proof of the corrupting influence of this neighbourhood, added Ben.[13]

The last two debates did not display the emotional intensity of the 1967 one. In June 1968, the Leader of the Opposition, Robert Nixon, asked the government about its action to prevent glue-sniffing. On behalf of the government, Attorney-General A.A. Wishart disputed Nixon's assessment that glue-sniffing had taken on 'dangerous proportions' in Ontario. Certainly, it gave cause for 'considerable concern' by the government, but the attorney-general reminded the Opposition of the province's limited powers to deal with this issue. The proposed solution of banning the sale of glue to minors was inappropriate, because the government did not have the jurisdiction to do so. Even if it could do so, Wishart doubted its effectiveness because it would incite a young person to use 'another substance such as gasoline, or nail polish, or vanilla extract or something else that would be used to create another sensation.'[14]

In 1969, in the final debate of this period under study, health minister Thomas Wells praised the work undertaken by ARF. There was one dissident voice, however, not on the work of ARF, but on the broader drug-abuse issue. MPP George Ben repeated his denunciations of illegal drugs. To give credence to his warnings, he quoted numerous American studies that illustrated the health dangers of marijuana use and other associated dangers, such as sexual diseases, physical violence, murders, and suicides.[15]

Discussions by MPPs about illegal drug use often took place in a scientific vacuum. In order to provide answers to questions emerging from the public debate on recreational drugs, and especially to fight some of the fears expressed by the public, interest groups, and elected officials, ARF was called upon for its advice.

'Living in the Age of Drugs': The Alcoholism and Drug Addiction Research Foundation of Ontario (ARF) and Its Views on Drugs

Created in 1949, ARF, which became the Alcoholism and Drug Addiction Research Foundation in 1961, is an arm's length foundation of the government. In the words of its executive director, H. David Archibald, 'it is – of the [provincial] government – but not in it.'[16] It was to be devoted to research, treatment, prevention, and education. Initially, its focus was on alcohol abuse, but in 1961, the government expanded ARF's mandate to include other drugs. With this change, it became the first organization to combine work on alcohol and other drug abuse.[17]

ARF believed that the scientific character of its activities inevitably conferred neutrality on its actions and recommendations. This was a belief held by many scientific institutions at the time.[18] Thus, it attached great importance to research aimed at better understanding the complexity of alcoholism and other drug addictions; these were, however, issues that still evoked numerous moral judgments, and research findings often met with controversy. Its action being based on a scientific approach, the ARF's social and government mandate was nevertheless to provide objective information.[19]

The ARF's construction of alcoholism and the non-medical use of drugs reflected this scientific conception of its mandate. Thus, recreational drugs and alcohol, when consumed in ways that were 'excessive,' 'abnormal,' or 'careless,' constituted a health problem for the user, and his or her behaviour had an impact on the familial and social environment. The result was addiction (the term was replaced by 'dependence' following the recommendation of the World Health Organization in 1964). Addiction was thus a health problem and a disease: 'An alcoholic or a drug addict is a sick person who can be helped by medical means.'[20] ARF tried 'to minimize the number of people who develop any such abnormal dependence on a substance' and 'to effect all possible improvement in the condition of those who, despite preventive endeavours, in the end become alcoholics or addicts to other chemicals.'[21] In June 1970 ARF retained the notion of disease but referred also to what was characterized as the mechanisms of adaptation to the social environment. 'Drug dependence,' it noted, 'occurs when a vulnerable individual adapts to environmental pressure by selecting drug use as his major adaptive behaviour.'[22] Consequently, it was necessary to help such an individual reduce his or her vulnerability towards drugs, while at the same time making society aware of social and other pressures that lead to drug use.

To be able to help these patients, it was important to conduct research into the causes of dependence, the effects of drugs on health, and the appropriate treatments. By doing its own research, and by maintaining links with universities, ARF hoped to contribute to the debate on these issues and, in this way, to advance knowledge.

ARF planned to approach the drug addiction/dependence issue in the same manner it had previously approached alcoholism. Indeed, it was in the middle of 1960s that the ARF succeeded in making alcoholism a public health concern. While this way of framing alcohol dependence did not obtain full support from the medical profession and society at large, ARF did at least manage to convince the provincial government. When health minister Dymond commented on his department's strategy on alcoholism, he recognized it as a health problem and no longer simply a lack of self-control or a matter of moral weakness.[23]

When the issues of LSD, and especially marijuana, were put before the government, ARF had an array of programs to help the state better understand recreational drug use in what it qualified as 'total objectivity.' The ARF's first area of action was thus the organization and dissemination of research.[24]

In 1966, ARF's director, H. David Archibald, pressed the minister of health to support his research projects, so the government would be ready when the time came to intervene in the field of recreational marijuana use. In his brief to the minister, he presented the drug user as a sick individual in search of treatment. 'The marijuana user has no conception that he may be "sick" and would seldom seek voluntarily an exposure to a treatment facility.'[25] Archibald's comments allow us to identify how the behaviour of drug users was constructed by ARF. At first, the Ontario organization tried to defend its traditional area of specialization. Thus, it reminded the minister of health that the therapeutic approach was preferable to a jail sentence. Canadian federal law made possession of marijuana for non-medical use a criminal act punishable by detention. In his letter to the health minister, Archibald proposed that his organization collaborate with the Department of Justice and receive convicted individuals, notably those found guilty of marijuana possession, in private hospitals overseen by his staff. 'A number of us felt that the traditional pattern of sending marijuana users [particularly the younger group] to jail or penitentiary under the provisions of the narcotic control legislation, was a somewhat uninspiring, fruitless, and probably damaging approach.' In fact, the director wished rather to treat young marijuana users. 'We approached the Deputy Attorney-General to see whether or not there was any possibility of arranging for young marijuana users to be placed on probation with the condition of probation that they attend our clinic for study.'[26] Naturally, the letter remained vague as to the proposed clientele. Who would be the focus? Young offenders who committed a first offence? Users who had a long criminal history? For long-time users, ARF judged that the time had come to offer them another choice, which was the treatment of their 'disease.' Doing that would make it possible to better understand the motivations of those who used marijuana.[27]

Besides its research in trying to quantify the drug phenomenon, ARF in 1969 demonstrated boldness by creating laboratories to test the composition of illegal drugs available in Ontario. In cooperation with Toronto radio station CHUM, which was very popular with young people, ARF diffused information about the drugs available in Toronto. An emphasis was placed on the composition of drugs available on the street.

This initiative resulted in a number of reactions and some criticism. The Toronto Metropolitan Police, for instance, urged ARF to cancel its initiative, claiming it would incite young people to experiment with illegal drugs. ARF defended itself by reminding its critics that it had a duty to test drugs available on the streets and to inform the users about degrees of toxicity.[28] ARF also stated that the drug phenomenon was a changing reality, and it was necessary to show 'innovation and flexibility as essential attributes in development of services.'[29] ARF did find some important allies, however. First among them was the Le Dain Commission itself. The Commission's interim report encouraged the federal government to set up regional laboratories to test drugs that were available in Canada. This recommendation was seen as a form of support for ARF's initiative.[30] Another important ally was the medical profession. At its 1970 meeting, the Ontario Medical Association supported drug analysis in laboratories and disclosure of the results. 'It is not unreasonable for such results to be known "on the street" in light of the well-known reality that such drugs are frequently widely available in the community.'[31]

According to ARF, the criminalization of marijuana was handicapping research, notably into its effects on users' health. From 1970 until 1972, with the permission of the Department of National Health and Welfare, ARF conducted studies on this question. In his letter presenting the project to the Le Dain Commission, Archibald explained that the research team would measure the effects of marijuana cigarettes on humans. The participants would receive $5 per day, and would, of course, be volunteers. One possibly interesting group was 'US draft dodging conscientious objectors.' For ARF, these people formed an ideal test group for several reasons. First, 'they [were] likely to be reasonably intelligent people'; second, 'they [were] likely to be appreciative of a place to stay for a few months'; third, 'they [were] quite likely to be impecunious and therefore, would welcome the opportunity to earn money for participating in the study at the same time as they receive the basic essentials of life'; fourth, 'they [were] likely to be in a desirable age range, that is, between 18 and 35'; finally, 'there [was] a high probability they would be physically and mentally healthy – if they [were] attempting to evade the draft they would most probably have been subjected to military medical examination.' In the end, ARF did not look specifically for this group, but the above criteria shed some light on the type of volunteer they sought.[32]

On 2 March 1972 an internal report produced for the ARF presented the preliminary results of this research project, and these appeared in several daily newspapers, such as the *Globe and Mail*, the *Ottawa Citizen*, and the *Montreal Gazette*. Who were the volunteers? They were about twenty healthy young men with no mental illness or history of hard drug use, aged between 21 and 35, who had the habit of consuming marijuana at least once a month for the previous two years. These volunteers agreed to participate in a ten-week study. What were the results? For instance, were there any effects on mental health? The report indicated that there were no 'gross behavioural changes,' no 'chronic mood change effects,' and the 'drug did not appear to induce hostility or aggression.' Furthermore, 'psychiatric examinations detected no adverse effects as a result of the experiment.' What about physical health? On this point the answers were that there was 'no clinical evidence of obvious physical damage' and 'no obtrusive evidence of a withdrawal syndrome.' In its conclusions, the study exercised cautious, notably because the experiment had lasted only a short period of time. The long-term health effects were not measured, nor were age-related effects explored, nor were the influence of previous marijuana use examined.[33]

Finally, ARF went to great pains to disseminate the outcome of its research, notably through its numerous publications, its journal *Addictions*, its pamphlets *Facts About ...*, and its short films. In June 1972 it launched a monthly publication, *The Journal*, dedicated to an examination of alcoholism and drug addiction in Canada and abroad.

ARF's second area of activity was the development of alcohol- and drug-addiction treatment and rehabilitation programs. ARF opened its first treatment centre for narcotic addicts in 1964. Although ARF had more than seven hundred employees and twenty-two regional offices at its disposal by the end of the 1960s, it quickly became apparent that the organization's limited finances and human resources could not handle all cases presented. As a result, it sought to coordinate the work of other health resources, such as hospitals, psychiatric institutions, and street clinics, by privileging flexibility and adaptability in strategies of treatment and prevention. This task of coordination led ARF to subsidize street clinics and other treatment and rehabilitation centres, such as Street Haven.[34] ARF also supported community initiatives, such as Project 70. This project, which was continuous with Project 69, coordinated services offered by new innovative youth services and by ARF, the Metropolitan Toronto Police, and the Toronto School Board. The focus of Project 70 was on helping young people, especially those dealing with drug use. In *A Plan for Action*, an internal paper produced for the Toronto Metropolitan Social Planning Council, its author used the following words to describe the initiative: 'Project '70 views drug abuse as symptomatic of other more complex problems' and its people worked 'at the so-called "street level."'[35]

The third and last realm of activity concerned education and prevention campaigns aimed at alcohol and drug addiction. Since 1953, ARF had developed an educational program based on 'an interest in public education, not propaganda.'[36] From 1966 on, it adapted its programs to include the issue of non-medical drug use. However, the information content to be passed on to young people worried ARF officials. Information campaigns were difficult to organize, because young people were aware that the drug phenomenon, in spite of media interest in some aspects, was much more widespread than the public had been led to believe. Furthermore, young people noticed the divergences among medical experts concerning health consequences for users. Taking these realities into consideration, ARF officials judged that it was crucial to avoid sensationalism, scare tactics, moralizing, and especially simplification of information in the development of anti-drug campaigns. The information on drugs had 'to be presented in a form that is comprehensible and meaningful to young people.'[37] The challenge for ARF was to pass on the most scientific information possible, underline the limits of the current knowledge on health effects and possibilities of dependence, and remind young people of the dangers posed by drugs.

ARF addressed the problem of credibility, often identified by young people as a deficiency of educational programs that intended to frighten rather than educate. Executive Director Archibald was not ashamed of supporting young people in their observations. 'Today's young people do not believe dogmatic statements – especially when it is so easy to find contradictory statements that are equally dogmatic. The "scare" technique – warning against dire consequences of drug use – is not very persuasive, since many young people are likely to know persons who have used these drugs without apparent adverse effects.'[38] Archibald based his educational strategy on a need to inform, and the perceived neutrality of his organization persuaded him that ARF could fill this credibility gab. Over time, and with the experience of its efforts to quantify the drug phenomenon, ARF refined its approach. In 1970, for instance, it asserted that its work with the Department of Education consisted of 'inform[ing] those who are not experimenting with or using mood-changing drugs about the effects of these substances,' as well as providing help to those who used drugs and had developed a dependency.[39]

These educational strategies targeted numerous groups. At first, ARF developed teaching materials for young people with the provincial Department of Education and distributed films, pamphlets, and books, such as *Drugs and People*, to school and public libraries. Then it developed materials for parents, such as *For Worried Parents* (available in French), *Handbook for Parents about Drugs*, *Clues for Parents about Alcohol*, and *Drugs and Man and Chemical Comforts*, as well as films describing the reality of drug use. The aim was not only to provide information but also to suggest that parents had some responsibility for this issue. ARF often noted, as it did in its publication *Handbook for Parents about Drugs*, that 'effects vary with user, dose, and setting.'[40] Finally, for school personnel and especially teachers, ARF lent assistance to the Ontario Teachers' Colleges and the Colleges of Education responsible for training future teachers in order to help them explain recreational drug use. For in-service teachers and other professionals concerned about this phenomenon, ARF offered its annual two-week summer course, in collaboration with universities. Private courses were offered for health care professionals.[41]

In 1970 the ARF set up 'Operation Drug Alert Week,' featuring workshops and other educational activities on recreational drug use. The target audience was not only young people and their parents, but also judges, police, pharmacists, and physicians.[42] ARF also developed a phone line called 'Connection,' which provided information about drug use to users, parents, teachers, and others who wanted to know more about this new socio-cultural phenomenon.

Assessing the ARF's Influence: Science Serving Public Policy

ARF's symbolic capital was based on its credibility as a widely recognized health organization in Canada and abroad. Besides its links with various departments and state institutions in Ontario, ARF developed a close relationship with the national health and welfare department and the Le Dain Commission. Outside Ontario, several provincial education departments used its publications on alcoholism and illegal drug use. Finally, at the end of the sixties, ARF's director served as a member of the World Health Organization Committee on Drug Dependence, and its organization became one of the two World Health Organization centres for research and training on drug dependence in North America.[43]

ARF believed that the state had the power, and sometimes the obligation, to intervene in the field of non-medical drug use. State action was tripartite in nature, because it focused on the users, the drugs, and the social environment. Given the nature of the federal system, the central government intervened in the first two areas, which did not exclude provincial action aimed at users and the social environment. Thus, ARF embarked on a mission to sensitize provincial and federal governments to the limits of the repressive approach in dealing with recreational drug use.[44] Often, education and treatment/rehabilitation proved to be more appropriate, as ARF reminded the Ontario government at the time of the discussion of glue-sniffing.[45]

From December 1967 to January 1968, different alarmist requests reached the Ontario government concerning glue-sniffing by young people. Although these were not based on quantitative scientific studies, those sending them had credibility based on the legitimacy attached to members of municipal governments, such as the Toronto City Council. The latter sent a copy of a resolution, approved on 31 January, 1968, urging the federal government to adopt the drastic gesture of amending the Criminal Code in order to forbid sales of glue to young people under eighteen years of age. This measure, it was felt, would 'prevent the practice of glue-sniffing by young people.'[46]

The glue-sniffing issue worried Premier John Robarts to the point that he pressured his health and justice ministers to suggest possible recourses if the federal government refused to act. In its opinion offered to the provincial minister of health, ARF pleaded for a cautionary approach. According to ARF, for reasons unknown the number of young people involved in glue-sniffing was declining. In the face of the inaccuracies and exaggerations surrounding the issue, ARF defined glue-sniffing as a health problem. The repressive approach, that is, a ban on the sale of glue and jail sentences for those arrested and convicted, would be inadequate, because young people – notably those who developed dependence – needed treatment, not jail. ARF clearly favoured a curative and educational approach. Rather than an outright ban on the sale of glue, it proposed several concurrent solutions: an educational program sensitizing young people to the dangers of glue-sniffing, another program destined to help those who had developed dependency, and a possible limit on the quantity of glue one could buy at a given time.[47]

In his answer to the City of Toronto Municipal Council, Premier Robarts repeated several of ARF's arguments. These were already familiar to the Municipal Council because they had previously sought ARF's opinion.[48] First, the power to amend the Criminal Code was not within provincial jurisdiction. Even if Ontario had this power, the government would hesitate to do so. Was a ban on glue sale to young people an adequate solution, in fact? 'To restrict the use of airplane glue,' Robarts wrote, 'might only promote the use of the other substances.'[49] The premier's reaction was perceived as government unresponsiveness; consequently, the Toronto City Council and the Municipality of Metropolitan Toronto encouraged the Toronto School Board in 1969 to implement an educational program intended to inform young people about 'the injurious effects' of glue-sniffing.[50]

When marijuana use for non-medical purposes became part of public discourse, ARF officials had a precise set of objectives in their interventions, notably those aimed at politicians and interest groups. First, it was necessary to force the legislator to recognize marijuana use as a health problem. Second, it was crucial to convince the government that heavy use was a symptom of dependency. Finally, the government had to finance research projects on controversial aspects, such as the short- and long-term effects on human health, the circumstances that led to experimentation with illegal drugs, as well as the characteristics of dependence. In this way, ARF suggested challenging the accepted belief that marijuana use inevitably led to experimentation with other drugs. Conducting studies on this last question constituted a serious challenge, because the ARF was clearly fighting the tide of current opinion.

In 1968, ARF published its evaluation of the marijuana issue. Entitled 'Marijuana and Its Effects: An Assessment of Current Knowledge,' the document was summarized by health minister Dymond in the Legislative Assembly, and in doing so, he helped to lay certain myths to rest. For instance, marijuana use had no particularly fatal effects for the individual if this substance was taken in small quantities. The health minister reminded legislators that the development of dependence on marijuana was not inevitably harmful, because the history of the individual, the frequency of consumption, as well as the individual's environment had to be taken into consideration. Finally, there were not enough studies to confirm that marijuana use incited people to try other drugs, especially hard ones. Although the minister insisted on the benefits of a therapeutic approach in the elaboration of a strategy to fight drug use, following the example of ARF, he did not support the movement in favour of legalizing marijuana. At most, he considered that a legislative change transferring marijuana from the Narcotic Control Act to the Food and Drugs Act could facilitate the development of anti-drug strategy.[51] In its document, ARF mentioned that there were still many unknowns when assessing health effects on frequent marijuana users. It even suggested that dependence in itself was not inevitably bad, but 'whether dependence in a given case results in physical, psychological or social harm.'[52]

Throughout the public discussion on marijuana use, ARF did not recommend intensifying the punitive approach, nor did it ever recommend legalizing marijuana. It was concerned with the human, social, political, and economic consequences of the options put forward by various social actors, interest groups, media, and politicians. ARF's role was to disseminate its opinions and studies and hope that they would contribute to the debate and help decision-makers. Its view was that 'all relevant facts should be communicated to those who must ultimately decide whether or not the legal status of the drug should be altered.' Furthermore, 'it is our duty to provide our best scientific judgment as to the probable consequences [both good and bad] of different proposed systems of control including legalization.' In its assessment, ARF pointed out that the current repressive approach was unacceptable because it made young people who experimented with illegal drugs criminal. For its part, ARF believed that the legalization of marijuana would entail an important growth in the number of users and the quantity consumed by them. Furthermore, inevitable health problems would put increasing pressure on the health system. ARF based its assessment on alcohol use: since alcohol had become a socially accepted drug, the number of users had increased considerably, to the point of its becoming the drug of choice among the population at large. Ontarians' consumption of alcohol increased by 60 per cent between 1950 and 1975.[53] If the federal legislator opted for the legalization of marijuana, ARF noted, it would be necessary to modify international treaties that treated marijuana as an illegal drug.[54]

Did ARF opt for sitting on the fence? No, answered its executive director. It was not necessary to compromise ARF's mission by obliging it to take a stand with one camp or another; this would only diminish its capital of influence. Archibald argued that, in the spirit of objectivity, it was necessary to present all the facts and to let people formulate opinions by themselves. For Archibald, the role of his organization consisted of providing 'society as well as the policy maker all the tools they need in making sound decisions.'[55] He continued:

> It is not our job as a scientific organization to decide whether the probable benefits outweigh the probable costs. Our tasks are to try to identify accurately what the consequences may be, and to see that this information is adequately communicated to the decision-makers. In my view we have never deviated from this position either in our exchanges with the Le Dain Commission or in any public statements endorsed by the Foundation.[56]

ARF studies supplied arguments to groups favourable to the legalization of marijuana; there was, however, one organization that attempted to limit ARF's action, at least in education. This group, CODA, pressed the Ontario government to support its own endeavour. As mentioned in the previous chapter, ARF expressed its strong opposition to CODA's educational initiatives. Yet, in spite of ARF objections, CODA was invited to nominate one of its own to ARF's board of directors.[57]

Besides seeing its educational strategies come under fire, ARF saw limits imposed on its political influence. Indeed, ARF was a creation of the Ontario government; thus the Cabinet was, in a sense, the ultimate judge. Those who attempted to convince Premier John Robarts and Ministers of Health Matthew B. Dymond and Thomas Wells of the merits of marijuana legalization did not find these individuals very sympathetic to their cause. Publicly and privately, the premier and the ministers of health expressed their strong opposition to legalization. However, Wells did consider the transfer of marijuana from the Narcotic Control Act to the Food and Drugs Act as an acceptable alternative.[58] John Robarts also expressed his firm opposition to the legalization of marijuana during a fundraising activity for the provincial Tory party in March 1970.[59] Even if dissenting voices from the provincial state apparatus (Ontario Supervising Coroner Dr H. Beatty Cotnam), or from the judicial system (Juvenile Court Judge William Little), pleaded for the legalization of marijuana or, as an alternative, its inclusion in the Food and Drugs Act or a separate act, and its distribution by the government, these voices by no means reflected the feelings of the Robarts cabinet.[60] When William Davis became Ontario premier in 1971, he did not say much on the legalization of marijuana or its inclusion in the Food and Drugs Act, at least during the legislative debates.

The Ontario government favoured cooperation when it came to federal–provincial relations on health issues. The defence of provincial autonomy, an argument used notably by the Quebec government and its civil servants during interprovincial and federal-provincial conferences of health ministers, was not a concern of the Ontario government. Already in 1968, health minister Dymond recognized that the federal government was an important actor that could not be ignored, simply because it was responsible for law enforcement and the classification of drugs. Certainly, he wished that Ottawa would involve more provinces in its initiatives, because recreational drug use was clearly an issue that implicated both levels of government. Consequently, cooperation was to be favoured. In 1969 Dymond encouraged the federal government to coordinate a national response to the drug issue with the cooperation of the provinces. Cooperation was also desirable because of the costs that addict treatment imposed on provincial health budgets. At the 1968 Interprovincial Health Ministers' Conference, the Ontario minister reminded participants that it was necessary to explain this cost to the federal government.[61]

The attitude of the Ontario government could be explained by the fact that the federal government, notably the Department of National Health and Welfare, collaborated closely with ARF. Consequently, unlike other provinces, the Ontario government had some influence, at least through ARF staff, on the orientation of federal programs. ARF remained a player that (with several others) tried to influence the federal government.

A New Player in the Arena: The Office for the Prevention and Treatment of Alcoholism and the Other Toxicomanias (OPTAT)

Unlike their Ontario colleagues, the elected members of the Quebec National Assembly between 1965 and 1975 were not vocal on the non-medical use of LSD and marijuana. When, in July 1971, a MNA asked the government about Ottawa's intentions regarding the legalization of marijuana, not only did the question provoke no discussion, but the Speaker of the Assembly went so far as to rule the member's question out of order as irrelevant to the Legislative Assembly.[62] In fact, only one debate surrounding the creation of OPTAT, in December of 1968, allows us to identify the MNAs' state of mind on recreational drug use. Their tone was in sharp contrast to that of Ontario MPPs.

During his intervention in the short debate on the bill creating OPTAT, Union Nationale MNA Maurice Bellemare welcomed this initiative by his government and indicated the importance for the Quebec state to help people who had developed, according to him, the vice of alcoholism. The former Liberal minister Émilien Lafrance reminded his colleague that alcoholism was now considered a disease and no longer a vice.[63] Lafrance's comments clearly reflected the consensus among MNAs, since the bill passed the various stages of the legislative process in a single day. In fact, those who intervened in the debate, in the spirit of comments made by the sponsor of the bill, Minister of State for Health Roch Boivin, reiterated that alcoholism was a disease that required appropriate treatment. The time had come for the Quebec state to intervene in this domain of public health, following the exam-

INFORMATIONS SUR L'ALCOOLISME

OPTAT

BULLETIN DE L'OFFICE DE LA PRÉVENTION ET DU TRAITEMENT
DE L'ALCOOLISME ET DES TOXICOMANIES (OPTAT)

VOLUME 2 - NO 3
JUIL. - AOÛT 1966

DANS CE NUMÉRO

Editorial:
L'Optat fait ses premiers
pas
André Boudreau

•

Donnons une petite pous-
sée
Albert Forcier

•

Organigramme de
l'Optat

•

Clinique de Réadaptation
pour Alcooliques (Brome)

•

Pour aider le conjoint
Alcoolique

Le Ministère des Pos-
tes à Ottawa, a autori-
sé l'affranchissement
en numéraire et l'en-
voi comme objet de la
deuxième classe de la
présente publication.
Ce numéro a été tiré à
15,000 exemplaires.

Siège Social de
L'OPTAT

EDIFICE STE-FOY – 969 RTE DE L'EGLISE, QUEBEC (10e) Tél.: 418-653-8771

Source: *Bulletin de l'Office de la prévention et du traitement de l'alcoolisme et des toxicomanies* 2:3 (July–August 1966), 1

ple of other provinces and American states.[64] The creation of OPTAT thus became part of the state-building process in the health sector, as Gaumer et al. show in their study of the Montreal municipal health service.[65] For practical purposes, it meant that some of the church-controlled organizations in the field of alcoholism treatment were taken over by the Quebec state. The new institution, called OPTAT, was the result of the merger of two governmental bodies, the Service médical sur l'alcoolisme of the Health Department and the Comité d'étude et d'information sur l'alcoolisme of the Family and Welfare Department, created in 1959 and 1961 respectively, as well as the Association des cliniques et des unités de réadaptation pour alcooliques, known until 1965 under the name of *Fondation Domremy*, and the Institut d'études sur l'alcoolisme.[66]

The parliamentary debate is remarkable because the MNAs were unanimous on the issue. No MNA disputed the state-building process and the idea that alcoholism was a disease. Notably, little was said about the use of drugs other than alcohol. The rare MNAs who talked about recreational drug use, three of the ten speakers in all, urged the population to question the belief that the drug phenomenon was rampant, and one MNA urged the public not to give in to panic. Former Liberal minister Émilien Lafrance criticized those who asserted that drug use was an 'endemic state in schools. I believe that it is exaggerated.'[67] He reminded the Assembly that the use and abuse of drugs was not limited to young people. Inspired by the analysis of OPTAT director Dr André Boudreau, Lafrance stated that drug use was indicative of a more important social illness, that of managing tensions generated by competing sociocultural values. Because existing institutional coping mechanisms, such as families, youth organizations, churches, and the workplace, were being questioned by youth, it was not surprising that some young people took refuge in drug use. Hence, young people did not 'find in the grown-up world models capable of responding to their feelings of being overwhelmed.'[68] For his part, Liberal MNA Victor Goldbloom alerted his colleagues to illegal drug use, especially among young people, and, without going into detail, seized the opportunity to indicate his opposition to the legalization of marijuana because of its harmful effects. Goldbloom did not specify, though, whether he believed that marijuana led to experimentation with other drugs.[69] Finally, MNA Maurice Martel, a former pharmacist, pleaded in favour of education in order to deal with this phenomenon, while underlining the prevalence of drugs and the dangers of LSD and marijuana use for the health of young people and adults.[70]

The message 'not to panic' was further repeated outside the Legislative Assembly. On at least one other occasion, the sponsor of the OPTAT bill warned people against overreacting to illegal drug use. During the 1968 international conference organized by OPTAT and attended by more than 200 specialists in drug addiction, the Minister of State for Health, Roch Boivin, argued that 'panic in a situation like this ... was ill advised.'[71]

In spite of the rapid adoption of the OPTAT bill, the birth of this state organization was a slow one. On 1 April 1966 the four previously mentioned organizations merged. Dr André Boudreau, who obtained a degree in medicine from Université Laval in 1954 and a diploma in alcoholism studies from Yale University, became the first and only director of OPTAT. From 1959 he had been the general secretary of the Association des cliniques et des unités de réadaptation pour alcooliques. The team surrounding Dr Boudreau prepared the OPTAT bill in 1966, but the Legislative Assembly did not adopt it until two years later. It was only in 1970 that the lieutenant governor-in-council officially brought OPTAT into existence.

How can we explain this rather prolonged birth process, spread out over more than five years? Successive changes of government account for this lengthy gestation period. The Jean Lesage Liberals, who had encouraged the merger of the four organizations, lost power in 1966.[72] The death of Union Nationale leader Daniel Johnson, who formed the subsequent government, followed by Jean-Jacques Bertrand's arrival in 1968, disrupted the calendar of parliamentary work. It was necessary to wait for the 1970 election of the Liberals under Robert Bourassa for promulgation of the OPTAT Act.

Besides these difficulties, the drawn-out process was symptomatic of a debate on OPTAT's place within the Quebec's bureaucracy. The 1968 act put OPTAT in an awkward situation. On the one hand, OPTAT was part of the health department (Psychiatric Services). It was authorized to receive funds from both private and governmental sectors, to coordinate the action of private health centres (without controlling them, however), and to advise the Department of Health and the government on alcoholism and other drug addiction issues. On the other hand, OPTAT was not a foundation.[73] Dr André Boudreau and his staff tried to force the government's hand on this last aspect by transforming OPTAT's hybrid structure into a Quebec version of ARF. Already in

1964 a study for the Comité d'étude et d'information sur l'alcoolisme had pleaded for the creation of a foundation modelled on its Ontario counterpart. During the merger of governmental committees with private organizations, members of the latter agreed to cease to exist if the future OPTAT became a foundation.[74] Believing he had the support of health department officials, Boudreau submitted a proposal for the creation of such a foundation in March 1971.

Its proponents felt a foundation could receive funds from the private sector, but use them without seeking approval of the health department. However, it was the chance of receiving grants from the federal government that made the foundation proposal especially, and undisputedly, attractive. In 1968 more than $5 million was granted to ARF, while OPTAT had to be content with the modest sum of $11,600 because the federal government defined OPTAT as a state entity. Also, the creation of a Quebec foundation would help maintain links with several privately run organizations that worked in the field of prevention and treatment of alcoholism and other drug addictions, such as the Association Lacordaire, Drogues-Secours, and Société métropolitaine des amis de la sobriété. Finally – and this was in fact the heart of the debate – the proponents of the foundation wanted to protect OPTAT's autonomy by weakening its institutional link with the health department. They wanted an arm's length relation in order to protect OPTAT's autonomy and to facilitate its short- and long-term financial planning, so that OPTAT would not have to compete with other divisions of the health department during annual budgetary planning discussions. Proponents knew that the foundation option was a hard sell because it meant going against the current of state-building and greater state control over health organizations. Still, they presented the argument to senior bureaucrats that the creation of a foundation would strengthen the credibility of state action in the field of alcoholism and other drug-addiction prevention and treatment. How might this be? The Quebec government, like other provinces, profited from alcohol sales. By reporting directly to the health department, OPTAT officials feared, they would discredit government action: on the one hand, the cynics would argue, the state had a pecuniary interest to incite the largest number of people to buy alcohol, and on the other hand, via OPTAT, it tried to make the population aware of the dangers of alcoholism and other drug use. A final argument made to persuade senior health department bureaucrats to support the foundation proposal was the general North American tendency to create foundations instead of fully integrated governmental institutions.[75]

OPTAT, however, lost the battle. It failed to become a foundation because this idea collided with the state-building process of the 1960s in Quebec. This was a period of important growth of state activities and bureaucracy, notably in the areas of health and education. In health, state-building took place over several years, and the conclusions of the Commission d'enquête sur la santé et le bien-être social (Commission Castonguay-Nepveu) accelerated this trend. The Commission recommended a major reorganization of health services, based on the principle of bureaucratic rationalization and financial centralization for the benefit of a health department that became, under the Liberals, the social services department. This department implemented a new philosophy centred on the concept of community health. It consisted of approaching health from a broad perspective that included its physical, psychological, and social dimensions. It was in this context of reorganization, rationalization, and bureaucratization that the integration of OPTAT and the different alcoholism and drug addiction centres occurred. This process of integration was carried out in several stages: at first, the four organizations merged in 1966; then there was a partial integration into the government, which allowed private alcoholism and drug addiction treatment centres to remain operative; finally, in 1975, complete integration occurred when OPTAT was absorbed by the social services department as a result of the Health and Social Services Act.[76]

OPTAT and Its Construction of Drug Addiction

OPTAT went into action in 1966. At the outset, it was particularly interested in alcoholism, but the increased visibility of the recreational drug use phenomenon obliged it to revise its priorities. OPTAT was structured around three important divisions: (1) coordination of the organizations that worked in the field of alcoholism and drug addiction treatment; (2) research; and (3) prevention (including information and education), which included the work of scientists, sociologists, and anthropologists.

Use of legal and illegal drugs for non-medical purposes was defined as a health problem, and not as a sign of individual emotional weakness. The OPTAT Act, the preparation of which the director actively took part in, defined alcoholism as 'a pathological state connected to alcohol consumption and perturbing the physical and psychic balance as well as the social behaviour of the affected individual.'[77] This definition of alcoholism, plus the training of the OPTAT director and staff, shaped their conceptualization of the use and abuse of other drugs, since the behaviour was defined in terms similar to those of alcoholism – that is, as a 'pathological state.' Thus, this conceptualization illustrated well the transfer of legitimacy of knowledge about alcoholism now being applied to other drugs.[78]

OPTAT's first field of intervention was alcoholism and other drug-addiction treatment. In this domain, and contrary to ARF, OPTAT did not control any treatment centres; rather, private corporations operated dozens of them. OPTAT's role consisted of offering summer training courses, accredited by the University of Sherbrooke, to individuals working in this area and to police officers. Also, OPTAT disseminated information among organizations that dealt with alcoholism and other drug addictions. Finally, it was present at rock festivals, providing first aid to victims of overdoses and injuries, notably during the Manseau Pop Festival of August 1970.[79]

The second domain of intervention was research, for which OPTAT did not have the financial means enjoyed by ARF. In fact, it had to compete with other services within the Department of Social Services. OPTAT thus never conducted bio-medical research, because this was the responsibility of the Department of Social Services.[80] This did not, however, prevent OPTAT from conducting research into different aspects of alcoholism and other drug addictions. In the field of illegal drug use, OPTAT launched a series of studies that aimed at quantifying the number of young drug users. It also supported the publication of its research. In 1968, for instance, it organized an international conference on drug use. It was, however, its journal, Toxicomanies (founded in 1968, with more than six hundred subscribers in 1974), that became its best means of publishing not only its own research but also that conducted by other organizations and individuals. Moreover, in the first issue of the journal, OPTAT's director underlined the importance of creating a French-language space for the dissemination of scientific knowledge about alcoholism and other drug addictions.[81]

It was in its third area of activity, prevention through education and diffusion of information, that OPTAT distinguished itself. During a December 1969 conference on the drug problem and on drug use among young people organized by Quebec police forces, the director of the OPTAT Prevention Service, Marcel Bougie, defined OPTAT's

Two posters on the negative effects of drug use.
Source: *Action pédagogique* 25 (August 1972), 35, 25

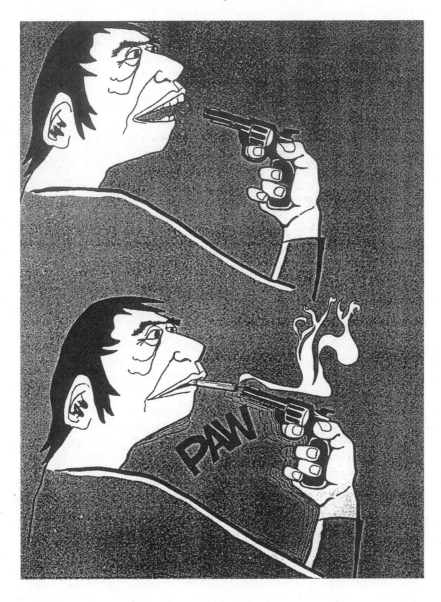

approach in the following way: first, it was necessary to circulate objective information on recreational drug consumption; second, OPTAT would appeal to the intellect rather than the emotions in its educational and information effort, because people were eager to learn about legal and illegal drug use (in this way, the population would become responsible with regard to drug consumption); finally, OPTAT emphasized that – contrary to the view presented by the media and certain interest groups – illegal drug use was not restricted to young people. Certainly, OPTAT was concerned about drug use by young people. The organization offered several explanations for this, such as curiosity, the desire to make a rebellious gesture, media influence, the religious vacuum in a society that had become materialistic, and the desire to follow a trend or to escape the difficulties associated with a fast-evolving society that had few adult role models to offer young people. It was also, however, necessary to educate adults about their own use of legal drugs before judging or condemning young people.[82]

These educational and informational efforts also emphasized that illegal drug abuse was symptomatic of social and cultural difficulties particular to the 1960s. In a context of conflicting values, of a society that was changing rapidly, and of concerns about these changes, OPTAT encouraged society to investigate the factors that favoured legal and illegal drug use. Moreover, it was necessary to 'direct' the public to understand that drugs were 'for patients, and those in good health did not need them at all.'[83] Dr Boudreau went so far as to assert that any drugs, even those for therapeutic purposes, were merely 'a palliative, a temporary help.'[84] Finally, it was necessary to convince society to favour the 'optimum' development of individuals by respecting others. This would be achieved by broad support for the implementation of 'educational, preventive and psychotherapeutic' measures.[85]

When OPTAT intervened in schools and CEGEPs, its staff suggested to teachers, school principals, and other staff that drug use was symptomatic of deficiencies in young people's environments. Illegal drug use by young people was an indication of a lack of variety of leisure activities, or of difficulties in the relationship between the school and students. In short, it was necessary to bring school personnel and principals 'to envisage solutions which not only contribute to the prevention of drug addiction, but also prevent drug use being replaced by something else that would be equally bad for the health of the school and those who attend it.'[86] It was also necessary to make school personnel aware of what OPTAT termed their mission and role of reassurance, since their interventions had an effect on young people and their parents. In summary, then, it was crucial to counter the climate of panic and strong concern about recreational drug use by speaking with school personnel and by encouraging them to exert a calming influence on society by circulating adequate, non-sensational, and relevant information. OPTAT also reminded educators that knowledge about drugs was incomplete and that rapid developments in research would periodically force them to update the content of their educational material. In this way, OPTAT hoped that young people would be made responsible and engaged 'in full knowledge of the facts' about illegal drug use.[87]

To fulfil its educational mission, OPTAT used multiple channels. Initially, there were the media. In 1970 OPTAT had a weekly ten-minute TV broadcast on the private network TVA. Other television stations, for example, a Quebec City private television station, offered airtime to OPTAT. With various partners, notably the police, the College of Pharmacists, and the College of Physicians, OPTAT operated a pavilion at Terre des Hommes (Man and His World – the former Expo 67 site) from 1968. The 1969 pavilion, in the former New York City pavilion, carried the name LSD–POT (La Science de la Drogue – Pavilion of Toxicomanias).[88] OPTAT collaborated with ARF, translated some of ARF's journal articles and distributed some of its material to Quebec's English-speaking population. ARF in return explored the possibility of using OPTAT material for Franco-Ontarians. In addition, OPTAT produced posters and pamphlets, but made no documentary films.[89] Finally, up until 1974, it published an information bulletin entitled *Informations sur l'alcoolisme et les autres toxicomanies*.

Assessing OPTAT's Influence: The Defence of Provincial Jurisdiction

Because OPTAT was a creature of the state, its first effects were felt within the Quebec bureaucracy. Although OPTAT lost the battle to define its institutional relationship with the social services department, its advice and opinions were considered seriously by both the latter and the education department. OPTAT's input was valued because of its staff's expertise and the legitimacy attributed to health specialists on alcohol and drug addiction questions. Moreover, in 1972, OPTAT's director chaired the Interministerial Committee on Drug Addiction appointed by the Quebec cabinet. Overall, OPTAT educated the Quebec political class (those officially responsible) and the Quebec bureaucracy, notably the health / social services and education departments (those unofficially responsible). OPTAT pleaded for a cautious approach. In 1969 it urged government officials to avoid any statement about illegal drug use by young people that would contribute to the climate of panic already created and maintained, it said, by the media, by other organizations (which it did not specifically identify), and by the public. This cautious approach was based on the fact that there were still no adequate answers to some crucial questions, such as the health effects of illegal drugs on users.[90]

As a Quebec state institution, OPTAT saw its scope of action limited by the federal system of government. Under federalism, the responsibilities of provincial governments in the field of non-medical drug use were numerous, and were sometimes in direct competition with those of Ottawa, which inevitably led to conflict. When the Quebec government interacted with the national health and welfare department, and in particular with the Non-Medical Drug Use Directorate, it was the social services department that was the spokesman. OPTAT acted as an adviser to the department. In this capacity, OPTAT pressed Quebec politicians and senior bureaucrats to remind federal officials and the other provinces that health and education were domains of provincial jurisdiction. Any federal initiative in education and treatment of drug users should be made in consultation with the provinces, rather than without them. OPTAT's position was that, if the federal government decided to initiate a policy or a program, it should do so through the Canadian Foundation on Alcoholism and Drug Addiction (the national organization located on the same premises as OPTAT's head office), or cooperate with either the Interprovincial Conference of Health Ministers or provincial organizations that worked in the field of alcoholism and drug use.

When the federal government announced its strategy on illegal drug use in June 1971, the Quebec government reminded Ottawa that the initiative should be integrated into the reorganization of the health sector centred on the creation of community services centres (CLSCs). In March 1972 Ottawa and Quebec formed a joint committee to study grant requests submitted by public and non-profit organizations under the program on non-medical drug use. Over the years, the Quebec government complained that the national health and welfare department paid little attention to the role of CLSCs, since it tended to support specific projects, thus increasing the quantity of resources offered to drug users, while the Quebec government was simultaneously trying to rationalize resources.[91]

OPTAT's positions were often in agreement with those of the Departments of Intergovernmental Affairs, Education, and Social Services. Thus, when these bureaucrats negotiated with the federal government on Quebec's behalf, they underlined the constitutional limits to the federal government's power over education and health.[92] However, there were exceptions. For instance, when the federal government appointed the Le Dain Commission in 1969, the director of OPTAT in vain urged the Quebec health minister to denounce what he considered a federal intrusion in an area of provincial jurisdiction, which was the collection of information about the phenomenon of illegal drug use.[93]

When OPTAT explained the Quebec position directly to federal institutions and departments, its influence seemed ineffectual. The root of the problem (unlike ARF's situation) might have been its weak network with federal bureaucrats. Thus, OPTAT was rarely involved with work undertaken by the Le Dain Commission. It was invited, as were any interested individuals and organizations, to submit its views to the commissioners. Moreover, in its evaluation of the last two reports by the Commission, OPTAT complained that the specific Quebec situation had been neglected.[94] OPTAT reproached the RCMP for the same reason; indeed, as will be outlined later, the RCMP preferred the approach of the Narcotic Addiction Foundation of British Columbia.

At the international level, the director of OPTAT participated in several international conferences and was appointed to international organizations related to alcoholism and other drug addictions. He was a member of the board of the *Ligua Catholica Internationalis Sobrietas* of Lucerne, and was one of the experts on the Alcoholism and Drug Addiction Committee of the World Health Organization. OPTAT also acted as the secretariat of the Alcohol and Drug Problems Association of North America and of the International Council on the Problems of Alcoholism and Other Drug Addiction of the World Health Organization.[95]

In the public domain, OPTAT contributed to the fact that legal and illegal drug use was viewed as a health issue. This approach reflected the convictions of OPTAT staff, but was also motivated by the material interests of its direction, because obtaining more human and financial resources would allow it to increase the services it offered, and thus guarantee its survival as an institution.

'The Drug Capital of Canada': British Columbia Politicians and the Drug Issue

While provincial politicians in Quebec were not particularly vocal on the phenomenon of recreational drug use, their counterparts in British Columbia certainly were. Between 1970, the year the publication of the legislative debates began, and 1975, members of the Legislative Assembly spoke repeatedly on drug use. It is must be said that the drug issue was not a new one for BC politicians. It had been ongoing in the province, but by the 1960s there was a sense of crisis and urgency. There was also a feeling that renewed efforts were needed against heroin addiction. In general, it was imperative to deal with a drug problem that, according to politicians, had reached epidemic proportions, remained a social evil, and was no longer limited in number of substances or of users.

Politicians did not hesitate to describe recreational drug use in dramatic terms. During a discussion on glue-sniffing in 1972, Member of the Legislative Assembly (MLA) Agnes Kripps maintained that sniffing nail-polish remover had reached 'almost epidemic proportions, particularly in the Raymur public housing project in Vancouver.'[96] Minister of Municipal Affairs Daniel R.J. Campbell, in turn, stated that drugs were bad because 'the whole drug culture is a bad scene, period, and should not receive any encouragement from any public people.'[97] These comments (attributable to political partisanship) became even more dramatic after the New Democrats formed the provincial government in 1972. Member of the Official Opposition Robert H. McClelland, for instance, described the drug phenomenon as 'a national tragedy' and 'a cancerous problem that we've allowed to grow.' Two years later, McClelland did not hesitate to describe his province as 'the drug capital of Canada.'[98] Liberal MLA Patrick L. McGreer wanted 'drugs out of our schools.'[99] The statements of Social Credit MLA Donald McGray Phillips are particularly striking. Besides his use of the term 'cancer' to describe recreational drug use, he did not hesitate to characterize it as the greatest threat for society and particularly for parents. 'Every parent who has a child, some time during the course of a 12-month period, has a great fear that that child will become addicted to drugs.' In order to deal with this cancer, he recommended the death penalty for pushers 'by firing squad.'[100]

While Ontario cabinet members were aware that provincial powers were circumscribed by federalism since they could not legislate on

criminal matters, the BC government, led by Social Credit Leader
W.A.C. Bennett, believed that the criminal law remained the best way
to deter young people from using drugs not prescribed by physicians.
Thus, in March 1967 it passed the Act Respecting Proscribed Substances. Marijuana was already a banned substance; the act now
rendered possession of it a criminal offence, and for the first time outlawed LSD. If someone was found guilty, he was liable, on summary
conviction, to a fine of a maximum of $2000 and/or six months in
jail.[101] Another law, the Act to Amend the Health Act, targeted LSD. In
this case, anyone in possession or aware of the presence of LSD should
inform police or a health professional. Someone in possession of LSD
could be condemned to pay a maximum fine of $2000 and/or serve a
six-month prison sentence.[102] It is worth mentioning that in 1967 the
Alberta legislature adopted a law that made the production, possession, and distribution of hallucinogenic drugs (including LSD) illegal.
The penalties included a prison sentence.[103] To the dismay of several
BC MLAs, the BC Act to Amend the Health Act was declared unconstitutional by the British Columbia Court of Appeal because the province
did not have the power to legislate in the field of criminal law.[104]

Repeatedly during the debates, several MLAs denounced the
division of powers preventing the Legislature from adopting laws
that would increase the repressive approach in the fight against non-
medical drug use. When politicians debated the glue-sniffing issue in
January 1972, the Social Credit government argued that not much
could be done because the division of powers bound the hands of the
province. Some members of the Opposition, including Liberal leader
Patrick Lucay McGeer, asked that glue-sniffing be outlawed as it had
been in several American cities and states. Furthermore, McGeer
requested that educational resources be allocated to warn young people about the health risks glue-sniffing posed to their 'brains, livers,
kidneys, [and] blood.'[105] Attorney-General Leslie Raymond Peterson
reminded everyone that it could not be done, not because the government did not want to, but because it did not have the constitutional
authority to do so, as the Act to Amend the Health Act had shown.
This government response frustrated certain MLAs who expected
more; some suggested that municipalities or the federal government
should ban the sale of glue to people under sixteen years of age. Others
argued during the debate that parents or the federal government
should acquaint children with the dangers.[106]

During the 1972 debate there were few dissenting voices to question the law-enforcement approach as a way to deal with glue-sniffing or any other drug problem. MLA Price tried to downplay reports about glue-sniffing by arguing that it was not as widespread as politicians and the public believed. MLAs Eileen Elizabeth Dailly and Dr H.R. McDiarmid questioned the repressive approach, not only in dealing with glue-sniffing in particular, but in dealing with recreational drugs overall. Banning LSD or marijuana, McDiarmid stated, 'is [not] in any way going to stop their distribution to juveniles who are intent on getting them.' Education seemed a more appropriate way to deal with the issues.[107]

The new NDP government created the British Columbia Alcohol and Drug Commission in April 1973. During his announcement, Minister of Rehabilitation and Social Improvement Norman Levi informed the Assembly that drug abuse was not restricted to illegal drugs. Moreover, the new state organization would coordinate work by agencies in the field of drug dependency.[108] The announcement marked a change of tone and approach, since the law was not to be used to punish, but to assist drug addicts to seek and obtain treatment. In the following years, the Opposition would denounce the work accomplished by the Commission. Its harshest critic, Social Credit MLA Robert H. McClelland, used every opportunity to portray the Commission's work as a failure.[109] He did not hesitate to introduce the Drug Addiction Rehabilitation Act, intended to force treatment upon drug addicts, though the government rejected it because compulsory treatment violated individual freedom.[110]

During this period, and regardless of which political party was in power, the perceived inaction of the federal government on the drug issue was often criticized. Because a majority of Canadian heroin addicts lived in British Columbia, provincial politicians expected Ottawa to help to deal with the treatment costs. Furthermore, the drug issue was defined, as stated by the Social Credit attorney general Leslie R. Peterson, as 'national in scope, not only in terms of the problem, but in terms of the constitutional authority to tackle the problem.'[111] Consequently, BC politicians would support any federal government initiatives, since the drug problem was, in their view, Ottawa's responsibility. Meanwhile, they could count on their provincial research body, the Narcotic Addiction Foundation of British Columbia, to develop anti-drug strategies, while the federal government studied the phenomenon of recreational drug use.

'Combating the Social Ill of Drug Dependency':
The Narcotic Addiction Foundation of British Columbia

Founded in 1955, the Narcotic Addiction Foundation of British Columbia (NAFBC) was a non-profit organization in charge of research, education, treatment, and rehabilitation. However, the particularities of the drug culture in British Columbia, and particularly in Vancouver, came to define the action of the NAFBC. In the 1960s there were about 4000 addicts in the country, and 61 per cent of them lived in British Columbia. Consequently, the treatment and rehabilitation division of the NAFBC expanded in order to deal with this particular group. From 1959 it had used methadone as a means of treatment. The federal government came to the aid of the NAFBC in its treatment activities. Starting in 1966, a grant of $800,000 from the Department of National Health and Welfare supported the NAFBC in its program of methadone distribution over a four-year period.[112]

The NAFBC's financial resources, however, limited its ability to conduct research. Until 1966, its overall budget was less than $200,000 annually; thanks to assistance from Ottawa, the budget doubled in the following years.[113] The NAFBC, like ARF and OPTAT, conducted studies of how widespread the use of illegal drugs really was, especially among youth. It did so as a direct result of the debate about the legalization of marijuana. According to the NAFBC, 'it suits the purpose of those who would press for the legalization of this drug to lead us to believe that "everyone is doing it"; conversely, those who oppose its use only through ignorance or fear would like to pretend a mere handful of persons use the drug.'[114]

Starting in 1967, the NAFBC allocated more resources to education, partly in reaction to strong concerns expressed by parents, teachers, and school officials about LSD and marijuana use. Its strategy, known as 'educating the educators,' targeted teachers in order to multiply the number of people able to teach about the dangers of drug abuse. The NAFBC suggested including drug-use education in the school curriculum in order to equip young people to make informed decisions when they were exposed to drugs. The educational approach also meant that parents had to be informed, so that they could engage 'sensibly and knowledgeably' in dialogue with their children. Finally, the NAFBC counted on the media to help educate the population.

The NAFBC produced booklets intended to inform and educate, as well. Besides producing such material and pamphlets, it organized seminars, sent speakers to organizations, and was vocal in the media in order to stop the number of drug users from increasing. It aimed, ultimately, as stated by the executive director Herbert F. Hoskin, to reverse the new trend. On the other hand, the NAFBC was aware, like the AFR, of the educational challenge due to the gap between what young people were told about illegal drugs such as LSD and what they found out by themselves:

> It was our hope that young people at long last were accepting the factual and objective information that these are highly dangerous drugs and were turning away from them, but now we are not so sure, and there is evidence that as the users become more familiar with the drugs and their effects, they become less and less willing to attribute any ill effects to the drug or to seek competent medical help.[115]

When H.F. Hoskin became executive director in 1964, he influenced the NAFBC's conceptualization of drug use. Beginning in 1965 a sense of emergency began to characterize the annual reports and other reports submitted to the provincial and federal governments. Subsequent events increased the feeling of urgency. What was the root of this sense of crisis? The first point of concern was the increase of drug abuse among young people. The second was what appeared to be a serious and changing pattern of drug abuse, since many people now used a wide variety of drugs without proper medical supervision. The management of the drug problem was no longer confined to heroin, a substance already familiar to the NAFBC. The third point of concern was a vocal 'minority' of people who pleaded for the liberalization of drug legislation while there was still so little known about the health consequences. The fourth point of concern identified by the NAFBC was the lack of means for education, research, and treatment to face this new and disturbing reality. Finally, the NAFBC denounced the absence of leadership, especially from the federal government, in dealing with this threat.[116]

In his 1968 annual report, Hoskin used the expression 'social ill' to characterize the problem of drug abuse and dependency. He was fighting the public tendency to discuss drug abuse by focusing on one drug in particular, that is, marijuana. For Hoskin, 'it obscures the real threat and issues we face: that adolescents and adults alike are increasingly abusing a wide variety of drugs.'[117] Consequently, marijuana's lack of harmful effects on users' health was a false excuse for softening drug legislation.

The NAFBC, led by Hoskin, concluded that there was a correlation between consumption of marijuana and that of other drugs that tended to support the theory that marijuana was a stepping-stone drug. This contradicted studies by John Russell concluding there was no relation between the consumption of marijuana and heroin use.[118] In its document submitted to national health and welfare minister John Munro in 1969, the NAFBC indicated that residents of neighbourhoods where illegal drugs circulated relatively freely were at risk of being introduced to hard drugs and being incited to use them. In fact, the 'known total user population ... together with the admitted evidence of users turning to other drugs such as the barbiturates, amphetamines and LSD, points out the very real possibility of progression ... All of which would indicate that we are on the verge of having an even more serious drug problem than we now have.'[119] The NAFBC was also concerned with the motives for drug use among youth. In 1969, a report by Ingeborg Paulus identified several causes such as a 'lessening of parental influence and control,' easy access to drugs, and 'pure enjoyment.'[120]

Some NAFBC studies on marijuana and other drug use confirmed Hoskin's fears. In the 1968 NAFBC annual report, Hoskin wrote that illegal drug use had attained such proportions in Canada that 'any adult, student or adolescent at some time will have the opportunity to obtain a non-narcotic drug, should he or she desire to experiment in this area.' What should be done to contain what Hoskin qualified as a 'social ill'? 'As an interim and emergency measure,' the director indicated, there should be 'a concerted effort to contain the problem by means of control legislation, treatment and education.' In the longer term, it was crucial to attack the root causes of drug abuse and to promote abstinence.[121]

For the NAFBC, the federal government and, more particularly, the national health and welfare department, had a crucial role to play. In the research field specifically, coordination of the work undertaken by the different provincial organizations was needed. The solution was 'a co-ordinated, nationally supervised programme [that] would obviate gaps and overlapping, with more effective research, based on regional capabilities and needs.' It was equally necessary to coordinate all the provincial organizations working in education. For the NAFBC, provincial jurisdiction over education and health was secondary to the need for national coordination. According to the NAFBC proposal submitted to minister John Munro in 1969, the national health and welfare department should coordinate the distribution of documents on illegal drug use produced by national and international organizations, in order to overcome the isolation that often plagued the activities of these organizations, to avoid duplication, and to favour the distribution of up-to-date factual information about drugs, 'particularly to educators and researchers,' as fast as possible.[122]

The NAFBC did not adopt the same position as ARF and OPTAT regarding federal regulation of the non-medical use of drugs, nor did it reject the repressive approach. Rather, it distanced itself from any suggestion of legalization of marijuana because there were too many unknowns about its effects on health, the composition of the drug, and the obligations that resulted from international treaties and conventions signed by Canada. However, the NAFBC did note that the penalties imposed on young offenders in cases such as possession of marijuana sometimes exceeded the crime. This assertion that punishment did not fit the crime reflected the doubts of the scientific community about the degree of danger and toxicity of this drug. While still maintaining the list of drugs listed in the Food and Drugs Act and the Narcotic Control Act, the NAFBC suggested a new categorization of penalties that would be more appropriate. What the organization proposed was dramatic: merging the Narcotic Control Act and the Food and Drugs Act in a new law called the Dangerous Drugs Act. This new act would contain two sections: opiates and other drugs. 'The Foundation has stated many times that it is unrealistic and unacceptable to base our approach to drug dependency solely on the point of "possession."' It was necessary to rethink the repressive approach and to ease its application by taking into account the results of scientific research on drugs. 'It is proposed that all [non-opiate] drugs be recorded, and escalated or de-escalated on the dangerous drug scale according to the objective evidence amassed from clinical and social research programmes available at the time.' This combination of repression and scientific and social research would lead to a new classification of drugs based on their toxicity and danger for the health of users. Compulsory treatment in rehabilitation centres or imprisonment would be prescribed accordingly. This proposed law, contrary to the current one, would allow the justice system to force an opiate addict to be sent to a drug treatment centre. 'Under existing laws, unless an addict is prepared to undergo a voluntary treatment programme, he cannot be helped unless he is apprehended in "possession," found guilty and sentenced to custodial care, at which point, on transfer to the Federal Matsqui Institution, he is directed into a treatment programme.'[123]

The state should accept the premise that an opiate drug user (as opposed to a trafficker or anyone involved in the sale and distribution of drugs) 'is a sick person.' 'He or she should be directed into treatment ... carried out in an authorized laboratory.' The NAFBC went on to state: 'To those who would object on the grounds of an invasion of human rights, we point out that control and compulsory treatment regulations already exist and are accepted by the Public for any communicable disease, such as, tuberculosis and venereal disease.'[124]

In the case of other drugs, such as marijuana and LSD, traffickers and those who sell and distribute these drugs would be sent to jail. However, the user would receive a penalty based on the drug used, its degree of toxicity for health, and the background of the user. This could be effected by making distinctions among 'beginner, experimenter, casual or compulsive/continuous user. The judge would decide on an appropriate penalty, such as jail term and/or treatment.'[125]

After Hoskin's departure and his replacement by Douglas A. Denholm, the NAFBC's budget increased, which led to the creation of new services, notably the 1972 opening of regional units in Prince George, Nanaimo, Trail, and Coquitlam. In 1970, the NAFBC opened The House, a drop-in medical and counselling centre for youth. Finally, to reach out to young people who were sometimes reluctant to go to official health establishments, NAFBC launched In Touch, an on-the-street referral agency.[126]

Assessing NAFBC's Influence: Some Strange Bedfellows

The construction of drug use put forward by the NAFBC bore a striking resemblance to the opinions of BC politicians, especially those in the Social Credit government. In short, the NAFBC presented the phenomenon of recreational drug use as a serious and looming crisis that had to be contained before it was too late. This alarmist tone was likely a result of strategic considerations. Because the financial resources of the provincial body were limited, a tone of urgency could encourage governments to attribute more financial resources to its activities. This is likely why, from 1967 on, the NAFBC received annual budget increases.

The relationship between the federal government and the NAFBC were tense. NAFBC Director Hoskin resigned in 1970, after national health and welfare minister John Munro mused about the possibility of legalizing marijuana.[127] Hoskin characterized Munro's reflection as irresponsible. He was also bitter about the Le Dain Commission, describing it as an 'unnecessary extravagance,' since both federal and provincial governments could deal with the issue.[128] In 1972 Hoskin released *Year of Decision*, a document supported by the CACP that pleaded for increased state measures aimed at making drugs hard to obtain. Hoskin also favoured a significant increase in the financial and human resources assigned to drug law enforcement, and argued for the implementation of an effective educational strategy on drug use. He believed that because an important segment of society was vulnerable to drugs, any state measure intended to increase the availability of marijuana would mean a significant increase of its consumption and a worsening of the situation.[129]

If the NAFBC, especially during Hoskin's tenure, had difficulty developing a good working relationship with the national health and welfare department, the opposite was true of its relationship with another constituent of the federal state apparatus, the RCMP. The national police force used NAFBC's studies and scientific credibility to support its opposition to the legalization of marijuana. Although I have been unable to ascertain for how long these two organizations worked and/or cooperated together, NAFBC and the RCMP were definitely allies on the marijuana issue, at least until Hoskin's resignation, and were determined to win over, or at least influence, public opinion and federal politicians to their understanding of the phenomenon of illegal drug use.[130]

With the arrival of a New Democrat government under the premiership of David Barrett, the NAFBC, like OPTAT in Quebec, essentially met its demise. Minister of rehabilitation and social improvement Levi announced the merger of NAFBC activities with those of Alcoholism of British Columbia. The BC Alcohol and Drug Commission would henceforth be responsible for issues that were previously dealt with by the NAFBC. With the defeat of the NDP government in 1975, Herbert Hoskin would be appointed by the newly elected Social Credit government to head the BC Alcohol and Drug Commission, led until then by former Le Dain commissioner Peter Stein.[131]

Small But Vocal: The Government of Prince Edward Island and the Drug Issue

Even if the PEI health minister maintained at the 1968 Interprovincial Conference of Health Ministers that the phenomenon of non-medical drug use was not a problem in his province, PEI played an important role in opposing individuals and interest groups sympathetic to the legalization of marijuana.[132] The case of PEI is fascinating, because unlike Ontario, Quebec, and British Columbia, it did not have a well-known state organization in the field of alcoholism and drug addiction. In fact, the province's role in the debate can be attributed to the indefatigable action of G. Keith Cowan, an adviser to the PEI government and an active member of the PEI Drug Education Committee. Cowan was engaged in a battle against what he called the pro-marijuana lobby – a vast and loose coalition in which he grouped the media (especially the CBC, the *Globe and Mail*, and the National Film Board), some scientists, and other groups. In 1971 he argued that national health and welfare minister John Munro's staff were sympathetic to a softening of penalties for illegal drug users.[133] Cowan fought hard against those who conveyed the idea that marijuana use was harmless. Several physicians opposed to the legalization of marijuana supplied Cowan with data and scientific evidence aimed at thwarting the pro-marijuana lobby whenever possible. Thus, Cowan quoted the opinions of Dr Conrad Schwarz, associate professor of psychiatry and head of the mental health section of the University of British Columbia, Dr F.W. Lundell, associate professor of psychiatry at McGill University, and Dr Henry Brill, head of the American Medical Association Drug Committee. These health professionals gave a list of serious health dangers for marijuana users, such as 'organic brain syndrome,' 'irreversible brain damage,' 'perception distortion,' 'reversal of social values,' 'memory [and] motivation loss,' 'movement to harder drugs' (the famous stepping-stone theory), and 'loss of I.Q. potential.'[134] Dr Lundell even drafted for the government of PEI a critique of the interim report of the Le Dain Commission.[135]

Cowan's activities were influential and varied. At first, as an educator, he made several tours of PEI, and sometimes New Brunswick, schools. During his speeches, Cowan made great efforts to convince young people, parents, and teachers of the risks of non-medical drug use, notably those associated with marijuana. Later, he intervened on the national scene by drafting the briefs of the PEI government for the Le Dain Commission. In 1975, he was also invited to appear as a representative of PEI before the Senate Committee that studied Bill S-19, which dealt with the transfer of marijuana from the Narcotic Drug Act to the Food and Drugs Act.[136] A year earlier, he had appeared before the United States Senate Committee on marijuana.

The PEI cabinet shared Cowan's views. Attorney General J. Elmer

Blanchard was very concerned by 'the apparent campaign underway in Canada, and other countries, to pressure governments into legalizing [marijuana].'[137] Perceiving a very active pro-marijuana lobby determined to present marijuana as harmless for users, Blanchard justified his action with the following words: '[I]t is now time for the feelings of the family people concerned with youth, and the general responsible public to be heard with conviction.'[138] In the PEI brief submitted to the Le Dain Commission in February 1970, he did not hesitate to assert that Ottawa was attempting to force 'upon us open use of this drug [marijuana] by legalization, where our children would be exposed daily to its use.' This was 'a totally unacceptable position' for the PEI government.[139]

In March 1970, Blanchard sent a letter to all provincial premiers, as well as to federal and provincial ministers of justice, education, and health, in which he denounced the pro-marijuana lobby. In fact, in his letter to the national health and welfare minister, Blanchard pointed an accusatory finger at Ottawa, denouncing what he termed the federal government's pro-marijuana campaign. In his letter, Blanchard enumerated a list of reasons to prevent the legalization of marijuana at all costs. Its legalization would definitely create a significant increase in use and thus pose health problems for its users. These health problems would be handled by hospitals, and the attorney general reminded his correspondents that PEI and the other provinces had limited financial means. The issue of increased health costs, however, served as a form of pretext for the presentation of Blanchard's objections. The minister urged his provincial and federal counterparts to join him in his opposition to marijuana, which was a 'hazardous' and 'unpredictable' drug. Without providing specific information, he asserted that evidence concerning the dangers of this drug were mounting. Indeed, Blanchard referred to the 1967 Massachusetts Superior Court decision that ruled marijuana dangerous. 'In the light of massive evidence presented by both sides,' Blanchard wrote, 'the court ruled unequivocally that marijuana was proven to be a socially and personally harmful and dangerous drug, a position which has not been subsequently threatened, but indeed has been increasingly supported by current research.' What else was there to say![140]

What were the solutions minister Blanchard proposed to halt recreational marijuana use? First, education was part of his arsenal. It was necessary, to summarize his opinion, to teach young people about 'the harm and problems of drug usage.' Second, legal repression was still appropriate, but it should be tempered with a certain leniency towards first- and second-time youth offenders.[141]

It should be noted that the bulk of the letter dealt with marijuana. A few lines were dedicated to other illegal drugs, such as speed and LSD. In the latter case, Blanchard opposed any softening of its status in the Food and Drugs Act. Nothing was said, however, about other socially accepted drugs such as cigarettes and alcohol.[142]

Blanchard's activities were not limited to forwarding the PEI briefs before the Le Dain Commission to his provincial and federal counterparts. The attorney general informed them about international developments in the struggle against marijuana. Blanchard applauded the decision of the British government to maintain its repressive approach towards marijuana, which was nevertheless accompanied by a softening in certain aspects. He publicized studies on the harmful health effects of marijuana, notably by quoting the results of an American study, 'Dr. Louria's work in New York,' which demonstrated 'that youth who experience more than ten sessions of using marijuana have one chance in five of going on to harder, more dangerous drugs, confirming general evidence from Dr. P.C. Whitehouse's study made at Dalhousie University recently.'[143]

At the beginning of 1971 Blanchard's successor, Gordon L. Bennett, continued his campaign. Bennett distributed PEI's brief to the Le Dain Commission in November 1970. The document summarized the main points contained in Blanchard's letter: denunciation of the pro-marijuana lobby (without being too precise on its membership), rejection of legalization and a recommendation of changes to the Narcotic Control Act to ease the judicial consequences for young offenders. Thus, the report, originally drafted by Cowan, featured both the stick and the carrot approaches. On the one hand, the brief pleaded for a certain leniency. 'We do not feel that first or even second offenders for possession of marijuana for personal use should be punished with jail sentences under normal circumstances.' 'Fines and other light sentences could be followed – after say two years of a clear record – with the complete removal of a person's name from a criminal record for court use.' The same applied to drug addicts. These people should be sent to treatment centres rather than jail. On the other hand, the brief recommended maintaining, if not increasing, the penalties for trafficking.[144]

The brief was, in fact, a critique of the interim report of the Le Dain Commission. Thus, it contained numerous passages about the dangers incurred by a marijuana user. Based on scientific studies, the brief insisted that marijuana was dangerous for the health of its users because it created an 'adverse personality alteration.' Marijuana use led to other drugs (no specific information was provided on this point), and constituted a traffic safety issue. Using an argument of authority, the brief went on to state that 'some authorities' (who remained unidentified) 'are of the opinion that the number of unexplained teenage and college-age driver accidents on the road are due to the fact that youngsters driving cars after a marijuana party have gone to sleep and run off the road.'[145]

In his letter accompanying the PEI brief, Bennett pleaded for a change to the membership of the Le Dain Commission by recommending the candidacies of F.W. Lundell from the McGill University psychiatry department, and Conrad Schwarz from the University of British Columbia, individuals who influenced the PEI government and provided legitimacy to its action. Bennett's proposals were not, however, adopted by the federal government.[146]

The actions of the PEI government were oriented towards influencing the public debate on marijuana. The impact of these actions remains doubtful, however, especially on groups and individuals who were sympathetic to the anti-marijuana cause. What is clear is that the attempts to persuade other provincial governments and especially the federal government, which had the responsibility for amending its drug legislation, were decidedly limited in their success. Certainly, the Social Credit governments in Alberta and British Columbia supported the anti-legalization campaign.[147] Yet other provinces showed their reluctance vis-à-vis the PEI campaign, and the tone of the arguments used by the PEI government certainly evoked negative reactions from OPTAT and ARF officials.

In its comment on the brief submitted by Blanchard to the Le Dain Commission in 1970, OPTAT denounced 'the blatant lack of objectivity' and the partisan and dramatic tone of the document. It did not hesitate to attribute this tone to the 'island mentality,' which led the attorney general to attempt 'to avoid the contagion of [his province] by the marijuana use phenomenon' which had already affected the continent. OPTAT conceded that the brief highlighted the need for changes in federal legislation, but what the PEI government suggested was unacceptable. In short, OPTAT cited the brief's evident and strong ideological bias as a reason for its lack of credibility. OPTAT pointed to the partisan commitment echoed in the choice of studies and quotes used to support the PEI view. Furthermore, OPTAT argued that the brief contained too many generalizations, with a resulting distorted view of the state of knowledge on marijuana and its health consequences.[148]

The director of ARF was equally unreceptive towards the briefs sent by minister Blanchard in March 1970. In his opinion, they were tinged with value judgments that ultimately undermined their credibility. 'It is reminiscent,' Archibald wrote, 'of the kinds of briefs that used to be prepared by temperance organizations – exhibiting a "fire and brimstone" attitude, which is precisely the sort of thing that tend[s] to discredit the so-called "establishment" among the young people of today.' However, he concluded his evaluation on a positive note by underlining to the federal health minister that PEI's opposition to the legalization of marijuana on the basis of a lack of scientific studies was a valid stance.[149]

For his part, G.K. Cowan found no allies among officials at OPTAT, at ARF, and least of all at the National Health and Welfare department. These bureaucrats faulted him both for the simplicity of his message and for his activism, which appeared too doctrinaire.[150]

Conclusion

Although some provincial politicians adopted the same tone, as revealed at the 1970 meeting of provincial attorneys general who opposed the legalization of marijuana,[151] the analysis of these four provinces presents some differences in their views of the phenomenon of recreational drug use. On this point, the Quebec politicians, at least those who participated in the legislative debates and made ministerial declarations, refused to give into panic. They also did not attempt to agitate public opinion by formulating alarmist comments to pander to interest groups.

In order to explain Quebec's views on social issues, analysts tend to focus on the cultural factor. For instance, the cultural factor is highlighted in studies of Quebec's response towards alcohol and its prohibition at the beginning of the twentieth century.[152] In her study on gambling, Suzanne Morton argues that cultural factors, rather than the particularities of Quebec political culture, lay behind the province's preference for the liberalization of lotteries. This preference cut across party lines. Quebec premiers Alexandre Taschereau, Maurice Duplessis, and Jean Lesage, who were otherwise ideologically very different regarding the role of the state in society, asked the federal government to allow the province of Quebec to organize lotteries. Morton notes that as early as 1949, Duplessis launched a campaign for the creation of a provincial lottery in the name of provincial autonomy.[153]

Perhaps an alternative explanation should be ventured, though, one that takes into consideration Quebec's political culture, its nationalist demands, and its cultural sensibilities, all of which found expression in politicians' attitudes. Quebec society was different from the rest of the country, and politicians, especially those who formed the Quebec government, did not hesitate to use these cultural differences as a basis to defend Quebec's constitutional jurisdiction. Thus, health ministers of both the Union Nationale and Liberal parties shared a desire to defend Quebec's jurisdiction over health, to pursue the tradition of promoting nationalist demands, to support state-building in the context of the Quiet Revolution, and to promote treatment as a more suitable approach for drug use. The intersection of these various factors and motivations came to characterize Quebec political culture, and gave momentum to a discourse centred less on repression and more on treatment, in contrast with the British Columbia, PEI, and, to a lesser extent, Ontario jurisdictions, where politicians did not hide their aversion to illegal drug users.

For those interested in federal–provincial relations, the four case studies demonstrate that there was little in common among provincial politicians, which made the management of the recreational drug issue especially challenging for the federal government. Moreover, cooperation among provinces was unlikely, since most jurisdictions except Quebec wished the federal government to assume national leadership on the issue. In the case of Ontario, the political class was aware of the close relations between ARF and the national health and welfare department. Thus, ARF could be invited to play a leading role, contrary to OPTAT. The provinces also disagreed on how to deal with the marijuana issue. PEI and British Columbia rejected the legalization of marijuana. Ontario, by contrast, was not necessarily hostile to a transfer of marijuana from the Narcotic Control Act to the Food and Drugs Act, whereas Quebec was more preoccupied with defending provincial jurisdiction over health and education. Still, the Quebec government felt that legal repression was an excessive means to deal with young users of illegal drugs.

Unlike the PEI government and the NAFBC, ARF and OPTAT viewed the drug issue primarily as a health problem. They propagated the idea that drug use was a pathological symptom. Following the example of gambling[154] and alcohol use, they favoured the medicalization of a deviant behaviour. Not only did they attempt to persuade politicians that illegal drug use was a symptom of a disease and not a proof of emotional deficiency, they promoted solutions that reflected a health-care approach. The medicalization of illegal drug use was also used to undermine myths such as those which maintained that drug experimentation inevitably led to dependence and that the use of soft drugs was a gateway to hard drugs such as heroin. For its part, the NAFBC was worried about the changing pattern of drug use. It raised concerns about the tolerance that was gaining momentum in society and promoted a reform of drug legislation that would ally science and legal repression. BC politicians and the RCMP largely shared these concerns.

The medical approach to the illegal drug use problem was also a political strategy. Because the legalization of marijuana aroused heated opposition both inside and outside the medical profession, ARF and OPTAT, and to a lesser intent NAFBC, favoured amendments to the Narcotic Control Act. These changes generally aimed at softening penalties for possession of marijuana, and at convincing politicians that treatment was definitely preferable to jail. Still, the medical community was divided on this question. Some physicians did not hesitate to lend medical legitimacy to arguments made by governments favourable to their views, such as the PEI's, in order for their message to reach a wider audience. The creation of the Le Dain Commission in 1969 led to increasing interest in the recreational drug issue and the mobilization of different interest groups and individuals. It was in this context that provincial governments and their respective organizations competed to influence the federal government on the drug issue.

4 Debating Marijuana Use: The Le Dain Commission, 1969–1973

On 1 May 1969, the minister of national health and welfare, John Munro, informed the House of Commons that the government was appointing a Commission of Inquiry into the Non-Medical Use of Drugs. The Commission's mandate was to gather data on the phenomenon of non-medical drug use, to 'report on the current state of medical knowledge' regarding drugs, to identify and report on the motivation and factors that led to the non-medical consumption of drugs, and to recommend to the federal government, 'alone or in its relations with government at other levels,' ways to reduce drug use.[1] In making this announcement, Munro echoed demands made by some MPs.[2] However, the Commission was a strategy designed by the federal government to handle the public debate on drug use.

This chapter will focus on three aspects. The first part deals very briefly with the circumstances surrounding the creation of the Commission of Inquiry and with media reactions. The core of the chapter analyses the views of interest groups and individuals presented to the Commission, with particular attention to the issue of marijuana. Thus, comments about other illegal drugs (plus alcohol and tobacco) have, for the most part, been set aside. The chapter concludes with a review of the Commission's interim report, the report on cannabis, and reactions to them.

Appointing a Commission of Inquiry

The appointment of a Commission of Inquiry into recreational drug use meant that the debate was broadened, for the Canadian public now would be invited to take part as well. The members of the Commission of Inquiry into the Non-Medical Use of Drugs – better known as the Le Dain Commission – launched a series of research projects, toured the country, and invited individuals and interest groups to express their views on drugs. With the creation of the Commission, the federal government had gained some time, and hoped that this would help to overcome its own internal divisions on marijuana, since major decisions would, of course, have to wait until the Commission submitted its conclusions.[3] However, in proceeding this way, the government would not be able to control the tone and nature of the public debate.

Before the announcement of the Commission of Inquiry, RCMP officials and senior bureaucrats from the federal Department of Justice and the Solicitor General's Office informed their colleagues at National Health and Welfare of their concerns about the creation of a task force – or any other strategy – designed to broaden public debate. Thus far, the debate had been confined to the media, to conferences, and to symposiums. In fact, Munro's approach in addressing the phenomenon of recreational drug use gave senior bureaucrats an opportunity to express their differences on the government's eventual course of action. Although the deputy minister of national health offered assurances that the Commission would take no more than eight months to submit its findings, some bureaucrats identified several causes for concern. Some argued that the provinces would be disturbed by this 'unilateral federal announcement.' However, other warnings were prompted more by fear of losing control over the debate. The Commission would 'be besieged by all manner of people who may want the short list of drugs legalized and ... put great pressures on the Government' to do so.[4]

At one point, senior Justice bureaucrats and RCMP officials questioned the political wisdom of such a commission. They wondered about the need to proceed this way, since everyone knew the drugs under investigation were dangerous. Hence, there was no point in soliciting advice from the public. In fact, the Department of National Health and Welfare stated that this strategy, designed to widen discussion, would only delay government action by two years at a time when action was needed right away. The RCMP's views were that 'with the knowledge in the Department [of National Health and Welfare] and the common knowledge among lay men ... the Government [was] in a position now to make such a statement.' It further disagreed with the Department of National Health and Welfare's insistence that the Commission would not tie the government's hands. It would not be politically sound, the RCMP maintained, to have 'a Royal Commission solely to have the Federal Government disagree with it.'[5]

These concerns fell on deaf ears, however: senior bureaucrats from the Department of Justice and the Solicitor General's Office were told that Prime Minister Trudeau supported Munro's initiative. The task force came into being as the Commission of Inquiry into the Non-Medical Use of Drugs.

When Munro announced the creation of the Commission of Inquiry in May 1969, he stated that an interim report would be submitted within six months, and a final report by 1971. The names of the commissioners were released a month later. At first, the chair was to be Justice Emmett Hall, who had chaired the Royal Commission on Health Care in the early sixties and co-chaired the Hall-Denis Commission on Education in Ontario. However, he declined the invitation. Gerald Le Dain, who was Dean of the Osgoode Hall Law School at York University, was then appointed in his place. Three men and one woman were also appointed commissioners. In his memorandum to the cabinet, the national health and welfare minister used two important criteria in selecting them. The first was that commissioners were to come from a variety of disciplines. The second criterion was age. In other words, commissioners should come from different age groups in order to establish credibility, not only among young people, but among older generations as well.[6]

One of the commissioners, Heinz E. Lehmann, was a health professional. Clinical director and director of research at the Douglas Hospital in Montreal and a professor of psychiatry at McGill University, Lehmann was well known for his research on the use of tranquillizers in medicine and psychiatry. The other two male commissioners were Ian Lachlan Campbell, a professor of political science and dean of the Faculty of Arts at Sir George Williams University (later to become Concordia University), and J. Peter Stein, a social worker in Vancouver who had joined the Company of Young Canadians in 1967. At thirty-one, Stein was the youngest commissioner. The French-speaking representative, finally, was a woman. (André Lussier, professor of psychology at the Université de Montréal, was briefly appointed but resigned in June due to numerous other commitments.) Marie-Andrée Bertrand, a professor in the Department of Criminology at the same university, replaced Lussier four months later. Although commissioners came from a variety of disciplines, as the minister had wished, none came from law enforcement.[7]

Commissioners Bertrand and Stein were not well perceived by the Department of Justice and the RCMP. Justice felt that Dr Bertrand in particular could not exercise objectivity, because of her favourable views on soft drugs. Moreover, these bureaucrats felt that there were too 'many academic persons who had insufficient immediate contact with' the drug issue.[8] The Commission of Inquiry, nevertheless, set to work.

Newspapers reported that the Commission had been instituted. For its part, the *Globe and Mail* issued a prophetic warning, stating that the government should not use it to delay action on the marijuana issue.[9]

Canadians and Their Views on Drug Use

The Commission became a forum for individuals, interest groups, and provincial representatives to express their views on drugs and thus influence the federal legislator. Reflecting on the experience of chairing the body, Gerald Le Dain wrote: '[T]he Commission conceived of its role as not merely to conduct a scientific study of non-medical drug use and to make recommendations for action by government, but also to make a contribution to public understanding and reconciliation. That was one of the reasons for its decision to conduct public hearings.' In order to encourage participation, people at the hearings were informed that their testimonies would not be used by law-enforcement officers and the press could not take any photographs.[10]

In his statement at the first public hearing, in order to stimulate public participation and probably also to facilitate reconciliation between young people and adults, the chairman offered a liberal definition of the drug issue. The scope of the Commission's work was on drugs taken without any medical supervision and used by young people, but also on drug consumption by adults as 'it relates to or affects the use of drugs by youth.' The adoption of this definition meant that socially accepted drugs, such as tobacco and alcohol, were included in the study's parameters. During its existence the Commission concentrated on factors that led to non-medical drug-taking and on its effects on people and society. In doing so, it took into account age, occupation, and any other factors that might be at issue. Finally, the Commission looked at the controversial stepping-stone theory, which held that certain illegal substances, especially marijuana, led to the use of others.[11] Despite this liberal definition, most of the submissions to the Commission focused on marijuana.[12]

"THE DRUG SCENE"

THE COMMISSION OF INQUIRY INTO THE NON-MEDICAL
USE OF DRUGS will be on campus

WHEN: FRIDAY, OCTOBER 17th

WHERE: THE DEBATES ROOM, HART HOUSE

TIME: 12:00 noon to 1. 1:30 p.m.

STUDENT OPINION WILL FORM AN IMPORTANT PART OF THE DATA WHICH
THE COMMISSION IS CURRENTLY GATHERING AND WILL BE INCORPORATED
INTO THEIR FINAL REPORT TO THE FEDERAL GOVERNMENT.

HERE'S YOUR CHANCE TO EXPRESS YOUR VIEWPOINT ON A HIGHLY
CONTROVERSIAL SUBJECT AND JOIN IN THE GENERAL DISCUSSION.

ATTENTION WOMEN STUDENTS!
This Is Not A "Men Only" Affair. Come Along And Get Into The Act.

Advertisement for a meeting of an inquiry into drug use.
Source: *The Varsity*, 17 October 1969, 10

The Le Dain Commission received more than 291 briefs and statements from various interest groups and organizations, and 304 from
individuals. Some were in fact a description of drug education initiatives or drug clinic treatments; this was the case with briefs submitted
by 'Tell It As It Is' from Montreal, 'Cool-Aid' from Vancouver, or the
North Toronto Youth Project, but what of the other interest groups,
organizations, and individuals who took part in this process?

Four groups dominated the submissions. It should be no surprise
that the medical profession was prominently represented. Not only did
various organizations related to the profession express their views, but
several health professionals did so on their own. The other three
important groups were educational institutions, religious organizations, and provincial ministries (with addiction research foundations).
Certain groups kept a low profile by submitting relatively few briefs.
Among these were police forces, student organizations, law and civil

liberties associations, and women's groups. No native groups and few French-speaking organizations submitted their views.

Health and medical professionals offered contrasting and competing views. Their definitions of drug abuse and views of how marijuana should be handled showed deep divisions. These rifts betrayed the debate raging in the medical community, as seen in the case of the Canadian Medical Association.

Besides the Canadian Medical Association, which was very active on the issue, other national health organizations submitted their views. The Canadian Psychiatric Association (CPA), for instance, submitted two briefs to the Commission. Its 1970 interim brief emphasized the importance of the spread of multi-drug use, such as LSD and glue-sniffing. The use of these two drugs greatly exceeded marijuana consumption, and yet the latter had received the lion's share of attention from the media and the public. The CPA described drug users as sick people who chose to harm themselves. It argued that those who opted to become drug users did so, despite being 'well aware of the evils and dangers of drug dependence.' Furthermore, drugs were 'not introduced against [their] will.' Consequently, drug users were 'neither mentally retarded nor initially psychotic: they may be immature or psychopathic.' Drug dependence was both 'a learned and contagious behaviour' that led 'drug users ... to group together for mutual support in' drug experimentation.[13]

Despite such comments about drug consumers, the CPA proposed several solutions. First, governments should pursue their efforts to support financially the treatment of addicts and to continue research. This last initiative was essential to shed some light on controversial questions such as the health effects of certain substances, and the causes that incited people to use them. On the subject of education, the CPA promoted an approach that appealed to people's intelligence rather than their fears: 'Educational efforts stressing the evils of drug dependence have not been very effective deterrents to drug abuse. New and better modes of educational approach await development.'[14]

In January 1970 the CPA did not yet have a firm stand on the legalization of marijuana. Nevertheless, it reminded the government that there were still numerous unknowns about this drug. Consequently, the legislator should maintain legal control but eschew a regime as stringent as those currently in place. This could be accomplished, according to the CPA, by transferring marijuana from the Narcotic Control Act to the Food and Drugs Act. This suggestion was seen as part of an overall evaluation of the repressive approach to marijuana use, with the CPA inviting the legislator to monitor the consequences of such a transfer and make the necessary changes.[15]

In its second brief, submitted in 1971, the CPA repeated some elements of its first, such as the importance of education. However, it emphasized a scientific approach to the treatment of those who had developed a dependency on legal and illegal drugs. On marijuana, the new brief added nothing to what was in the first. However, one of the authors, Dr Conrad J. Schwarz, indicated disagreement with the CPA approach, which was hardly surprising, since he was opposed to the drug's transfer. In his view, marijuana and cannabis had 'no known therapeutic use.' Furthermore, Schwarz recalled that the Narcotic Control Act had been amended in 1969 to reduce penalties for marijuana possession. Consequently, a transfer of marijuana to the Food and Drugs Act had no legitimacy. Furthermore, he argued, the classification of marijuana in the Food and Drugs Act was inappropriate, because it was not a food, and its effects on health users were still unknown.[16]

The CPA's briefs were very liberal compared with a working document submitted by its president, Dr Keith Yonge of the University of Alberta. Yonge was a strong supporter of the hard-line approach to marijuana. According to Yonge, who was the chair of the psychiatry department, marijuana presented serious health dangers. He suggested the establishment of 'work colonies for drug offenders.'[17] This proposal triggered strong reactions within the CPA, with certain members threatening to withdraw from the organization if this became the CPA's official position.

The Canadian Pharmaceutical Association offered a very different point of view. On behalf of the 9000 pharmacists across Canada (except those in Quebec), it formulated a specific construction of the drug use issue. Drug abuse was defined as the consumption of any drugs without proper medical supervision. The Association's report tried to exonerate pharmacists in cases that involved abuse of drugs prescribed by a physician and sold by pharmacists. Certain pharmacists were perhaps negligent, but the brief was quick to point out that some of them were manipulated by consumers. 'In their busy daily lives, they may be "used" by the addict who falsely describes migraine to obtain a new analgesic or by the vociferous pill-taker who trades symptoms and drugs with friends and relatives.' The brief also emphasized that many non-prescription drugs were abused and that pharmacists had no control over this phenomenon.[18]

As for the responsibility of the pharmaceutical industry in controlling drug abuse, the brief argued that the current mechanisms created by the industry in collaboration with governments were adequate. Certainly, these mechanisms contained some gaps, but 'leaks in distribution control ... have always been considered minimal.' Further, the organization was anxious to point an accusatory finger at criminal organizations. 'Street availability of drugs comes about through criminal channels having access to production facilities of one kind or another.'[19]

The Canadian Pharmaceutical Association's solutions to the drug abuse problem in fact supported the status quo. From the available range of options, the organization suggested the development of educational programs in which pharmacists should be involved. Of course, it did not neglect to mention the work accomplished by CODA with its Drug Information Centers in Ontario. On the legal front, the repressive approach was judged essential. The brief did not suggest any legislative change to the legal status of marijuana, since this drug was not harmless and had no usefulness in scientific research. However, the submission argued (without mentioning marijuana specifically) that the enforcement of the Narcotic Control Act should not be 'such as to give the curious, youthful, one-time experimenter a lifetime criminal record which prevents him from demonstrating responsible citizenship.'[20]

The BC and the Alberta Pharmaceutical Associations submitted briefs that presented some similarities with that of the Canadian Pharmaceutical Association. According to the BC association, pharmacists were opposed to 'permissiveness in the use of drugs, any drugs.' As a guiding principle, every drug should be 'controlled until proven safe.'[21] For its part, the Collège des pharmaciens du Québec emphasized the role of pharmacists as responsible health specialists who educated the public about the dangers of abusing prescription and 'over-the-counter' drugs, as well as illegal drugs. In agreement with the Canadian Pharmaceutical Association, the College believed that pharmacists were able to control drug use and abuse. On the marijuana front, the College did not support its legalization, because there were not enough studies done yet on its health effects. Because of this, and since caution was highly advisable, the federal government should restrict liberalization of the status of marijuana to its simple transfer from the Narcotic Control Act to the Food and Drugs Act.[22]

The Pharmaceutical Manufacturers Association of Canada also came to the defence of pharmacists and the drug industry in general. Submitted on behalf of the fifty-eight research-based companies, the Association's brief stressed the fact that control mechanisms had been put in place by the organization to prevent 'leakage into illicit channels' of pharmaceutical products. How? There was a numbering system of each product produced by pharmaceutical companies. Since the Association believed that these control mechanisms were sufficient, its recommendations on the drug issue did not favour a greater role for the state. On the contrary, the Association mentioned its support of CODA's work. If state intervention was necessary, it should be directed towards research in the field on non-medical drug use.[23]

The last health organization to present its views was the Canadian Mental Health Association. Similarly to the Canadian Pharmaceutical Association, it restricted its definition of the drug issue to substances consumed without medical supervision. Those who abused drugs did so because they suffered from 'imperfect or poor mental health.' The brief did make an exception for one specific demographic group: young people. These people were not 'unstable,' nor did they suffer 'from a mental disorder.' The motives of young people to consume illegal drugs were ascribed to curiosity and a desire to challenge societal values, and wore a form of 'social protest' and a sign of 'adolescent rebellion.' In terms of enforcement of federal public policy on illegal substances, the Association pointed out some of the negative impacts on drug offenders. For instance, a prison term could increase the risk that offenders would come in contact with other substances, notably hard drugs.

The Canadian Mental Health Association submitted recommendations favourable to the liberalization of the drug policy. In fact, it supported the recommendations of the Commission's interim report to transfer marijuana from the Narcotic Control Act to the Food and Drugs Act. It endorsed the creation of mandatory educational programs, which should avoid 'sensationalism' and 'emphasize the motivational factors that affect the students' decision to use drugs.' These programs should 'invite young people who have had experience in drug use to become involved in the educational process.' In addition, treatment and the rehabilitation of young drug offenders were seen as better approaches. Further, the federal government should support research projects on the drugs. Finally, television and radio media should be involved with the education of the population as a whole.[24]

These contrasting positions from the professional associations

reflected the debates within the medical and health professions. Moreover, certain physicians and other health specialists did not hesitate to
submit their own briefs to ensure that their opinions, not always
reflected by their professional organizations, benefited from the audience provided by the Commission. Three individuals are worthy of
attention, because their activism was not limited to submitting briefs.
On the contrary, each found ways to ensure that his views would
receive public attention beyond the Commission's hearings.

Fred W. Lundell, an associate professor of psychiatry at McGill University, argued in February 1970 that the legalization of marijuana was
'premature and dangerous': premature because the short- and long-
term effects of marijuana were still unknown; dangerous because there
was increasing medical evidence that indicated marijuana use caused
brain damage. Lundell based his findings on youth patients that he
had met. He reported that 'a significant number of chronic drug users
"drop out" and cease to be socially functioning unites.' In addition to
the problem of dependence, Lundell was concerned with the effects of
marijuana use on vulnerable young adults, at risk because of their age.
The decision to use drugs would impair their maturating process,
yet another reason for the state to resist becoming soft on marijuana.
'By using drugs to escape from pressing problems,' youth failed to
'develop an ability to tolerate a reasonable degree of anxiety or frustra-
tion in terms of future gratification.'[25]

Lundell wrote a critical analysis of the interim report that he submitted to the Le Dain Commission, repeating his arguments against the
legalization of marijuana. Although he favoured some 'flexibility' in
cases of possession, he remained very critical of how the Commission
collected its data and constructed the phenomenon of non-medical
drug use: 'The studies selected for discussion were highly edited and
hardly current ... Nonetheless those reportedly minimizing the effects
of marijuana do not on scrutiny give marijuana a clean bill of health.'
Lundell upbraided the Commission for a certain negligence in its handling of the marijuana issue. 'It requires more courage, under intense
group pressure, to adopt a cautious, scientific approach, particularly in
view of more recent scientific experience and research, to weigh the latter carefully and unhurriedly rather than to be stampeded into hasty
decisions from the pressures of lobbying and proselytization.' Lundell
regretted that the Commission did not attribute more importance to
the theory that marijuana was a stepping-stone drug: 'While cannabis
sativa appear[s] to have been identified as the major concern we must

weigh seriously the evidence of progression to other currently accepted as more dangerous substances and that we are really dealing
more and more with multiple drug abuse.' He felt the Commission
should concentrate on traditional thinking on the subject and
strengthen it by providing evidence.[26]

Through his work with the PEI government, Lundell was probably
hoping his views would reach a larger audience. A symbiotic relation
developed between these two social actors. Lundell now had an ally to
propagate his views, and the PEI government received Lundell's medical and scientific backing for its opposition to any attempt to legalize
marijuana or to overly liberalize its status.

The second health specialist was Conrad J. Schwarz, professor of
psychiatry at the University of British Columbia. Schwarz was very
active in his opposition to the legalization of marijuana or the liberalization of its legal status. He was also prominent within the Canadian
Psychiatric Association (CPA) and the Canadian Medical Association
(CMA).

Schwarz's battle against the legalization of marijuana took place outside the ranks of the CPA and the CMA. At the 1968 Loyola Conference
on Student Use and Abuse of Drugs, Schwarz argued that marijuana
was a dangerous drug, since it produced 'an acute state of intoxication
with alcohol.' He concentrated his efforts on dismantling the argument
used by proponents of legalization, that marijuana's effects were similar to, or less than, those of alcohol. Schwarz argued that an individual
under the influence of marijuana was 'not aware that he is intoxicated
to the same extent' as one under the effects of alcohol. He stated that
the marijuana user was 'in control of himself but then in the next sentence, he will admit that he is paranoid, that he is suspicious, that he
thinks people are playing tricks on him; he will admit that his sense of
time is distorted, that his sense of distance is distorted.'[27] Contrary to
the position of the LaGuardia Committee on Marijuana, in terms of
long-term effects, marijuana was not harmless. Schwarz reminded conference participants that much about marijuana was still unknown. It
was therefore prudent to state that marijuana was not harmless: 'I'm
giving an opinion, and I think there's enough evidence in my opinion
for me to say that I think marijuana is a dangerous drug.'[28]

Schwarz believed that it was crucial to counteract the pro-marijuana
arguments presented to the Le Dain Commission. Above all, he felt
that by remaining highly critical of it, he was warning commissioners against being seduced by the pro-marijuana lobby. To this end,

Schwarz wrote to Gerald Le Dain: 'I wonder whether the Commission might not serve a useful function in bringing the level of debate down from hysterical rabble-rousing by asking proponents of legalization whether they are aware of the following points.' He then provided a list of unknowns about marijuana, such as its chemical composition and its varying 'psychological and physical effects.' If the unknown health impacts alone could not silence pro-marijuana forces, Schwarz argued, there were Canada's international obligations, as well as the obligations of all countries having signed the Single Convention on Narcotic Drugs, an international agreement that required signatory states to suppress marijuana.[29]

In June 1970, Schwarz submitted a brief to the Commission that detailed his criticisms of the interim report. Schwarz denounced the construction of the drug issue by the Commission and its stand on marijuana. The Commission, according to Schwarz, should have restricted its definition of the drug phenomenon to illegal substances and hallucinogens. 'Alcohol and sedatives and stimulants can, of course, be used to produce states of intoxication but they are not "solely intoxicating."' The Commission should have also confined its study to illegal drugs used by youth because, unlike adult users, young people wished to advance a social agenda. 'The spread of sedative and stimulant drug use among adults, however, is by a much softer selling approach, and the individual who is involved in extensive abuse of these substances is more inclined to be secretive about it than to be a crusader. This also tends to apply to the alcoholic.' In Schwarz's opinion, the Commission should focus on young people because of their immaturity. The drug crisis was symptomatic of the rebellious stage in normal human development; it was therefore incumbent upon the Commission to acknowledge this and deal with drug abuse accordingly: 'Adolescents have, as yet, incomplete personality development and their drug usage may precipitate a movement towards further immature, or even pathological behaviour, may cause significant interruptions in educational processes and in development of satisfactory relationships with others.' Finally, Schwarz denounced the weak evidence provided by the Commission to support its stand on marijuana. 'In my opinion the Commission is being unrealistically optimistic in inferring that we will know almost everything there is to know about cannabis some time next year.' According to Schwarz, not only was the scientific evidence insufficient, the Commission did not understand the full implications of Canada's international obligations.[30]

These were by no means Schwarz's final words. He wrote again to the commissioners to remind them of the health dangers that accompanied marijuana use.[31] It was his action within the Canadian Medical Association, however, that underlined the firmness of his convictions to the Commission and to those favourable to the reduction of criminal penalty for marijuana use.

The final individual contributor worth mentioning is Lionel Solursh, a psychiatrist at Toronto Western Hospital and a psychiatry professor at the University of Toronto. Solursh was very active within the Canadian Medical Association and also submitted his own views to the Le Dain Commission. In his written brief, Solursh recommended the legalization of marijuana because of the particularities of the socio-political context of the late sixties in Canada. His stand was based on his medical expertise resulting from 'sufficient evidence from wide street observations, office practice and these acute studies which have been performed to state that marijuana, in specific, is an intoxicant.' Based on this expertise, Solursh argued that marijuana was no more dangerous than alcohol but this depended on 'how it is used, in what circumstances and by whom.' He even stated, '[W]e have observed thousands of people who have smoked marijuana for two to five years, with no obvious social, intellectual, personality or psychological deterioration, and no evident medical complications.' He justified his new stand (in the past he had advocated the transfer of marijuana to the Food and Drugs Act) by making reference to the social reality created by rendering marijuana illegal. The enforcement of the Narcotic Control Act created conflicts between police forces and drug users, many of whom were young people. According to Solursh, police actions had resulted in rising violence and soured relations between them and drug consumers. In order to put an end to police violence and these deteriorating relations, the time had come for the government to adopt a courageous new public policy. The state should legalize marijuana for a two-year trial period while the Le Dain Commission pursued its study. During this trial, the government should take control of marijuana cultivation and distribution; furthermore, possession should be legal for anyone over twenty-one years of age. At the end of the trial period, the Commission should make a recommendation to extend this policy or not.[32]

As seen in chapter 2, Solursh used his role as chair of the Sub-committee on the Misuse of Drugs to favour the adoption of a liberal stand by the Canadian Medical Association. Solursh was aware that the

CMA carried more influence than an individual voice, but his position stirred debate within the organization.

Various school boards and some parent federations, mostly from English Canada, answered the invitation issued by the chair of the Le Dain Commission to express their views on non-medical drug use. Except for the briefs from the PEI Federation of Home and School Associations and the Administrative Staff of Charlottetown Public Schools, which opposed the legalization of marijuana, most school boards did not deal specifically with this issue. In their submissions, many stressed the fact that education was an important part of any strategy to counter drug abuse. In order to provide accurate information and strengthen education programs, not only for students, but also for their parents and the community at large, governments had the responsibility to support research on the effects of illegal drugs.[33]

Church groups and institutions constitute the third largest social actor to submit formal briefs or short written statements. Although some of them were discreet, in that their views were not in written form – such as the Catholic Church of Canada[34] and the Anglican church – those who did write formally expressed a variety of opinions, ranging from strong opposition to support for legalization or even liberalization of Canada's drug policy. Among the religious institutions opposed to the legalization or the reduction of marijuana penalties, the Toronto Stake of the Church of Jesus Christ of Latter-Day Saints justified its stand by stating that there was a lack of 'conclusive' medical research results and that the option of legalization was pushed by a minority, which did not reflect the views of the majority.[35] While being cautious, most religious groups that submitted written documents were favourable to the liberalization of marijuana laws in the form of reduced penalties. This could be achieved by transferring marijuana from the Narcotic Control Act to the Food and Drugs Act. Religious organizations supported their position either by questioning the depiction of marijuana as a dangerous drug or by pointing out that the penalties, in the case of those convicted for marijuana possession, exceeded the crime. Accordingly, the law should be amended to avoid long-term penalties for marijuana use. After all, many young people had tried marijuana out of simple curiosity or a wish to experiment. Also, some briefs argued that treatment was a better approach in certain circumstances.[36] Many also agreed that more effective educational programs on drug use for youth were essential.

The last group consisted of the provinces. They expressed their

views through provincial ministries or addiction research organizations. As mentioned in the previous chapter, the PEI government's
strong opposition to the legalization of marijuana predated the Le Dain
Commission and was expressed outside the Commission's purview,
even during its existence.

Although the Quebec Department of Education was invited to submit a brief, it did not do so. Instead, it suggested that the Commission
contact Quebec school boards; however, none of them submitted written views. In the end, it was OPTAT that provided a brief reflecting the
government's position. Its submission repeated arguments, seen in the
previous chapter, about the definition of drug abuse and the causes
that led youth to consume drugs, and stressed the importance of pursuing research on the drug issue and its support for the transfer of cannabis from the Narcotic Control Act to the Food and Drugs Act.[37]

The NAFBC forwarded various briefs to the Commission that it had
already sent to the minister of national health and welfare. These documents invited the government to revamp its drug legislation on non-
opiate drugs by combining scientific expertise and law enforcement to
establish specific penalties according to the toxicity of each drug. The
NAFBC opposed the legalization of marijuana, pleaded for a stronger
federal role in supporting drug research, treatment, and educational
programs, and argued for the prohibition of drug advertising in the
media.[38]

The state organization most actively involved with the Le Dain
Commission was ARF. During public and private meetings, ARF was
a strong supporter of the Commission, which is hardly surprising
considering the cooperation between the two organizations.[39] Its preliminary brief is a good example of how the Ontario organization perceived its role: in short, it felt it could enlighten the debate. In this
document, ARF stressed the fact that the drug problem in the country
was not restricted to marijuana. Furthermore, the state had the right to
implement legal mechanisms to control the drug supply. In the context
of the sixties and the phenomenon of recreational drug use, however,
the time had come to review the legal approach and to weigh its benefits and drawbacks. In order to do this, scientific assessment of all
available data on drug use and its consequences should be carried out,
in order to help decision-makers rectify public policy, if need be. The
organization noted that value judgments often prevented a fair assessment of the drug issue. Indeed, ARF stressed the benefits of taking
drugs: it enhanced 'sensual pleasure,' facilitated 'social interaction,'

'mystical experience,' and 'self-understanding,' and even alleviated pain in certain circumstances. Still, drug consumption also had decidedly harmful aspects, such as 'toxicity,' 'intoxication as a factor in accidents,' 'psychiatric damage,' 'anti-social behaviour,' and criminal records, in some cases. For the state, nevertheless, it was important to eliminate the positive or negative value judgments of different interest groups that clouded perceptions of marijuana. By putting aside value judgments, the state could see with objectivity that it had two choices: either increase control mechanisms over the drug supply or allow more freedom for individuals to use drugs. If the state chose the former, it had to develop better control mechanisms, since current legislation was inadequate. If it opted for the latter, the state had to help individuals who suffered from health and psychological consequences of drug use by funding treatment and rehabilitation facilities. This decision would then affect provincial governments and their management of the health care system. The assessment of these choices should be based on factual evidence and scientific assessment.[40]

Briefs from the provinces of Saskatchewan and Manitoba emphasized alcoholism and its treatment. For their part, the Alberta minister of education and youth, the Nova Scotia Department of Public Welfare, and the Newfoundland Alcohol and Drug Addiction Foundation opposed the legalization of marijuana. Although the Alberta minister suggested that penalties for possession of marijuana should be proportional to the offence, the Nova Scotia Department of Public Welfare rejected any change to the law whatever, especially with respect to youth. The Nova Scotia brief stated that young people, as opposed to adults, were incapable of making sound decisions and therefore should be discouraged from using drugs. Although the New Brunswick Interdepartmental Committee on Drug Abuse did not specifically address the issue of marijuana, it did suggest a change to law enforcement by arguing that drug abuse was a social problem. Consequently, education and treatment had important roles to play. Echoing the recommendation of the Alcoholism and Drug Addiction Foundation of Newfoundland, the New Brunswick Interdepartmental Committee on Drug Abuse called upon the federal government to assist the provinces financially in drug treatment and in the development of educational strategies. The New Brunswick group also recommended that the federal government support research on drugs.[41]

As previously stated, there were many more other groups that did not necessarily use the Le Dain Commission to express their views.

Among these were police forces. With the exception of the Vancouver police force, the Montreal Police Department,[42] and the RCMP, most did not submit their views.

In its brief to the Le Dain Commission, the Vancouver City Police Department focused on the non-medical consumption of soft drugs and depicted their use with a very alarmist tone. According to the police department, soft drugs, particularly marijuana, were easily accessible, and their use led to experimentation with other substances and eventually heroin. 'It is our hypothesis that a person who uses marijuana and other soft drugs, form [sic] personal associations that expose him to heroin: and a person predisposed to the use of soft drugs is also predisposed to the use of heroin. This person then will commit crime to support a drug habit and will then come to the attention of the police.' In its attempt to counteract the pro-lobby marijuana, which it associated with universities and members of the artistic community, the Vancouver police department stated, '[T]hey offer no evidence to prove the effects harmless but base their arguments on the lack of convincing evidence against drugs.' The Vancouver police department's recommendations covered a range of issues: they called on the state to support research on the effects of marijuana and the 'relationship between it and aggressive behaviour and crime, ... and use of other drugs,' then pressed the federal government to create an education program for youth and finance treatment. Nothing specific was stated regarding the marijuana issue, but the brief did call for an examination of current drug legislation 'with a view to establish a more effective framework for control and law enforcement.'[43]

It was the RCMP that introduced the point of view of law-enforcement agencies. In fact, the RCMP had a privileged access to the Commission, since several documents were submitted and private meetings took place between commissioners and RCMP officials. The RCMP's initial strong opposition to the idea of a Commission of Inquiry had to be put aside, since the prime minister supported Munro's endeavour. Wanting to 'do everything within [its] power, not only to convince the Committee of [its] point of view, but also to present to that Commission all the known facts,' it therefore tempered its message and closely followed the Commission's work.[44] However, the RCMP instructed its officers not to attend the Commission's hearings unless invited to do so by the Commission itself.[45] Finally, it tried to throw its force behind the anti-marijuana lobby.

In its briefs, documents, and private meetings with the Le Dain

Commission, the RCMP stated that drug use was an extremely serious problem in Canada. Furthermore, the international community had condemned marijuana consumption by restricting its use to medical and research purposes. Consequently, the RCMP opposed legalization. In fact, it pursued two important goals in attempting to convince Commissioners to adopt its views on drugs and the need for law enforcement.

The first goal was to depict marijuana use as a dangerous practice by providing as many health-related facts as possible, in order to convince the Le Dain Commission, which had, according to the RCMP, a 'very enquiring mind.'[46] Although new research was still needed, the RCMP stressed the fact that previous investigations had demonstrated serious health risks. To support its point, the RCMP referred to Henry Brill, who testified before the Superior Court of Massachusetts in 1967 that the 'psychological dependence' that resulted from cannabis use 'is a much more serious medical problem than physical dependence.' Why? Because 'physical dependence to heroin could be cured within one or two weeks, whereas psychological dependence is susceptible to periodic relapses even through the entire life of the individual.' In its first brief to the Commission the RCMP also referred to the Commission on Narcotic Drugs of the Economic and Social Council of the United Nations. In 1968 this group stated that cannabis use provoked serious health effects, such as impairment of judgment and memory, distortion of sensation or perception, inertia, lethargy, and self-neglect.[47] In its second brief, the RCMP referred to Lundell's research. 'One of his important findings,' the brief stated, 'is that some of the metabolic substances in Marihuana have a lasting effect of six months to a year, compared to alcohol with its effects of six to twelve hours.'[48]

Marijuana was also dangerous because it was a stepping-stone to harder drugs. In its first brief, the RCMP argued (with little evidence to support its claim) that 'in many cases a transition from Marihuana to Heroin does take place,' but conceded that it was 'not necessarily directly, and certainly not in every case.'[49] In its second brief, the RCMP adopted a firmer stand by citing several studies conducted in Great Britain and the United States, and in Canada by the NAFBC and the RCMP itself. They all proved that heroin addicts, or users of LSD or speed, admitted that their first drug of abuse was marijuana. Consequently, 'the abuse of non-opiate drugs, which may be considered as being transitory to the opiate drugs, is a much more serious and pertinent problem than the final transition to opiate drugs.'[50]

If that was not enough to demonstrate the dangers of marijuana use, the RCMP also reminded commissioners that marijuana users adopted criminal behaviours such as robbery. Referring to studies in Greece and in the United States, as well as data collected by the RCMP, the brief concluded that 'cannabis intoxication can induce acts of violence.' For instance, thirty-two individuals arrested for possession of cannabis in 1967 and 1968 were also in possession of firearms, which was not the case for those engaged in the trafficking of heroin.[51] Since this claim was not very convincing, the RCMP tried to give some authority to the stance in its second brief. This time, the RCMP told the story of a Montrealer who committed an armed robbery in November 1968. During their search, police officers found marijuana and hashish on him. 'It is significant ... that during the last three years at least 32 persons arrested for Marihuana offences were found in possession of firearms and in some cases were prepared to use them,' as opposed to drug addicts, who were not 'known to carry firearms as a general rule.' Because marijuana opened the door to a variety of drug abuse and to criminal behaviour, leniency was unacceptable as a public policy.[52]

The second goal pursued by the RCMP with the Le Dain Commission was to undermine the arguments put forward by pro-marijuana forces. In its first brief, the RCMP went on the offensive by depicting recreational drug use as 'a vice of the young middle class.'[53] In order to prevent its spread, which encouraged youth to lead a 'life of indolence,' the brief did not hesitate to compare what could happen in Canada with the case of India, a society that had, according to a study quoted by the RCMP, a serious drug problem: India was an example of a society that 'produced one of the sickest social orders ever created by mankind.' The RCMP hoped that this reference would discredit pro-marijuana forces.[54] However, the Mounties had to readjust their strategy. Instead of leaning toward moral judgments and racism, their second brief strove to minimize the importance of the pro-marijuana lobby by questioning its representativeness. Pro-marijuana forces, the RCMP argued, spoke for a minority in society. Addressing the fact that some scientists and other professionals argued in favour of marijuana, the RCMP responded darkly that often a 'so called expert is deeply involved in the abuse of Cannabis himself.'[55]

The participation of the RCMP in the Le Dain Commission represented only one facet of its strategy to counteract the pro-marijuana lobby. As an apparatus of the federal state, the RCMP had other means to convey its views to elected politicians, cabinet ministers, and the prime minister. In fact, it was within the federal bureaucracy that the battle of influence would be waged.

In its brief to the Commission, the Department of the Solicitor General entered the debate by stating that marijuana was a dangerous drug. Although its brief was not as provocative as those submitted by the RCMP, it emphasized the health and psychological dangers associated with marijuana use and the fact that marijuana was a stepping-stone to other drugs. Furthermore, it opened a new line of defence in trying to counter the argument that marijuana use, if dangerous, was no more so than that of alcohol or cigarettes. The government had demonstrated its concern with alcohol abuse and resulting traffic accidents by amending the Criminal Code 'to authorize a peace officer to require anyone whom he suspects of being impaired by alcohol or a drug to supply a breath sample.' In terms of cigarettes, it was now acknowledged that smoking was 'deleterious to health and does add to the social and hospital costs of the nation.' These examples led the authors of the brief to ask the Commission if Canadians wanted 'to allow themselves to use "soft" drugs indiscriminately when all the social effects seen so far lead one to believe that they are no better than alcohol or tobacco and probably worse and more disabling when used indiscriminately by the undiscerning.'[56]

The Department of the Solicitor General justified its opposition to the transfer of marijuana from the Narcotic Control Act to the Food and Drugs Act by referring to government-instigated change and enforcement of the former. Since 1969, most first-time offenders convicted for simple possession of marijuana were being fined instead of being sentenced to jail. Under these new conditions, the department argued that no further amendment was required. Furthermore, Canada's international obligations resulting from the Single Convention on Narcotic Drugs required the state to limit marijuana use to medical and scientific purposes.[57]

Although many briefs referred to young people, youth representatives did not provide many submissions to the Commission. Approximately seven university student organizations and youth wings of federal political parties presented briefs or written documents, but none came from official representatives of the Quebec or national student movements. The submissions frequently repeated arguments already made public, such as the one proposing that marijuana be treated in the same manner as alcohol. It argued that the drug should be legalized and its distribution handled by the government.[58] For instance, the UBC Law Student Association denounced the fact that marijuana was a criminal substance, since it was 'no more a physical or mental danger to its user than orange juice is to the women who just can't let a morning escape without the habitual early morning glass of juice.' For the law students, marijuana was illegal due to the actions of the US government and 'some unprincipled men who were put out of work when prohibition ended in the U.S. [and] set out to find a new job of a similar nature. Mr Harry Anslinger, using the office of the Federal Bureau of Narcotics, successfully carried out an amazing campaign to scare the Congress of the U.S. into passing the 1937 Marijuana Tax Act.'[59] Although there was no specific recommendation regarding the legalization of marijuana, a representative of the University of Toronto's Rochdale College – a contemporary experiment in university education – believed that drug laws would change anyway because governments would be unable to enforce them in face of increasing drug use. The Rochdale brief largely concentrated on efforts by the institution to deal with drug use among its residents and sojourners, which included setting up a drug clinic and disseminating information about drugs and their quality in order to inform and educate.[60] The youth wing of the federal Liberal party and the Quebec wing of the Progressive Conservative party favoured the legalization of marijuana. As some student associations had done, they questioned the rationale behind the depiction of marijuana as a dangerous substance, since both the 1893–4 Indian Hemp Drugs Commission and the 1944 La Guardia Committee Report provided evidence that marijuana was not addictive and did not entail the terrible consequences described by opponents to legalization. Moreover, alcohol, if indeed it had any ill health consequences, was as dangerous as marijuana. The time had come to put an end to the tragedy that affected the lives of many young people who were convicted by drug laws 'irrelevant to today, arbitrary in action, and confused in rationale.'[61]

Although many student organizations did not make their views known to the Commission, others did so by submitting survey results. For instance, a survey at the CEGEP de Trois-Rivières showed that 42.5 per cent of the 830 students polled were generally in favour of the legalization of drugs, without being more specific, but 40.6 per cent were opposed.[62] A different portrait emerged at Dawson College, where a poll of 200 students was 'unanimous' in demanding that soft drugs be legalized and 'put under government control.'[63] At Memorial University, 50 students – 25 users and 25 non-users – were surveyed, and all agreed that a medical approach to narcotics was more suitable than a legal one. Consequently, 76 per cent favoured the legalization of marijuana – 100 per cent of users agreed – but only 44 per cent of non-users and 8 per cent of users supported the legalization of hallucinogens. Most survey participants believed that information about drugs (in particular marijuana) and their health consequences was inadequate.[64] At the University of Western Ontario, 62 per cent of the 487 participants surveyed approved the idea that marijuana should be handled by the state in the same manner as alcohol. Those who took part in the survey also complained about how drug laws were enforced.[65]

The tobacco industry was not a prominent voice during the Le Dain Commission. Studies on recreational drug use in the United States highlighted a significant increase in the sale of cigarette rolling papers, and many American manufacturers of such papers advertised in magazines and the underground press. For instance, 'in 1973, the makers of Acapulco Gold rolling papers – named after a type of marijuana – were advertising in *Rolling Stone* magazine for the end of marijuana prohibition and soliciting for membership in a pro-pot organization ... supported in part by sales of the rolling papers.'[66] There were also rumours that tobacco companies had purchased large fields in Mexico to cultivate marijuana in anticipation of marijuana's decriminalization, following the release of reports by the Committee for Youth in Canada and the American Presidential Task Force on Marijuana.[67] In Canada, the action of tobacco companies seems to have been more discreet. The president of Imperial Tobacco Company of Canada, Paul Paré, rejected the claim that his company was interested in producing marijuana cigarettes.[68]

Law and civil liberties organizations also kept a low profile. There was no official brief submitted by the Canadian Law Association. The Young Lawyers Conference of the Alberta Section of the Canadian Bar Association pleaded for an amendment to the Narcotic Control Act because 'it places the onus on the accused proving his innocence rather than the usual presumption of innocence which exists. It is our opinion that this section should be amended to reflect the usual philosophy of law.' Regarding marijuana, no specific recommendation about its legalization was put forward, but more research was required, since the authors of the brief felt that 'present investigation is inconclusive and on the basis of this alone it is our opinion that another intoxicating agent should not be legalized until such time as we have more conclusive information as to the effects of this drug on the user.'[69] Elsewhere, the BC Civil Liberties Association favoured the transfer of marijuana from the Narcotic Control Act to the Food and Drugs Act, since the current law-enforcement approach was not working.[70]

In looking at social actors, one must also examine women's organizations. Approximately 8 per cent of briefs and other submissions came from women's groups. It is noteworthy that three categories were predominant: temperance associations (three submissions), religious organizations (nine), and secular bodies (twelve) such as the Provincial Council of Women of Saskatchewan or the Provincial Council of Women of Ontario. It is equally important to note that national organizations such as the Quebec Federation of Women or the National Council of Women of Canada did not submit any documents to the Commission.

Women's groups were divided over the legalization of marijuana. The majority (21 of 24 submissions) were opposed.[71] The authors of these briefs justified their position by citing reports about the dangerous health and behavioural effects on youth. Their opposition was also based on moral and social values. Since the consumption of marijuana for recreational purposes was perceived to be symptomatic of a wider social malaise, women, or at least their leaders, were presented as the first line of defence against this social ill. Their combative role was supported by the fact that marijuana consumption was defined as a problem affecting young people in particular. Thus, writers of the various briefs appealed to women's maternal qualities, to lend aid to a group perceived as being endangered. The following tone is typical: 'As a Council representing thousands of Saskatchewan women, we are anxious to do our part, enlisting Mothers and Grandmothers and all women who are deeply concerned, in finding a solution to this problem before it becomes more deeply entrenched in our way of life.'[72]

Among the women's groups opposed to the legalization of marijuana, one stands out for its zeal and attention to documenting briefs. The Vancouver District of the Woman's Christian Temperance Union (WCTU) presented three documents, two of which dealt with the moral and medical dangers of marijuana use. It stated: 'Mothers who live in a chaotic and unpredictable environment as these hippies do, and subject their children to such a life, are creating a generation so psychologically scarred that the damage may never be undone.'[73] The organization went on to argue that marijuana caused damage to the brain and to the nervous system. Moreover, according to Dr Howard Boughey, a sociologist at the University of British Columbia quoted in the brief, marijuana consumption destroyed young people's lives. 'Among the problems associated with [its] use,' Boughey stated, were 'homosexual acts, distraction of career and education, and loss of ability to make rational decisions.' Finally, marijuana consumption entailed serious economic costs. Referring to a statement by a British Columbia cabinet minister regarding the growth in treatment costs of mental illnesses, the Vancouver group wrote: '[A] person would have to be extremely naive if he did not believe these costs were ... in large part due to drug and alcohol misuse.'[74]

The activity of the Vancouver District of the WCTU was not limited to sending briefs to the government body. When the Commission published its interim report in 1970, this group wrote a letter to the CMA expressing its annoyance at the fact that the Commission had ignored its briefs.[75]

Among opponents to the legalization of marijuana, nine briefs advocated some vague legislative change. Certain submissions give a much more realistic portrait of the consumption of legal and illegal drugs, even if age was not always a factor (some of these women themselves were not young). First-hand experience and repeated contact with habitual or experimental drug consumers tended to define their positions. For instance, the reports of the Toronto branch and the British Columbia branch of the Elizabeth Fry Society, groups devoted to the welfare of women in prison, encouraged lawmakers to revise federal drug laws. These reports stated that criminalization of drugs encouraged criminal behaviour among women. The Elizabeth Fry Society of British Columbia argued that young women arrested for possession, who spent time in jail, came into contact with drug addicts. These addicts then 'influence the girl to proceed to more dangerous drugs and lesbianism through associations made in prison.' Furthermore, 'these contacts undoubtedly harden their attitudes and make rehabilitation more difficult.'[76] Certainly education offered the best hope for the prevention of these behaviours, but a change in the legislation would make the task much easier. In short, marijuana should be taken out of the Narcotic Control Act. Some women's groups argued that the current punishment for marijuana possession was too harsh, especially for young people, who made a mistake by using marijuana and ended up with a conviction for possession, a jail term, and a criminal record. Although this behaviour was judged reprehensible, it was understandable, because young people were still developing and were not yet capable of making mature decisions.[77]

The option of reducing penalties for possession of marijuana was criticized by other groups, such as the WCTU of British Columbia, as well as the WCTU Vancouver District. These two groups emphasized the social costs that had accompanied the end of alcohol prohibition: alcohol consumption increased, and society had to pay for treatments of alcoholics. Given this history, it made sense to oppose the legalization of marijuana, since it would entail similar consequences: 'Legal liquor did not solve the alcohol problem. Presumably, legal marijuana will not solve the marijuana problem. Rather, the problem most likely will be magnified, resulting in physical, mental, social, spiritual and economic waste.'[78] For its part, the WCTU of British Columbia reminded the Commission about the tragic events surrounding thalidomide, which was 'available for medical use before the dangers [for the foetus and mother] were fully understood.' As a result, caution regarding the marijuana question was recommended: '[P]revention is more economical than a belated effort to effect a cure.'[79] The reference to thalidomide represented an implicit criticism of medical experts whose erroneous assessment of its dangers had tragic results for many women and their children. Not only was caution required, it was also necessary to heed scientific opinion, which contradicted those who asserted that marijuana did not constitute a health danger for users.

One submission questioned the logic of the laws and other measures that restricted the consumption of legal and illegal drugs. The Victoria Voice of Women, a peace-activist group concerned from the beginning of the sixties with nuclear warfare, pointed out that the federal government favoured a repressive approach in regulating certain drugs, but not others. Thus, the question of classification had to be revisited. For instance, LSD and marijuana were considered illegal, whereas tranquillizers and other mood-modifying drugs were not, even though the latter could cause health risks if consumed in large enough quantities. Also, the Victoria group asked, why was marijuana illegal, while cigarettes and alcohol, both dangerous to health, were not only legal but benefited from publicity campaigns? According to the Victoria Voice of Women, this illogicality was explained by the fact that 'we feel more secure with long-established, traditional "drugs" that are now identified with our North American way of life and are afraid of new drugs with strange, foreign-sounding names.'[80]

Finally, one document was especially noteworthy. The Sudbury Young Women's Christian Association (YMCA) lifted the veil on the drug culture of female adolescents and agreed with scientific findings indicating a gender gap. The knowledge garnered by the group came first-hand, as the group had managed a shelter for young women since 1955. The authors emphasized that drug consumption was a more complicated issue than many believed. First, there were differences between men and women in terms of consumption, as women tended to use tranquillizers. Indeed, they noted that the consumption of tranquillizers resulted from ease of access through prescriptions. Thus, without entering into the question of the social construction of gender roles, the Sudbury YWCA demonstrated the complexity of drug issues through its own observations.[81]

Although women's groups disagreed on the best course of action on marijuana, many of them reminded the Commission of the importance of setting up educational programs for youth. Parents, departments of education, the media, and – as the National Council of Jewish Women of Canada suggested – even volunteer organizations like the National Council should take part in the educational process.[82]

After reviewing the various positions expressed by interest groups and some individuals, it is possible to identify at least three competing arguments. Each jockeyed to dominate the debate and thus win the maximum number of supporters and allies.

The first, which favoured the legalization of marijuana, did not enjoy the support of a majority of individuals and interest groups that submitted written documents to the Le Dain Commission. Those supporting it were young people's groups, some women's organizations, other bodies (such as the Legalize Marijuana Committee),[83] and at least one health professional. They sought to build credibility for their solution, at first scientifically and with medical evidence, referring, for instance, to the Indian Hemp Drugs Commission at the end of the nineteenth century and to New York Mayor LaGuardia's 1944 Committee on Marijuana. These documents argued that marijuana use contained few health dangers, or so few that they compared easily with those of a socially accepted drug such as alcohol.

Scientific credibility was only one aspect of this approach that challenged the status quo. It was imperative to identify the weaknesses, contradictions, and limits of established positions. In this way, those favourable to the legalization of marijuana pointed to inconsistencies in the classification of legal and illegal drugs. This classification, they maintained, reflected moral rather than scientific judgment. Although most of these groups failed to offer an alternative method of classifying drugs, they preferred to denounce the status quo, especially as it applied to marijuana.

The last aspect of this discourse dealt with the practices of law-enforcement officers. Individuals and groups favourable to the legalization of marijuana denounced police work that targeted young people. In this regard, they frequently referred to anecdotal evidence and witnesses of police action and repression.

The argument in favour of legalizing marijuana disturbed many, since it was seen as a trigger for social change. The second competing argument put forward by certain groups agreed with the criticism of unfair law enforcement and illogical drug classification, yet did not support legalization because of the many unknowns about the short-term, and especially the long-term, effects of marijuana use. Thus, certain medical organizations pleaded for limited legislative change, but pushed their own definition of the drug phenomenon as a medical, rather than a legal, issue.

Other groups, such as religious institutions, women's groups, and law organizations that supported the liberalization of drug legislation, agreed on the necessity of controlling the non-medical use of drugs. In the case of marijuana, and especially for possession by young offenders, they pleaded for leniency. The solution advocated was the transfer of marijuana from the Narcotic Control Act to the Food and Drugs Act. They considered the legal consequences for possession excessive, especially when it was due to a 'youthful mistake,' such as smoking an occasional joint. In fact, the notion of teenagers not being fully conscious of their actions became an argument for softening the law, there being no justification presented for harsh repression.

The third discourse was put forward by proponents of preserving state controls on the non-medical use of drugs. They were eager to make their views attractive in order to win maximum sympathy, or, at least, to oblige opponents to reflect on the consequences of transferring marijuana to the Food and Drugs Act. Reacting to the strategy of those supporting the legalization of marijuana, those favourable to the preservation of legal controls refined their arguments. Thus, the pro-marijuana lobby's criticism of medical expertise was answered by a reaffirmation by some medical experts that there were still many health unknowns, and therefore the state could not confidently legalize it and should be cautious about its liberalization. Certainly, this position was justified by the fear that any modification of the status of marijuana would inevitably lead to liberalized control of other drugs.

Regarding the allegations of some pro-marijuana forces that law-enforcement officers were biased in their practices, proponents of legal control, among them the RCMP, replied that these claims were not based on close study and often relied on individual, inevitably slanted testimonies. Naturally, the RCMP never made public what young people and other groups suspected, which was that young people were indeed targeted. In spite of certain errors, the RCMP stressed the fact that law enforcement was imperative because of government policy on the use of certain drugs. The RCMP countered the argument that the classification of drugs was inconsistent by recalling that this classification was sanctioned by the international community; furthermore, using the weight of numbers, they showed that many states adhered to these classifications. Finally, in their attempt to undermine the credibility of the pro-marijuana groups, proponents of legal control stressed the fact that it was a minority that supported the legalization of marijuana, as demonstrated by the briefs and other written submissions to the Le Dain Commission.[84]

As for advocating a reduction in penalties, which essentially meant the transfer of marijuana from the Narcotic Control Act to the Food and Drugs Act, proponents of legal controls underlined the fact that accommodations had already been made. In their opposition to the transfer, they argued that members of the medical profession were the best judges for the management of drug use.

The pharmaceutical industry, through its association and allies (the Canadian Pharmaceutical Association, the BC and Alberta provincial associations, the Collège des Pharmaciens du Québec, and CODA), did not favour major change to public policy on drugs. In fact, they feared that it would trigger state intervention in their domain. Indeed, they were careful to restrict their definition of the drug abuse problem to substances used without proper medical supervision. Any comments about the abuse of legal drugs were dealt with by reassuring commissioners that control mechanisms were in place. It was only a matter of reminding pharmacists and drug manufacturers to comply with them.

The Le Dain Commission Reports and Ensuing Reactions

In her study of the Royal Commission on the Status of Women, Barbara Freeman analysed in detail the tensions within the Commission during the drafting of the recommendations. The challenge at this stage was to attain an 'internal consensus' by overcoming disagreements among the commissioners.[85] The Commission chair, Florence Bird, did not hesitate to resort to the media to exert pressure on male commissioners who had difficulties with some of the recommendations. In his recollection of his experience with the Addiction Research Foundation, H. David Archibald wrote that he received an invitation from the government of Bermuda to chair a commission of inquiry into drug and alcohol problems. He decided to seek Gerald Le Dain's advice. Le Dain's reply was, 'Make sure that you are a commission of one.'[86]

As Gerald Le Dain discovered, the commission he chaired was not a 'commission of one.' Perhaps he wished that it was so when the Commission reached the critical phase of agreeing on recommendations. The search for an 'internal consensus' was difficult and failed, since some commissioners opted to sign dissenting reports.

Between 1969 and 1973, the Le Dain Commission released four reports. Its 'Interim Report' was submitted to the minister of National Health and Welfare on 6 April 1970, but was tabled in the House of Commons on 19 June 1970. The reports on 'Treatment' and 'Cannabis' were submitted in January and June 1972, respectively. The final report was made available in December 1973. The following analysis deals mainly with the interim report and the report on cannabis, as the debate triggered by interest groups and individuals before, during, and after the Commission overwhelmingly focused on this particular drug. Although the Commission tried to broaden understanding of the drug issue and use the opportunity to revamp public drug policy as a whole, reaction to drug consumption in general was often affected by views on marijuana in particular.

The interim report reviewed the role of the state, as well as the instruments used to control the supply and demand for drugs. Although it recognized that the state had a responsibility to regulate drug use through legal means, it was critical of law-enforcement practices. The report deplored 'the use of entrapment and physical violence to obtain evidence.' It insisted that the view which held that marijuana (cannabis) inevitably led to the use of other drugs, and that there was a link between marijuana consumption and criminal activity, had not been 'adequately' studied.[87]

The interim report attributed a role to the federal government that went beyond law enforcement. A public drug policy that aimed to limit the non-medical drug supply required the federal government to intervene in fields of provincial responsibility, such as the establishment of regional facilities for drug analysis and research on non-medical drug consumption – notably marijuana – and its effects on humans. In other circumstances, federal initiatives should be implemented with the cooperation of the provinces. For instance, information and education campaigns should be organized and based on facts instead of fear. They should be developed with the provinces or through a federal-provincial institution. The Commission even suggested that young people should be involved with drug education. It also envisioned a role for the media by encouraging the federal government to inform them about drug use. The report also urged the federal government, with the cooperation of provinces, to provide financial assistance to street clinics and treatment facilities.[88]

On the marijuana issue, the interim report argued that there was still a lack of research about its health effects and of information about the implications of legalization. Consequently, the legalization option was rejected. Furthermore, the Single Convention on Narcotic Drugs prevented Canada from legalizing this drug. Commissioner Bertrand dissented when she recommended that possession of cannabis no longer be considered a criminal offence. However, the report recommended easing penalties. In this regard, commissioners suggested a series of actions that targeted not only marijuana, but also other drugs. Cannabis, for example, should be transferred from the Narcotic Control Act to the Food and Drugs Act. As an interim measure, pending the submission of the Commission's final report, it was proposed that, upon summary conviction for possession of narcotics and other restricted drugs, an offender should not be sent to jail, but be asked to pay a fine of $100. Criminal records should be erased after a certain period of time, and trafficking should be redefined in order 'to exclude the giving, without exchange of value, by one user to another of a quantity of cannabis which could ... reasonably be consumed on a single occasion.' In this particular case, trafficking should become subject to a penalty for possession.[89]

Reaching an internal consensus on the cannabis issue was difficult. The debate focused on the role the law should play in the control of the drug supply. In January 1972 Le Dain shared with the other commissioners his views on the legalization of marijuana. Although he believed that legalization could happen in five or ten years 'because of the voting power of the younger generation,' Le Dain could not support it at this moment. He judged that it was simply too difficult to counteract the RCMP's argument 'that an offence of simple possession is vital to law enforcement against trafficking.' Le Dain wrote:

I believe that the offence of simple possession has to be retained in more or less the form suggested by the Interim Report – no imprisonment, moderate fine, conditional discharge, destruction or records, etc. – because of (a) the need to continue to stigmatize use; (b) the relationship of the possessional offence to enforcement against trafficking; and (c) the desirability of a uniform legislative approach towards the possessional offence that will assure that there is no imprisonment.

... Briefly, the elimination of the offence of simple possession will not eliminate the criminalization of most cannabis users and might actually aggravate the situation because it would take an important element of flexibility out of the law.[90]

As with the interim report, commissioners could not reach a consensus on the marijuana issue. This time, three different approaches to legal control of the drug supply were recommended. A majority of commissioners (Le Dain, Lehmann, and Stein) supported repealing the offence of simple cannabis possession, reducing penalties for importing, exporting, and trafficking, and removing penalties for cultivation 'when there is a reasonable doubt.' In their justification, they insisted on the social costs of criminal conviction for cannabis users, but rejected legalization because of health concerns, such as the impact of cannabis on the maturing process of adolescents, safety – such as driving while under the influence of cannabis – and the theory that cannabis facilitated the use of other drugs, though not heroin. Speaking individually, Bertrand recommended the 'legalization of cannabis distribution through federal-provincial agreement,' arguing that legalization would 'be less harmful than the evils of prohibition.' Campbell opted for maintaining possession for personal use as a crime, but with reduced penalties (a fine instead of imprisonment upon summary conviction), since any reduction could send the wrong message, particularly to young people, that the Commission believed that cannabis was harmless.[91]

Reactions

Newspaper opinions about the interim report varied. The *Globe and Mail*, the *Montreal Gazette*, the *Toronto Star*, and the *Vancouver Province* welcomed the report. In its editorial, the *Globe and Mail* expressed the hope that the government would move on the marijuana issue by abolishing jail terms for possession and putting it under the Food and

Drugs Act.[92] Among French-language dailies, *Le Devoir* welcomed the report and argued that the fact that it was inconclusive on the key issue of drug effects and health consequences demonstrated the commissioners' intellectual honesty and reflected the current state of knowledge about drugs.[93] This inconclusiveness, however, bothered *La Presse*. This reflected, according to its editorial, divisions among the cabinet and the Commissioners on the drug issue and signalled a victory for those in society who favoured reducing penalties for marijuana and other drugs.[94]

When the report on cannabis was released, newspapers noted the divisions among commissioners. For the *Toronto Star*, the majority report was 'the best advice we have, but whether it is acceptable to the public is another question.'[95] The *Globe and Mail* welcomed the three reports, but encouraged the government to proceed with a new law that would not give a criminal record for the offence of possession. Once the new law was implemented, it would be possible to proceed with recommendations of the other reports.[96] Although *La Presse* limited itself to inviting the government to act without giving any practical advice on how to proceed, *Le Devoir* praised the commissioners for the quality of their report and identified the areas of agreement, one of which was the need to change the status of cannabis. *Le Devoir* hoped that the government would be as courageous as it had been in 1968, when it introduced the omnibus bill that decriminalized contraception devices and homosexuality. This time, it pressed the government to implement the main recommendations of the report.[97]

Among the interest groups studied here, CODA and university student associations did not send any documents about either the interim report or the cannabis report to the Le Dain Commission or the Department of National Health and Welfare. For its part, the CACP publicized its views on soft drugs in October 1972, as mentioned in chapter 2.

The interim report confirmed the worst fears of the RCMP about this exercise in public consultation. In its second brief to the Commission, the RCMP rejected the criticisms of police violence contained in the interim report. On the contrary, the RCMP argued there was no excessive use of violence, but that 'force is used when required.' The RCMP categorically rejected the interim report's recommendation to reduce the penalty for possession. Such a move would render law enforcement irrelevant, which was not an option. 'To lessen or downgrade the seriousness of a possession charge to where there is no possibility of enforcing it is to virtually legalize illegal possession of a drug.' The

RCMP argued similarly against the recommendation to transfer cannabis to the Food and Drugs Act, stating that 'it may be dangerous at this time to completely remove the deterrent of a minimum sentence, and the provisions of extradition.' In short, the possession of marijuana should remain an offence.[98]

The CMA, by contrast, approved the recommendations contained in the Le Dain reports. However, the reports became part of the divisive debate on the legal status of marijuana. Some health professionals and physicians made their opposition to the Le Dain Commission and its work public. A group of ten health professionals, among them Dr Fred Lundell, rejected the interim report and characterized it as a 'highly permissive, fact-hiding, and vacillating report.' For this group, the document contained 'both bias and social and scientific irresponsibility.'[99] The CMA, however, was divided. The Council on Community Health Care, which had submitted a report on the issue, was opposed to both the CMA board and its members, as the adoption of Schwarz's proposal during the 1972 CMA General Assembly revealed.

The four provinces under consideration had varied reactions. PEI pursued its campaign against the legalization of marijuana. In addition, Lundell wrote a critique of the interim report, helping the PEI government in its opposition to marijuana use.

The NAFBC's reactions to the Le Dain Commission were negative. In its evaluation of the interim report, NAFBC officials criticized the functioning of the Le Dain Commission, its use of public hearings, and the scientific quality of its report, notably the evaluation of, and reference to, scientific studies on drug use, and in particular marijuana. The NAFBC regretted that the Commission was not very critical of certain briefs, while it was overly critical of those of the RCMP and the NAFBC. It could not hide its annoyance that the Commission did not take seriously the theory that marijuana was a stepping-stone drug. The NAFBC considered the recommendation to eliminate jail terms for possession of any drug inappropriate, especially for a substance such as heroin. In brief, the British Columbia organization noticed and deplored the fact that its recommendations did not influence the Le Dain commissioners, an analysis shared by the executive director of ARF, H. David Archibald.[100]

As a private individual, not on behalf of the NAFBC, H.F. Hoskin submitted a long critique of the interim report. He urged the Commission to halt its activities, since its report did much damage to the whole issue of drug use because it failed 'to come to grips with the complexity of the situation.' What were his main criticisms? First of all, the interim report did not contain any 'evaluation of any of the drugs.' Nevertheless, it recommended reducing penalties. This prompted Hoskin to ask if the Commission was 'saying that people have the right to use drugs regardless of [its] assessment of the consequences?' Hoskin believed that law enforcement was a valid option in dealing with non-medical drug use. Furthermore, he recommended that drugs be reclassified according to the suggestions made by his organization.[101]

The Quebec government, through evaluations produced by OPTAT, welcomed the work undertaken by the Le Dain Commission. OPTAT highlighted the quality of the research and the concern for objectivity, while regretting that the Quebec reality was not considered in the treatment report and the final report.[102] It was delighted with the recommendation, following its own advice to the Commission, favouring transfer of cannabis from the Narcotic Control Act to the Food and Drugs Act. As for recommendations that the federal government do more in education and treatment, OPTAT repeated a position well known to the provinces and the federal government, that health and education were matters of provincial jurisdiction. Consequently, the federal government should provide funding to provincial organizations dealing with the education and treatment of drug addicts.[103] OPTAT's position also reflected deep reservations expressed by the Quebec Department of Education. Reacting to the interim report and the report on cannabis, bureaucrats from the department denounced the distinction made by the Commission between education and information. The first was certainly a matter of provincial jurisdiction, as the Le Dain commissioners acknowledged, whereas the second did not belong exclusively to any level of government because information campaigns took place outside the education system. For Quebec bureaucrats, the distinction made by the Commission was an attempt to justify the unjustifiable, which was the possibility of federal intervention in education. One could not, they maintained, dissociate education and information, because they were fully integrated.[104]

OPTAT praised the numerous qualities of the report on cannabis, notably the fact that the report dealt with the health dangers of marijuana use. While reviewing the different options, the head of OPTAT rejected the legalization of marijuana, since it would 'entail an increase in consumption and, consequently, significant health and social problems. Medicare costs will certainly increase.' In short, OPTAT felt that the solution proposed by a majority of commissioners was the best in the present context.[105]

The favourable reaction of the Ontario government to the interim report was largely due to the positive judgment rendered by ARF. In its comments, ARF qualified the report as an 'outstanding document,' identified some issues and questions that required further investigation, and encouraged discussions about the benefits and drawbacks of drug use. Despite ARF's reservation about the report's suggestion to include young people in drug education programs, it supported the Le Dain recommendations concerning the transfer of cannabis to the Food and Drugs Act and the reduction of penalties for cannabis possession. It also encouraged the Commission to identify the ideal solutions in terms of public drug policy and 'then point out which parts of this ideal response they consider politically and socially feasible, which parts are not yet attainable, and the reasons for the difference.'[106]

Inspired by ARF's positive evaluation, the Ontario government supported the recommendations, although it asked for further explanation about the 'nationally co-ordinated system of education and information.' In Ontario's view, however, the liberalization of the status of marijuana should be put on hold and the Commission should pursue its research on this drug.[107] Determined to encourage cooperation between the provinces and the federal government on the drug front, Health Minister Wells invited his federal counterpart to include the interim report on the agenda of the 1970 Federal-Provincial Conference of Health Ministers.[108]

When the Commission's report on cannabis was released in 1972, divisions that plagued ARF concerning the most appropriate current public policy to adopt on marijuana prevented it from presenting a position to the Ontario government. Although ARF favoured the report submitted by a majority of the commissioners, some of its employees preferred the minority reports. Besides, ARF's executive director, also a member of the interdepartmental committee set up by the government, supported Ian Campbell's minority report. In its submission to the cabinet, the interministerial committee recommended supporting the transfer of cannabis to the Food and Drugs Act, since current drug legislation was inadequate. However, committee members could not themselves reach a consensus on the changes required in controlling the cannabis supply by legal means. They agreed that further studies were required, since the solutions in the cannabis report were judged unacceptable.[109]

Federal political parties said nothing about the cannabis report in the House of Commons. However, it was a different story with the interim report. The leader of the Progressive Conservative Party, Robert Stanfield, welcomed the report. He was at ease with the fact that the Le Dain Commission did not recommend the legalization of marijuana. However, Stanfield supported the proposal to reduce penalties for possession of marijuana and pressed the federal government to act, with the provinces, on education, treatment, and research. The New Democratic Party was extremely favourable to the report, especially about the transfer of marijuana from the Narcotic Control Act to the Food and Drugs Act.[110]

Conclusion

On reviewing the work undertaken by the Le Dain Commission, one gets a sense of déjà vu. The divisions within the CMA became public when CMA members, such as Lundell and Schwarz, independently submitted their views on the dangers of marijuana use. Other professional health organizations faced internal disagreement about what constituted drug abuse and which legal, educational, and health mechanisms should be put in place in order to deal with abuse of legally obtained drugs. Students and their allies repeated the same arguments put forward by various groups advocating reductions of punishment for marijuana possession. Besides, the Le Dain Commission allowed groups to speak up and to use the divisions within the medical profession to promote their views. Finally, there were some absentees, such as native groups; others were under-represented, such as Quebec, the manufacturing industry, and police forces. The influence of the latter would be exercised within the federal bureaucracy and the government itself. As part holder of the monopoly in the legitimate use of physical force, and as part of the federal government, the RCMP exercised considerable influence there. Its power was not unlimited, however, because other departments also competed to influence the government's course of action. The divisions that characterized the reports submitted by the Commission gave ammunition to bureaucrats and politicians anxious to gain the attention of the cabinet and the prime minister. When the Le Dain Commission submitted its report on cannabis in 1972, the time had come for the federal government to make its position known to Canadians.

5 A Small Step beyond the Status Quo: The Federal Government and Recreational Drug Use

In July 1968, J.N. Crawford, the deputy minister of national health and welfare, wrote that his department was 'very much concerned with the problem of drug abuse and particularly the increasing use of marijuana in Canada.'[1] About six years later, an official from the same department declared that the drug scare, and in particular the one about marijuana, was almost over, and that alcohol abuse had become the new priority.[2]

By 1975, it seems that marijuana was no longer an issue. Since in the end the federal government did not significantly alter its drug legislation, at least in regard to marijuana use, it may seem that status quo forces won the battle or that those who pushed for change were not influential enough. But other factors besides lobbying from interest groups and individuals interfered in the public policy process. For instance, there were constraints on the federal government. Among other things, Canada's choice has to be considered within the context of the international community and the country's obligations resulting from international agreements.

This last chapter is divided into five parts. The first one deals with the construction of the phenomenon of recreational drug use by politicians before the appointment of the Le Dain Commission. The conceptualization of this phenomenon by politicians reflected some of the concerns expressed by the media and social actors, but also those of bureaucrats who were anxious to defend their views on recreational drug use. In fact, the second section of the chapter deals specifically with the reactions of bureaucrats (mainly those from the Departments of National Health and Welfare and Justice, as well as from the RCMP) to recreational drug use. These bureaucrats echoed opinions expressed by interest groups, but also voiced their own concerns and under-standing of the issue. Indeed, they were part of the state apparatus and thus enjoyed a certain degree of autonomy and control over how politicians understood the debate. But the international community, and in particular the United States, came to bear on the issue, as will be seen in the third section. Ultimately, ministers and the cabinet, which constitutes the fourth section of the chapter, adopted a stance that took into consideration the context and pressures resulting from domestic, continental, and international factors. The last part of this chapter looks at the fate of the bill transferring marijuana from the Narcotic Control Act to the Food and Drugs Act, legislation that was introduced in 1974 but never adopted by the House of Commons.

Federal Politicians and Recreational Drug Use

Before the appointment of the Le Dain Commission in May 1969, federal politicians had occasionally voiced their opinions about the phenomenon of recreational drug use. In the House of Commons, however, the issue of recreational drug use generated no important debates. When in 1969 members of Parliament debated Bill S-15, which amended the Criminal Code to legalize the sale and advertisement of contraceptives devices – and at the same time made LSD a restricted drug – they did not extensively comment on the drug issue. Most of the comments recorded refer to contraception.

For a comprehensive discussion of the drug issue, we must look to the Senate. There, a series of debates between 1967 and 1969 revolved on the amendment to the Food and Drugs Act. The senators' discussions let us reconstruct their understanding of the drug culture, one influenced by their own knowledge and experience, as well as by media coverage.

During these debates on drug use, senators perceived youth and the counterculture movement as threats. In their opinion, a line had to be drawn to prevent a collapse of the social order. They believed society was threatened by abortion, the sexual revolution, and now the phenomenon of recreational drug use.

Bill S-60, which was introduced in April 1967, amended the Food and Drugs Act by making LSD a restricted drug and by making LSD's possession, possession for trafficking, and trafficking criminal offences. When Senator A. Hamilton McDonald introduced Bill S-60, he invited his fellow senators to look again at drug regulation, an issue with which some of them were already familiar. In 1961 Parliament had approved a bill hardening the laws on narcotics. For instance, the possession of any narcotic, including marijuana, became punishable only by indictment and for a prison term of up to seven years. In 1967 most of the comments by senators were restricted to LSD, but some used the opportunity to condemn the phenomenon of recreational drug use.

The suicide of a young Toronto man in March 1967, attributed by his father to LSD use, prompted the federal government to introduce a bill amending the Food and Drugs Act.[3] But other reasons forced the federal government to act. For instance, the Minister of National Health and Welfare had come under fire for inaction after the provinces of Alberta and British Columbia had introduced legislation outlawing the possession of LSD.[4] Furthermore, Ottawa acted as a result of pressure from the United Nations Economic and Social Council. At its May 1967 and 1968 meetings, this organization adopted resolutions pressing states to implement national control over the importation, exportation, production, and distribution of LSD. Essentially, states were henceforth obliged to restrict LSD to research and medical purposes.[5]

This was the second time that Parliament looked at the LSD issue in the 1960s. In 1962 the Food and Drugs Act was amended to make LSD a prohibited drug and its sale illegal. In 1967 Bill S-60 opted for repression as part of a strategy to discourage LSD consumption without proper medical supervision. In the proposed bill, punishment included a maximum of three years' detention for simple possession and ten years for trafficking. Senators and daily newspapers, which occasionally chronicled the debate,[6] felt that reinforcement of the federal government's policy of punitive legislation remained the best method of deterrence. In short, social control through legal means was judged the most effective strategy to check this social threat. The comments of Senator J. Harper Prowse demonstrate that no participant in the parliamentary debate challenged this underlying assumption. Prowse stated that 'when we tell the young people of Canada that ... to have anything to do with [LSD] puts them in the position of having committed a crime for which society is going to put them away for a period of up to ten years, we will have made the point more effectively and more usefully than the use of all the logic from old men to young men ever could.'[7] In fact, some senators deplored the fact that LSD was not included in the Narcotic Control Act. If it were, penalties for possession and other offences would have been harsher. But it was impossible to do so; J.D. McCarthy, a legal adviser for the Department of National Health and Welfare, reminded senators that LSD was not a narcotic and had not been 'recognized internationally as in that group of substances.'[8]

Senators supported the repressive approach because of their construction of recreational drug use. First, they equated this new phenomenon with a specific group of people: youth, especially high school and university students. Senator A. Hamilton McDonald strove to add to this list 'a class of anti-social persons commonly known as the beatniks.'[9]

In their construction of the drug use phenomenon, senators insisted on the social dangers of LSD use. To exemplify this reality, some senators cited Toronto's well-known Yorkville neighbourhood. According to Senator Walker, a former lawyer who had a long career as a prosecutor under the Narcotic Control Act, a casual stroll through the neighbourhood gave one the opportunity to see first-hand LSD's dire impact on the young. 'You can see by the faces of the people you meet that they are either taking goof balls or LSD.' Unable to verify exactly what they used, Walker commented, '[T]hey are certainly taking something.'[10]

Senators highlighted in particular the health dangers of LSD and other drugs for recreational users. They held LSD responsible for suicides, deaths, and mental disability. Colleagues with a medical background, such as the physician Senator Gershaw, provided many examples to support these views. Gershaw stated, '[O]ne drop in a cup of coffee has caused a woman to jump out of a window and kill herself.' Moreover, 'just one very, very small dose caused a man driving his car to feel that he was driving into the river just at Niagara Falls.'[11] Intent on denouncing women who took LSD, senators also pointed to the genetic damage mothers could cause their unborn children. The opinions of Senators Gershaw and Sullivan, both of whom had medical backgrounds, were highly valued by their peers since they reinforced their own views about the dangers of LSD use. When senators debated Bill S-21 in the fall of 1967, Senator Sullivan once again emphasized the grave dangers of LSD use. Senator Flynn thanked Sullivan by saying, 'I consider the Senate is most fortunate to have an expert as highly qualified as [he is].'[12]

In their attempt to identify the causes of LSD use, members of the upper house were quick to blame journalists, some media personalities, and the CBC for what they qualified as their irresponsible promotion of LSD and other drugs. Senator McGrand attributed to the CBC an extensive power of influence by arguing that when the national television network had programs on LSD use, 'young people wanted to get in on the act.'[13] Others pointed an accusatory figure at the well-known unofficial leader of the counterculture movement in the United States, Dr Timothy Leary. Senator Joseph A. Sullivan even suggested that Leary 'should be locked up.'[14]

During the discussions on the bill in the Standing Committee on Banking and Commerce, Senator Molson convinced his colleagues that promotion of LSD, which had been identified as an important factor in its consumption, should become a criminal offence and that the offender, upon conviction on indictment, be sent to jail for ten years.[15] This would effectively halt Leary and others of his kind who freely advocated LSD use.

Molson's amendment created a commotion in the newspapers. They felt that they were being unjustly targeted. In its editorial, the *Globe and Mail* denounced this attack on freedom of expression by mentioning that the amendment was 'one of the severest restrictions on freedom of expression and freedom of the press that has ever been contemplated in this country.' It invited MPs not 'to conspire' with senators 'to lay such violent hands on freedom.'[16] Yet the Toronto daily newspaper was not the only one preoccupied with Molson's amendment. Department of National Health and Welfare officials, and in particular Robert Curran, who had developed an extensive expertise on drugs and international treaties, felt that this amendment was going too far. In fact, the amendment prompted the Pearson government to introduce a new bill, S-21, in the fall of 1967, in order to kill the amendment on promotion. But this new bill did not become law due to the prorogation of Parliament and the 1968 June election.[17]

It was only in 1969 that the Food and Drugs Act was finally amended as part of the omnibus Bill S-15 on contraception devices and abortion. Parliament approved the new classification of LSD as a restricted drug; furthermore, LSD possession, possession for trafficking, and trafficking became offences. For possession, a first offence upon summary conviction carried a fine of $1000 or a six-month jail term or both. For subsequent offences, the fine was $2000 or a one-year jail term or both. If the Crown decided to proceed by indictment, the offender could be condemned to a fine of $5000 or a three-year jail term or both. In cases of trafficking, the penalty was ten years in jail and if the Crown proceeded upon summary conviction, the jail term was eighteen months.[18]

Discussion in the Senate and the House of Commons focused on the legalization of the sale and advertisement of contraceptive devices, yet Bill S-15 included an amendment to the Narcotic Control Act that offered, according to National Health and Welfare minister John Munro, flexibility in 'both procedure and penalties' to Crown prosecutors and judges in cases of individuals charged with simple possession of narcotics. The amendment gave a choice to Crown prosecutors: to proceed by way of either summary conviction or indictment. The former carried for a first offence a fine or a six-month jail term, or both; for subsequent offences the penalty was a fine or one-year jail term, or both. The latter carried a maximum jail term of seven years.[19] This amendment, according to Munro, was 'a first step' in the revision of the law-enforcement approach.[20] It reflected the contemporary discussions and debates among senior bureaucrats from several departments on how to handle the phenomenon of recreational drug use and its legal consequences for youth.

Federal Bureaucrats and Recreational Drug Use

In his study on the development of public policies, Lemieux demonstrates that their complexity derives from the involvement of multiple social actors in the process. As seen in previous chapters, individuals and social actors outside of the federal government intervened in the issue of recreational drug use, with the hope of shaping the views of federal bureaucrats and especially those of politicians. Any analysis of the development of a governmental response to the drug issue should pay attention to those whom Lemieux refers to as the 'agents,' that is, actors within the governmental apparatus such as bureaucrats and governmental agencies, and those whom Lemieux calls 'responsible' for developing and implementing a solution, such as ministers and their immediate advisers, the cabinet and the prime minister.[21]

The 'agents' or federal bureaucrats became aware of the reality of drug use, as a social practice and a challenge to dominant values, through data collected on the number of arrests and the penalties imposed under the Narcotic Control Act. In 1961 the number of drug arrests was 15; by 1967, it had reached 1577.[22] Because this new social phenomenon was constructed on the basis of criminal data, no wonder the proposed solution tried to counteract what appeared to be an exponential growth in drug use! Some judges adopted lenient policies and others exercised their prerogative to mete out harsh penalties. In his review of some cases of young people arrested and condemned for possession of marijuana in 1967 and 1968, Whitaker points out the inconsistency of the courts: some youth were condemned to a suspended sentence while others received jail terms.[23] For instance, in Ontario, judges chose the option of suspended sentence; in Manitoba and New Brunswick courts preferred a jail term.[24] The issue of the prosecution of young people with no prior criminal record under the Narcotic Control Act and the consequences of a conviction on their future triggered discussions and debates among bureaucrats on how to handle this new social phenomenon.[25]

Three departments played a role in the discussion of recreational drug use: National Health and Welfare (the Food and Drug Directorate), the RCMP, and Justice. The first pleaded for the introduction of a health-oriented approach based on prevention and treatment in order to discourage demand for drugs, while the last two believed that legal repression was still required, since the criminal justice system had been selected by the state as an instrument of control of the drug supply. Consequently, the law represented a deterrent. Moreover, any calls to soften the range of penalties had to be weighed against Canada's international obligations.

The Food and Drug Directorate within National Health and Welfare administered the federal drug legislation, which comprised the Food and Drugs Act and the Narcotic Control Act. The Food and Drug Directorate determined the type of control required for drugs based of the five categories under which the two acts classified drugs: controlled (barbiturates and amphetamines), prohibited (thalidomide), restricted (LSD), narcotic (cannabis, heroin), and prescription. The listing of drugs such as heroin and cannabis in the Narcotic Control Act obliged the state to exercise control through a licensing system of manufacturers, wholesalers, and retailers. For instance, the federal government had to implement a system of licence and permits that allowed hospitals and pharmacies to keep narcotics. The state was also obliged to cooperate with the United Nations in suppressing the illicit use and trafficking of narcotics by supporting a licence system for export and import. On the domestic front, this suppression task was a shared responsibility between the Food and Drug Directorate, the Division of Narcotic Control, and the RCMP. The government also had the responsibility to collect data on illegal drug use and send them annually to the International Narcotics Control Board. The data covered issues such as illicit trafficking in narcotic drugs, domestic consumption of narcotic drugs, number of drug addicts and seizures, and the quantity of illegal drug seized.[26]

The Food and Drug Directorate and senior bureaucrats of the Department of National Health and Welfare were looking for a complement to law enforcement in terms of a drug-use public policy. Although law enforcement had been an important feature of Canada's approach to drugs, National Health and Welfare bureaucrats, like other medical health specialists in Britain, Canada, and the United States,[27] felt that the time had come to offer alternatives, such as treatment, prevention, and education, in the face of the changing reality of drug users. Drug consumption was more than a legal problem; it was also a social and medical one. Consequently, other means had to be found to discourage demand for illegal drugs, since young people used them, in particular marijuana, and were prosecuted. Prosecutions and convictions of youth meant that in some cases their future, for instance, when it came to finding a job or travelling abroad, was seriously handicapped. Furthermore, research on the effects of drugs on users was required in order to design appropriate and effective educational programs and treatment. Although the deputy minister of health informed his minister in 1968 that marijuana was a dangerous drug, it seems that it did not stop some in the department from questioning the law-enforcement approach as a deterrent. In fact, the arrival of John Munro as National Health and Welfare minister, following the June 1968 federal election, set a course in the department towards the development of arguments for the transfer of marijuana from the Narcotic Control Act to the Food and Drugs Act. This preference was outlined in the brief submitted to cabinet and in Munro's speech to the Canadian Pharmaceutical Association in August 1968.[28]

The Department of National Health and Welfare rejected the legalization of marijuana because the 1961 Single Convention on Narcotic Drugs prevented Canada and any country that had ratified it from doing so. However, it was felt that the Single Convention would allow the transfer of the offence of possession of marijuana to the Food and Drugs Act, while keeping trafficking and cultivation under the Narcotic Control Act. Why would such a move be contemplated? Department officials developed a series of arguments to give their case credibility. First, they argued that 'on medical grounds' cannabis (which includes marijuana, THC, and hashish) was not a narcotic but 'a mild hallucinogen or intoxicant,' an opinion that contradicted the views of the World Health Organization. For this reason, cannabis 'logically belonged with restricted drugs ... in the Food and Drugs Act.'[29] However, they were quick to point out that hashish possessed 'a potential for health hazards greater than that possessed by marihuana.' In the case of THC, control measures were necessary. For these reasons, hashish and THC would not be included in the transfer.[30]

Department officials insisted on the social costs of convictions. The transfer offered an acceptable legal solution (the terms of the discussion with other departments were often legalistic) to the issue of criminal records incurred by youth for simple possession of marijuana. It was imperative to reduce the impact of the law for the crime of simple possession in order to demonstrate that the government was adapting its legislation to the new reality. The government had to 'bring legal and social penalties related to [marijuana] into proper relationship with hazards to the individual and to society from the use and abuse of the drug.'[31] However, even this solution was not welcome by everyone.

Within the Department of National Health and Welfare strong voices were opposed to any reduction of penalties for marijuana users. Among them was Robert E. Curran, a legal adviser for the Department of National Health and Welfare, who from 1963 until his retirement in 1968 was a special assistant to deputy ministers of national health and welfare. He was a well-known figure among Canadian and foreign bureaucrats due to his long career strengthening the international drug-control apparatus. Curran was a member of the Canadian delegation to the 1953 conference to adopt the Opium Protocol and was the head of the Canadian delegation to the 1961 Conference on the Single Convention on Narcotic Drugs. During that conference, he was the chairman of the drafting committee, which produced the convention. From 1962 to 1969 he was Canada's representative on the United Nations Commission on Narcotic Drugs, being elected its chair in 1968.[32]

In the midst of the controversy generated by the phenomenon of recreational drug use, Curran used his international connections to influence Canada's ability to design its own drug policy. In January 1968 the UN Commission on Narcotic Drugs, and in May of the same year the UN Economic and Social Council, adopted resolutions pressuring states to pursue their fight against the non-medical use of marijuana due to its health dangers. According to the wording of the resolution approved by the UN Economic and Social Council, marijuana was known 'to distort perception of time and space, modify mood and impair judgment, which may result in unpredictable behaviour, violence and adverse effects on health, and ... it may be associated with the abuse of other drugs such as LSD, stimulants and heroin.'[33]

Curran's strategy consisted of obtaining a resolution from these international organizations to give more ammunition to those who opposed the pro-marijuana lobby, and so circumscribe the action of states that signed the Single Convention on Narcotic Drugs. Curran wrote the following to the director of the Division of Narcotic Drugs at the United Nations office in Geneva: 'One of the great difficulties that we have in combating publicity regarding the harmlessness of marijuana, is the fact that so many young people have used it without being exposed to or experiencing all of the dangers which are pointed out.'[34] In his letter to the deputy minister, Curran explained his action by the need 'to obtain' from international institutions 'some strong authoritative statement that would be wholly supportable condemning the use of marijuana, and this statement would prove valuable to enforcement authorities and to magistrates and others in showing that an international authority did not agree with loose professional thinking extolling the virtues of this drug.'[35] In 1968 he informed the participants at the Montreal students' conference that Canada could not modify its stand on marijuana because of its international obligations.[36]

Within the state apparatus, many sought Curran's opinions because of his involvement and his networking capabilities at the international level. Despite Curran's stature, Munro would favour the advice of Ross Chapman, director general of the Food and Drug Directorate; indeed, after Curran's departure, Chapman became an influential figure within and outside the Department of National Health and Welfare. Chapman, who became the assistant deputy minister, was the delegate to the United Nations Commission on Narcotic Drugs. Because of his new responsibility, he was a member of the Canadian delegation at the United Nations Conference to Adopt a Protocol on Psychotropic Substances in 1971 and headed the Canadian delegation at the Conference of Plenipotentiaries to Consider Amendments to the Single Convention on Narcotic Drugs in 1972.

The RCMP was the other important actor in the debate. The force's capital of influence was substantial because of the expertise it had acquired over many years in the domain of drug law enforcement. It was the RCMP, rather than the Food and Drug Directorate, that had the responsibility of controlling the illicit traffic of narcotics and other drugs classified as illegal. Until they created their own drug squads, municipal and provincial police forces relied on the RCMP. Finally, the RCMP was a member of Interpol (the International Criminal Police Organization), and in September 1971 the RCMP commissioner, W.L. Higgitt, was elected Interpol Vice-President for the Western Hemisphere.[37]

With the development of the counterculture movement and recreational drug use, the RCMP, in particular its drug squads, were busy. Data collected by the drug squads in Vancouver, Toronto, and Montreal demonstrated a clear trend: a sharp increase in the number of individuals convicted for drug offences, drug addicts, and the quantity of drugs seized. Police forces targeted soft-drug use by the end of 1965.[38]

The enforcement methods used by the RCMP (and indeed those favoured by municipal police forces and similar to those of the FBI in the United States) raised criticisms. Throughout the sixties, university campuses were under surveillance by RCMP officers who sought to detect and measure communist influence, as did the FBI. In the case of the FBI, New Left activists and sympathizers were targeted. In order to undermine their support, FBI officers leaked information discrediting them in the media and arrested them on drug charges. With the development of the counterculture movement, New Left, Black Power, and student activism, the RCMP increased its intelligence-gathering activities. Although the force could not recruit individuals on university campuses, it relied on a variety of sources, such as its own officers and students who took university courses, on the cooperation of other police forces, but also on university administrators and professors who volunteered to inform the RCMP about the extent of drug use within their institutions.[39]

Even though drug use meant that the user could cause self-inflicted harm but not necessarily harm to others, the RCMP did not always get the cooperation of victims, as opposed to the case of crimes against people and property. Consequently, drug enforcement mobilized important human and financial resources. The use of force to get access to premises and to recover evidence, and of informants and undercover officers who sold or bought drugs from people, and the arrests of drug users were denounced before the Le Dain Commission and fed the discussion about police methods used to reduce the availability of illegal drugs. In 1969, for instance, an Ottawa judge rejected a charge of possession against a young person on the grounds that an undercover RCMP officer had for two months attempted to obtain the name of the drug supplier. The young person was forced to reveal the name of his drug supplier 'after the agent borrowed money from him and refused to pay it back, unless the student got him some hashish.'[40]

In reaction to the way that the RCMP enforced the Narcotic Control Act, certain groups such as OPTAT, but especially ARF, were of the opinion that repression should remain one of the objectives of an anti-drug strategy, but that imprisonment was not the solution. Others such as CODA and NAFBC emphasized the importance of law enforcement in any public drug policy.

Drug law enforcement meant that more human and financial resources were required to face the increase in the number of drug users. The RCMP thus created drug squads in major Canadian cities, and police officers previously assigned to hard drug use were tasked with the repression of soft drugs.[41] The federal government complied with demands by the RCMP to allocate more resources: the manpower dedicated to drug enforcement increased from 105, in 1968, to 256, in 1972.[42]

The RCMP maintained, before the House of Commons Standing Committee on Justice and Legal Affairs, the Le Dain Commission, and the Interdepartmental Committee to Study the Le Dain Commission Interim Report, that the repressive approach was the best means suited to reduce, in the long run, the non-medical use of drugs.

The RCMP was especially concerned with marijuana. Its choice reflected the dynamics of the public debate on drugs, which was focused on marijuana. It also obeyed a strategic consideration: there was a fear that any reduction in the penalties for marijuana would open a breach in the legal anti-drug bulwark, which had been incrementally put in place through the twentieth century. Such a reduction in legal consequences could, perhaps, trigger the collapse of the repressive approach towards illegal drugs. In softening the status of marijuana, the RCMP judged, the state would have no choice but to reduce penalties for other drugs classified in the Narcotic Control Act and the Food and Drugs Act.[43] Thus it was crucial to avoid making a distinction between marijuana and other illegal drugs under the excuse that the former was not as dangerous. The message was spread that any drug, used without any medical supervision, was dangerous.[44] The RCMP made great efforts to explaining to the deputy solicitor general that the Le Dain Commission was on the wrong track. At a meeting of senior bureaucrats, the deputy solicitor general pointed out that the interim report of the Commission had broadened the terms of reference of the Commission in order to justify their recommendation of weakening the Narcotic Control Act.[45] To prevent any softening of penalties for marijuana use, the RCMP argued that the increase in the number of arrests for marijuana, which in 1962 was 20 and by 1967 had reached 1678, testified to the obligation to remain firm and to assign more resources to law enforcement.[46]

This plea for firmness in law enforcement relied on emphasizing the danger of marijuana use in order to counteract the influence of individuals and social actors who opposed legal repression. The construction of this danger was based on medical evidence. Because of its lack of expertise on this aspect, the RCMP drew its scientific legitimacy from scientists opposed to the legalization of marijuana and from its collaboration with the NAFBC. Naturally, the RCMP said little about the division of the medical community on the health dangers of marijuana. This construction of danger did not, however, ignore its social aspects. Thus, the RCMP argued, it was false to pretend that marijuana users caused harm only to themselves. Marijuana use brought about negative consequences for society as a whole. First, marijuana was a stepping-stone drug, since it led inevitably to the use of hard drugs, especially heroin. Before the members of the Standing Committee on Justice and Legal Affairs in 1968, RCMP commissioner F.A. Lindsay insisted on the stepping-stone theory, although he could not provide any accurate data apart from what his forces reported to him. The RCMP had estimated that '70 per cent of those who have died or become chronic addicts on hard narcotics started on marijuana.'[47] Therefore, the RCMP stated, marijuana use triggered addiction problems that, in turn, affected society since it had to pay for the treatment of drug addicts. Finally, marijuana incited users to commit acts even more reprehensible such as hold-ups. In this way the RCMP argued before the Le Dain Commission that there was a link between crime and marijuana use.[48]

The RCMP's construction of marijuana use paid close attention to young people. But why was this demographic group of users singled out? It was crucial, the RCMP insisted, to discourage youth through legal means from consuming marijuana because if they started with marijuana they would inevitably become drug addicts and cause serious social problems. In February 1968 the RCMP commissioner described the youth situation in the following terms: 'the lawless "beat" generation will create a mounting fear of anarchy in Canada unless it is met firmly by police with massive public and governmental support.'[49] Naturally, one group was singled out: hippies. RCMP offic-

ers depicted hippies as social parasites with no aspirations and no purpose in life. If these people represented the future of society, the RCMP
did not want to be part of it. The RCMP thus constructed a link of cau-
sality between the legalization of marijuana and the threat of a widespread social adoption of the hippie lifestyle.[50]

In the face of pressure from interest groups, social actors and individuals, as well as to counteract attempts by the Department of
National Health and Welfare to win the support of cabinet ministers to
its own proposal, the RCMP argued that legislative change had in fact
already taken place. Indeed, the federal government had already done
what many were asking it to do, that is, reduce penalties for possession
of marijuana. Starting in August 1969, the possibility of a fine, rather
than a jail term, was introduced in the Narcotic Control Act as a punishment option. In 1969, prior to the August amendment, about 74 per
cent of the 349 individuals convicted for possession of marijuana in
Montreal, Toronto, and Vancouver had received a suspended sentence.
'While the law formerly provided for severe penalties ..., these penalties were seldom imposed.' Consequently, the law was already lenient,
and as far as the RCMP was concerned, nothing more needed to be
done on the part of the state. Otherwise, the Narcotic Control Act
would lose its deterrent effect. In 1968 deputy RCMP commissioner
W.H. Kelly told the members of the House of Commons Standing
Committee on Justice and Legal Affairs that it was important to keep
possession of marijuana as a criminal offence in order to inform Parliament 'when there is a subsequent offence' committed by an offender.
The main point made by Kelly, however, was that keeping possession a
criminal offence gave police a tool that was 'essential in the enforcement of the drug act.'[51] This argument would be repeated again and
again in order to prevent any fundamental change to the Narcotic Control Act.[52]

The position of the RCMP reflected the state of mind and views of
police forces, notably those who attended the Interpol meetings. The
RCMP was an essential link in the international action against drugs.
As a member of Interpol, the RCMP reminded the federal government
of its obligations towards the international community. In the context
of the counterculture movement, Interpol emphasized the necessity of
preserving the repressive approach; indeed, it was imperative not to
let one's guard down in the face of actions orchestrated by the pro-
marijuana lobby. Thus, in reaction to probable change in the status of
marijuana in several countries, participants at the 1967 Interpol meet-

ing repeated the obligation to continue not only the repression of marijuana traffickers, but also those who possessed marijuana for recreational purposes. Indeed, the resolution 'urged' all Interpol members to remind governments which had signed the Single Convention on Narcotic Drugs of their obligations and to communicate the opinion of the World Health Organization (WHO) Expert Committee on Drug Dependence, namely, that 'cannabis is capable of producing drug dependence and that harm to society is caused by abuse of cannabis.'[53] In 1970, and again during the 40th General Assembly of Interpol held in Ottawa in September 1971, Interpol members renewed their call for the repression of illegal drugs. There is a sense of urgency in the wording of the 1971 resolution that stated the phenomenon of recreational drug use had reached 'epidemic proportions' in certain countries. It denounced the pernicious effects of the pro-marijuana lobby and urged the scientific community to reiterate the health dangers of marijuana, most notably that it led to the use of more dangerous drugs. Finally, the resolution invited countries to redouble their efforts to eliminate the culture of cannabis: 'large-scale publicity campaigns [should] be launched or relaunched, aimed not only at young people but also at parents and the general public, and designed to show the direct and indirect dangers of the consumption of cannabis and its derivatives.'[54]

The justice department was an ally of the RCMP in that it judged that law enforcement, as a method of control of the drug supply, was at issue. At the Interdepartmental Sub-Committee appointed to study the Le Dain Commission interim report in 1970, representatives of the justice department stated that the 1969 amendments to the Narcotic Control Act made the law very lenient, since first-time offenders for simple possession of marijuana received in most cases a fine instead of being sent to jail. Under these circumstances, the transfer of marijuana from the Narcotic Control Act to the Food and Drugs Act, a solution being considered by the cabinet, 'would be superficial and in form only, no change in substance will result.' Justice officials also disputed the claim that cannabis was not a narcotic. Marijuana, hashish, and THC all fell under cannabis, and it would be difficult to justify the transfer of the first substance but not of the last two. Either the argument that cannabis was not a narcotic had 'to be abandoned or for logical reasons, hashish and THC would have to [be] transferred' as well.[55] Furthermore, the justice department expressed the concern that by focusing on marijuana consumption, the government risked dealing with the drug problem in a piecemeal fashion. Drug abuse was not limited to marijuana, and this had to be taken into consideration when contemplating any review of the drug legislation.[56]

International Obligations: Any American Pressure?

Throughout the discussion on the marijuana issue, bureaucrats insisted on Canada's international obligations. In 1961 Canada had ratified the Single Convention on Narcotic Drugs, which took effect in 1964. This international agreement consolidated previous international drug-control treaties and conventions negotiated between 1912 and 1953. It classified narcotics into four schedules, and the level of control varied accordingly; the most stringent controls applied to opium, coca, heroin, and cannabis.[57] Canada therefore had an obligation to repress narcotics. Section 36 of the Single Convention stipulated that the cultivation, possession, importation, exportation, sale, and distribution of cannabis constituted an offence 'liable to adequate punishment particularly by imprisonment or other penalties of deprivation of liberty.'[58] Signatory parties were obliged to prohibit the non-medical use of cannabis, except for countries such as India and Pakistan that permitted non-medical use of marijuana, because they made 'specific reservations when signing, ratifying, or acceding to it.' Canada had not raised any reservations because marijuana was a non-issue in the country in 1961. But any country that opted for specific reservations had 'no later than 25 years from 1964, the year of entry into force of the 1961 Convention' to suppress it.[59] Moreover, the United Nations Commission on Narcotic Drugs, of which Canada had been a member since its creation in 1946, recommended 'that all countries ... increase their efforts to eradicate the abuse and illicit traffic in cannabis.'[60] For their part, the 1968 and 1969 meetings of the WHO Expert Committee on Drug Dependence reminded the international community that marijuana had no medical purpose and consequently control measures were required.[61]

Yet there were more issues than Canada's international obligations that had to be taken into consideration in any revision of the federal public policy on drugs. Drugs were an element of discussion among states and had become part of international diplomacy. At the beginning of the twentieth century, some states enrolled the international community in their fight against recreational drug use and pushed to make some substances illegal. These states responded to domestic pressure by temperance groups, anti-opium missionaries in Asia, and other organizations concerned with social regulation that constructed drug use as a reprehensible behaviour to be discouraged by the state. Because the targeted drugs originated from Asia, the 'apparent' inaction of Asian states, and in particular China, on the drug front had consequences in countries such as the United States and Canada. In fact, these two countries played a leading role in the creation of international agreements. Once the first convention on opium was signed in 1912, the goal was to broaden its scope by regulating more drugs and declaring many of them illegal, unless the drugs concerned had medical or scientific research applications. Throughout the twentieth century, efforts were made to classify existing or new drugs as illegal and to increase control mechanisms by creating a legitimate drug trade. Through treaties, the international community created a legitimate drug trade by restricting the production and distribution of certain drugs to specific countries. For instance, the 1953 Opium Protocol limited the production of opium to seven countries, including Afghanistan, Turkey, and Yugoslavia. If signatory counties of the protocol required opium for medical and research purposes, they could import it only from one of these seven countries.[62]

Following the Second World War, and especially with the development of the counterculture movement and recreational drug use in the 1960s, renewed efforts were made, primarily initiated by the United States, to reduce the international supply of drugs by strengthening the international system of drug control. To achieve this goal, states could use diplomatic pressure, develop new international agreements, or opt for domestic and international repression. However, the context of the Cold War interfered with these efforts; indeed, certain states in the sphere of influence of either the Soviet Union or the United States did not see their production of illegal drugs such as opium much affected, despite the fact that the International Narcotics Control Board targeted them. This organization was responsible for supervising international trade in narcotics and for estimating, with the cooperation of signatory countries, national requirements of drugs. In these efforts to strengthen the international system of drug control, the interests of drug-producing (such as Afghanistan, India, Iran, Turkey, Thailand, and Yugoslavia), drug-manufacturing (such as France, Germany, United Kingdom, and United States), and drug-consuming countries (such as Canada), as well as those of the pharmaceutical industry and medical research, interfered in the process. The pharmaceutical industry opposed 'narcotics-style regulation with great vigor,' but was forced to agree to certain measures in order to protect its market and profitability.[63]

In this renewed context of activism, Canada made its voice heard by taking into consideration domestic and international pressure and interests. Canada subscribed to the overall objective of reducing the overall drug supply, while ensuring the supply for medical and research activities. But in order to achieve this goal, multilateralism was necessary. Any country was free to regulate drugs and to classify them as they wished. However, the drug trade and especially drug smuggling affected countries such as Canada that classified certain drugs as illegal, and therefore they were obliged to take appropriate control measures. Since many of the illegal drugs originated from outside Canada, the federal government believed that only through a concerted effort by the international community could the objectives of reducing the drug supply, ensuring the drug supply for medical and scientific activities, and increasing international control over the production and movement of drugs be achieved. However, national sovereignty conflicted with these objectives. States had to be persuaded of the merits of control mechanisms and repression, a prerequisite to successful negotiations that would lead to an international agreement. This approach would make it possible to circumscribe state sovereignty on the drug issue. Still, a good international control mechanism would never replace a good national one, which Canada believed was the cornerstone of controlling the supply and movement of illegal drugs in the legitimate trade. As Robert Curran noted, '[I]f countries were not prepared to deal with the problem at the national level, there seemed to be little reason to think that they would be prepared to consider any form of international control which, in turn, would require as a basis national control.'[64]

As many specialists of Canadian foreign policy have observed, Canada would use the functionalist principle to make a difference in international relations in the post-1945 era. Canada participated actively in the United Nations Commission on Narcotic Drugs, the organization set up to advise the United Nations Economic and Social Council on the application of international treaties on narcotic drugs. In this way Canada hoped to reduce the overall supply of drugs and place control mechanisms on illegal drugs using state organizations, and thus circumventing smugglers and other elements of the underworld. Within the multilateral framework that guided its Cold War foreign policy, Canada supported the United Nations' work in the field of drug control and repression. For instance, it was among the first countries to ratify the Single Convention on Narcotic Drugs in 1961. It encouraged other countries to sign in order to achieve the threshold of forty signatory states required to enforce the Convention. By doing so, Canada's activism strengthened its reputation for responsibility in the international control of narcotics.[65]

In its geopolitical evaluation of the drug issue, Canada took into consideration its southern neighbour. In terms of U.S.–Canada relations, Prime Minister Trudeau was anxious 'to use [Canada's] limited resources in the most efficient way possible.'[66] In these circumstances, how did the Canadian government use its 'limited resources'? Was there diplomatic intervention at the highest level, that is, direct or indirect pressure from the American president on the Canadian prime minister? Unfortunately, I did not find any documents that referred to a phone call made by U.S. president Nixon to the prime minister, nor a letter or any indication of a meeting between the two men during which Nixon expressly told Trudeau that Canada should not legalize marijuana use.

From the appointment of the Le Dain Commission in May 1969 to the tabling of its report on cannabis in 1972, Trudeau and Nixon met on two occasions: in December 1971 and in April 1972. During these meetings, officials from the Department of External Affairs emphasized in their notes to the prime minister the importance of reassuring the American administration about the orientation of Canada's drug policy. It was necessary to reassure the American president of Canadian support in the war on drugs by explaining that Ottawa supported Nixon's new initiatives in terms of international agreements. Although Canada could not make any official statement about new international agreements (to avoid undermining the work of the Le Dain Commission before it had submitted its final report), it did support the new American goal of strengthening the international system of drug control. Officials from the Department of External Affairs insisted that legalization of marijuana was a non-issue for the government, since it did not intend to legalize the drug, despite appeals by some individuals and interest groups. At most, the federal government could make some legislative changes, which included reducing penalties as far as international agreements allowed. And in addition to using legal mechanisms, Canada's commitment to fighting recreational drug use was underscored by its funding of information and prevention campaigns and treatment facilities.[67]

Legalization of marijuana was not an option for the Nixon administration. The Canadian embassy in Washington forwarded to the Department of External Affairs a copy of Dick Parker's article, published on 11 February 1970 in the *New Jersey Journal*. Parker wrote that if the legalization of marijuana became a reality in Canada, it would create tensions with the United States. 'The fact that legalization is even being considered in Canada,' Parker mentioned, 'will surely add to this country's growing reputation as a "hippie Utopia," a country that has no draft, no pretensions of world power, lots of wide open spaces, and now – maybe – legalized "pot."' In October 1970 officials from the Department of National Health and Welfare stated clearly before the Liberal parliamentary caucus that the legalization of marijuana was impossible not only because of Canada's obligations stemming from the Single Convention on Narcotic Drugs, but also because the United States was opposed to this course of action.[68]

Shall we conclude that Canada's policy on marijuana was influenced, or even dictated, by the United States? The answer to this question is complex because the American influence in the debate took multiple forms. American influence was benign or malign, depending on where individuals, interest groups, bureaucrats, and politicians stood on the issue of legalization of marijuana.

Canadian citizens used American data when they wrote to politicians. For instance, in letters to Ontario premier John Robarts, some quoted American studies favourable or hostile to the legalization of marijuana.[69] As mentioned in the first chapter, Canadian newspapers and magazines published articles on the United States and its approach to the drug issue; in addition, Canadians often preferred American magazines to Canadian ones and were therefore exposed to American constructions of the phenomenon of recreational drug use. Several interest groups and school boards used American educational and information material and resources in order to make their arguments more appealing or to give more authority to their position. The best example of this practice is CODA, whose pedagogical materials were sometimes from the United States. CODA pleaded against legalization and often opted for simplicity in its anti-marijuana message with the aim of appealing to the emotions of its audience. On the other hand, the positions of the American Medical Association or reports from US Senate and presidential commissions and the 1944 La Guardia Committee on Marihuana report received favourable echoes among groups supporting the legalization or the decriminalization of marijuana. Some American proponents of LSD use urged Canadian senators to reconsider the repressive approach of Canadian drug legislation when they were discussing the bill that criminalized the possession, possession for trafficking, and trafficking of LSD.[70] Finally, in 1975, when senators debated Bill S-19, which foresaw the transfer of cannabis from the Narcotic Control Act to the Food and Drugs Act, both proponents and opponents of marijuana legalization cited the Oregon state law that had decriminalized possession of small quantities of marijuana. Senators invited the president of the Drug Abuse Council, Dr Thomas E. Bryant, and J. Patrick Horton, Lane Country District Attorney (Eugene, Oregon), to speak before members of the upper chamber. Both spoke favourably of the Oregon law, since it offered an alternative to jail for recreational users of marijuana.[71] Therefore, we can conclude that American influence in the public domain was multi-faceted.

Ottawa's drug policy in relation to the United States cannot be labelled as one of subordination. Through the century, both countries had developed close cooperation at both the bilateral and international levels. In fact, Canada supported the United States in the development of international agreements in order to reduce the drug supply and regulate drug trade among nations. This cooperation among bureaucrats who took part in negotiations of international agreements was one of the aspects of the Canada–U.S. collaboration. Since the 1925 U.S.–Canada convention on drug trafficking and smuggling, law-enforcement agencies worked closely together and exchanged intelligence on drug trafficking and smuggling. The RCMP worked with the US Bureau of Customs and Bureau of Narcotics (which in 1969 became the US Bureau of Narcotics and Dangerous Drugs).[72]

However, the federal government had to take into account the new context initiated by U.S. president Richard Nixon. When Nixon became American president in 1969, he declared that a war against drug abuse would be one of the priorities of his administration. He did so because he considered that illegal drug use was the number-one problem afflicting American society. In order to put an end to this abuse, strong action was required, and American embassies throughout the world were instructed to enlist other countries in the initiative.

The American administration launched a multi-dimensional war on drug abuse. On the domestic front, Nixon instituted the Special Action Office for Drug Abuse Prevention and the Office for Drug Abuse Law Enforcement, and increased funding of various organizations in charge of drug education and prevention programs and the treatment of drug users and addicts. In 1973 drug-enforcement organizations were brought under one body called the Drug Enforcement Agency.[73] Nixon's vigorous domestic campaign was accompanied by strong activism at the international level. The ultimate goal of this American activism, forcing producing countries to control or suppress their production of drugs, was characterized by various strategies. The overall objective was to reduce the international supply of drugs and to restrict the movement of illegal drugs in the legitimate trade to medical and research purposes.[74] To that end the United States employed unilateralism, bilateralism and multilateralism; the choice of strategy depended on the evaluation of the best way to achieve the overall goal.

A good example of this approach is Operation Intercept. Most marijuana and some heroin in the United States came from Mexico; as a result, the U.S. Bureau of Narcotics and Dangerous Drugs closed the American-Mexican border from 29 September to 2 October 1969. The border closure was a unilateral gesture of the American administration: it was felt that the Mexican authorities were not serious about halting the illegal importation of marijuana across the U.S.–Mexican border. Thus, the American government put pressure on Mexico to tighten its surveillance on marijuana smuggling. Having thus forced the hand of the Mexican government, the Americans obtained Mexico's agreement to cooperate and Operation Intercept became Operation Cooperation. Both countries agreed to work together in order to stop the importation of marijuana through the shared border. US unilateralism then gave way to bilateralism.[75]

Turkey is an interesting case in the study of US multilateralism. The American administration considered that deaths in their country caused by heroin resulted from the importation of this drug into the States from Turkey via France. But Turkey was both an ally and a NATO member, which made unilateral action, as in the case of Mexico, more problematic. However, Turkey was in American sights because American administrations had wanted to force the hand of the Turkish government by suppressing poppy cultivation. From 1961 Washington pressured successive Turkish governments to act, but without success. The Nixon administration redoubled its efforts beginning in 1969 by multiplying the number of participants involved in pressuring Ankara. In this vein, the American administration indicated that economic assistance could be cut off if nothing concrete was done. Although Canada subscribed to the objective of reducing the supply of opium at the international level, officials from the Department of External Affairs and the Canadian ambassador in Ankara were uncomfortable with the American tactics. After all, as exchanges between the Canadian embassy in Ankara and the Department of External Affairs reveal, some Turkish farmers depended on poppy cultivation, and it would be necessary to compensate them for lost revenues. Despite their reservations, Canadian diplomats used 'quiet diplomacy' in order to contribute to the American objective. At the Americans' request they congratulated the Turkish government for its eventual support of the U.S. government in its fight against drug abuse. Following the announcement by Turkish officials of a reduction in poppy production, the US government granted $3 million to buy up poppy crops and finance the creation of a 700-man enforcement force in Turkey.[76]

American activism at the international level translated into pressure to create new international treaties in order to deal with the consumption of recreational drugs, such as LSD. In 1968 discussions began for the Convention on Psychotropic Substances at the United Nations Commission on Narcotic Drugs; the U.S. government signed the convention following the plenipotentiary conference to adopt the Protocol on Psychotropic Substances held in Vienna in January and February 1971. This international agreement obliged signatory parties to limit the use of several hallucinogens, such as LSD, to medical and research purposes. In addition, governments agreed to regulate hallucinogen production, manufacturing, and distribution. These substances had not previously been subject to international control. Washington was also the driving force behind strengthening the Single Convention on Narcotic Drugs by giving to the International Narcotics Control Board the power to carry out on-the-spot investigations. Finally, it pushed very hard for the creation of the United Nations Fund for Drug Abuse Control, financed by voluntarily contributions, which was in charge of developing education campaigns on drug abuse, setting up treatment of drug addicts and conducting research, and limiting the production of illegal drugs. It expected Canada to contribute, which Ottawa agreed to do by giving $400,000 for the 1971–3 period.[77]

Certain elements of the American multilateral approach to the war on drugs enjoyed the support of Canadian bureaucracy. For instance, the negotiations that led to a new international agreement to control hallucinogens and that strengthened the 1961 Single Convention on Narcotic Drugs were strongly supported by Canadian bureaucrats, especially those who had been involved in these issues. However, Canadian delegates sent to the 1971 Vienna conference on psychotropic substances and to the 1972 conference of plenipotentiaries to consider amendments to the Single Convention on Narcotic Drugs were informed that they could not sign the new international agreement, or the amended Single Convention. Rather, in the case of the 1971 conference, they were instructed by the federal cabinet to influence the protocol in a way that would ensure that 'sufficient flexibility be built into the protocol to accommodate present Canadian legislation relating to the control of drugs which are liable to abuse, as well as any changes which might be made by the government based on' the Le Dain Commission's recommendations. In practical terms, this meant that the delegation was to attempt to convince participants that possession of amphetamines should not be deemed a criminal offence, as it was not an offence under the Canadian Food and Drugs Act.[78]

The Protocol on Psychotropic Substances also imposed a control mechanism on researchers because it restricted medical research on LSD, and required 'special authorization' for the export and import of amphetamines, hallucinogens, and other synthetic psychotropic substances, and obliged signatory states to ensure, 'as an alternative to conviction or punishment ... that abusers of psychotropic substances undergo measures of treatment, education, aftercare, rehabilitation and social reintegration.'[79] But Canadian senior bureaucrats who took part in the conference judged that the new international agreement did not impose controls that were not already in place in Canada. Furthermore, the document offered the flexibility sought by politicians.[80] However, as long as the Le Dain Commission had not submitted its final report, Canada would not sign the new international agreement or the amended Single Convention. This position raised some concerns among American officials. In 1972, a diplomat from the American embassy informed External Affairs that this would have a negative impact on Canada's ability to rally other states. He argued that 'in terms of influencing other countries to similarly ratify' these international agreements, Canada's influence 'would be substantially reduced' if it chose not to sign them.[81]

Other aspects of American activism created some problems for Canadian government officials. Although Canadian bureaucrats agreed with the objectives, they criticized the means and the tone of the arguments used by the American government to rally the international community. Canadian objections concerned the justifications used by Americans, notably the deputy attorney general, Richard G. Kleindienst. For them, the war on drugs was a battle between good and evil, of strength and morality versus laziness and dependence. For the Canadians, this approach was overly simplistic. In fact, it led Canadian bureaucrats to reject American overtures to put pressure on Pakistan, West Germany, or France to curb heroin smuggling.[82]

In North America, the Nixon administration encouraged Canada and Mexico to increase their efforts on drug repression. Washington intended to crack down on Mexico, a policy to be succeeded, in return for cooperation, by economic aid assistance. Invited by the Mexican government to be part of the US–Mexico cooperation agreement regarding drug smuggling in 1971, Canadian bureaucrats reluctantly became involved in the drug issue. Their hesitation to join the U.S.–Mexico group was based on the fact that Canada simply did not have a drug problem with Mexico. Canada also feared that cooperation between the three countries would translate into greater American control over domestic drug policy and law-enforcement in Mexico and Canada. Despite these concerns, Canada took part in these meetings. This tripartite cooperation did have certain advantages, among which were opportunities to exchange intelligence among law-enforcement organizations, emphasis on the importance of educational and preventative drug campaigns, and increased diplomatic relations with Mexico.[83]

In revising its drug policy, the federal government saw its sovereignty restricted or circumscribed by obligations resulting from international agreements that it had freely signed. National sovereignty was also at issue in diplomatic circles, even though Canada had been a proponent of international control and, since 1946, had been a member of the United Nations Commission on Narcotic Drugs. Any move on the domestic front on marijuana was closely monitored by other nations that were dealing with recreational drug use. Finally, Canada had to take into consideration its southern neighbour. The United States was putting pressure on the international community to ensure the success of its anti-drug war. Time was precious because the Nixon administration knew that it had only four years, or eight at most (assuming re-election in 1972), to implement its policies.

The Government's Choice: Reducing Penalties

Amidst the discussion about criminalizing LSD possession that took place in the Senate in 1967 and 1968, Allan J. MacEachen, minister of national health and welfare, proposed a significant change vis-à-vis marijuana to Solicitor General Larry T. Pennell. He argued that legalizing marijuana was impossible, but reducing penalties was. In fact, he hinted that his department was leaning towards the transfer of marijuana from the Narcotic Control Act to the Food and Drugs Act.[84]

Why such a solution? Was MacEachen of the opinion that marijuana was not dangerous for human health? This particular issue generated a divisive debate among health and scientific experts. But in 1968 the minister of national health and welfare could not mention any health benefit. It is intriguing that even though MacEachen stated that 'marijuana is a drug that distorts time and space and affects behaviour as well as impairing judgment and is capable of producing violence,' and could lead to using hard drugs, he wanted the government to reduce the penalty for its possession. In order to justify his position, he lamented the negative judicial consequences for young people who used marijuana. 'Personally I think it is unfortunate that possession, at least for a first offence, should require being punishable only on indictment.' He stated that a 'suspended sentence, in the case of a young person, with strict conditions attached can result in a more effective deterrent punishment than a brief term of imprisonment.' And what about Canada's international obligations, arguments put forward by bureaucrats and some interest groups? MacEachen was persuaded that it was possible to proceed because the transfer of marijuana to the Food and Drugs Act would not 'have the effect of legalizing the non-medical use of this drug.'[85]

The hypothesis that the Department of National Health and Welfare worked on became public at the annual meeting of the Canadian Pharmaceutical Association in August 1968. The new minister of national health and welfare, John Munro, informed participants that the government was considering placing marijuana in a new act or transferring it from the Narcotic Control Act to the Food and Drugs Act. What could justify such an initiative? The first argument was that the punishment exceeded the crime because it affected the lives of youth who made, according to the minister, a foolish decision to try an illegal drug. 'The teenager who tries pot at a Saturday night party because someone has some and passes it around and everyone else tries it, may be very foolish, but he isn't a criminal – at least not in the sense that I think of criminals.' The time had come to make the penalty correspond to the offence. The second argument was more controversial. Munro maintained that marijuana was not a narcotic, an opinion contrary to the stand of the World Health Organization and the Single Convention, which obliged countries to consider marijuana as a narcotic.[86] For his part, Trudeau informed the House of Commons that the Criminal Code could be amended as it related to marijuana, but the Prime Minister remained vague on specific actions.[87]

The federal cabinet was divided on the issue of reducing the penalty by transferring marijuana from the Narcotic Control Act to the Food and Drugs Act. National health and welfare minister John Munro had to overcome the opposition of Solicitor General George McIlraith and justice minister John Turner. In March 1969 McIlraith expressed opposition to the transfer due to 'certain' health dangers for marijuana users. Furthermore, regular users tended, according to the brief submitted by the solicitor general to the cabinet, 'to show basic defects of personality.' Besides health concerns, McIlraith stressed the fact that Canada had international obligations to respect and any change could reduce the deterrent effect of law enforcement. The solicitor general countered with his own suggestion, which was to amend the Narcotic Control Act by giving the option to the Crown to prosecute either on indictment or by way of summary conviction. Justice minister Turner warned his colleagues that such a transfer could send the wrong message by affecting the overall anti-drug strategy and the symbolic place marijuana occupied within it. Making such a transfer 'might be interpreted as indicating that the Government is taking a less serious view of the cannabis problem.' This move could be seen as the first step towards legalization. A better solution would be for the government to enact new drug legislation called the Dangerous Drugs Act in which drugs would be ranked according to their danger. This proposal mirrored that sent by the NAFBC to the Minister of National Health and Welfare. In the present context, justice minister Turner supported both McIlraith's suggestion and a program of public education.[88]

In the 1969 March cabinet meetings, national health and welfare minister Munro appeared to have lost the battle, but not necessarily the war, over the transfer of marijuana to the Food and Drugs Act. Cabinet agreed to amend the Narcotic Control Act as part of Bill S-15 that was then being debated by senators. By doing that, Cabinet followed the suggestion made by the solicitor general and supported by the justice minister as the best solution in the present context. However, the discussion about the transfer would continue and be enlarged with the appointment of a commission of inquiry on the non-medical use of drugs.[89] By taking this step, the national health and welfare minister and his officials hoped to broaden the support for their solution. In 1969, Munro hinted at the possibility of further reducing the penalty for possession of marijuana and perhaps abolishing 'laws which ban possession and use of marijuana.' However, this would not be done before the Le Dain Commission had submitted its interim report.[90]

In 1970, delays in the release of the interim report of the Le Dain Commission stimulated rumours that the government had opted to keep it secret and that Gerald Le Dain was contemplating the possibility of resigning. The fact that *Time* magazine published some parts of the interim report in June 1970 gave more fuel to these rumours.[91] The Interim Report was submitted to the minister of national health and welfare on 6 April 1970, but the report was tabled in the House of Commons only on 19 June 1970. Why such a delay? During the intervening months, the minister of national health and welfare and his officials were preparing the governmental strategy not only to respond to the report but, more importantly, to win the support of the cabinet for the proposal to transfer marijuana. The department's approach was to divide the interim report recommendations into two categories: controversial and non-controversial, or recommendations that the cabinet would agree upon (non-controversial) and those on which important divisions still remained. Recommendations labelled as non-controversial referred to support for research on non-medical drug use, the establishment of drug analysis laboratories, information strategies, and innovative treatment and rehabilitation programs. In its response to the interim report, the government would stress the fact that it had already implemented some of these measures. The controversial recommendations, such as that the possession of narcotics and of restricted and controlled drugs should be subject to a maximum $100 fine, would be referred to an interdepartmental committee of senior bureaucrats. However, to avoid being accused by the media and interest groups of doing nothing on the marijuana front, Munro recommended placing marijuana, and not cannabis as the interim report suggested, under the Food and Drugs Act, no longer sentencing offenders to a jail term for simple possession of marijuana, and instituting a system of fines for simple possession. These fines would 'be on a graduated scale for first and subsequent offences.'[92]

At its June meeting, the federal cabinet approved the approach devised by John Munro, except for his proposals on the marijuana issue. Munro's suggestion was referred to the interdepartmental committee. By doing so, the cabinet acknowledged the concerns expressed by the justice minister and the solicitor general.[93] This also meant that the battle would be waged among bureaucrats.

In June 1970 the national health and welfare minister announced that the government would not amend the Narcotic Control Act as recommended by the Le Dain Commission. Munro justified the decision of the government on the basis of 'current medical and sociological information.' But he argued that this decision was not a sign of hesitancy or inaction. On the contrary, the government would 'consider' the possibility of transferring marijuana from the Narcotic Control Act to the Food and Drugs Act. Outside the House of Commons, Munro was more forthcoming; he told journalists that the government would introduce a bill to transfer marijuana before Christmas. But he rapidly had to deny any such legislative intent. Later in the House of Commons Munro apologized for the confusion and confessed that he 'got carried away and went too far.' The position of the government was 'to consider' such a transfer.[94]

Due to fundamental differences of opinion among the Department of National Health and Welfare, the RCMP, and the Department of Justice, the interdepartmental committee did not reach a consensus on the transfer of marijuana from the Narcotic Control Act to the Food and Drugs Act.[95] However, the committee reminded the minister of national health and welfare that the government could wait until the Commission's final report, which was due in 1971, before making any announcement. Since the government would be close to the end of its term, 'this timing' for any announcement 'could prejudice the taking of action which might be socially sound but politically difficult.'[96]

The Le Dain cannabis report was tabled in the House of Commons in June 1972. A month later, the cabinet rejected the recommendation by a majority of the members of the Le Dain Commission to legalize possession of cannabis. This decision was not surprising, since legalization was never considered an option.[97] In his brief to Cabinet, national health and welfare minister John Munro listed several reasons to justify the rejection of legalization: among them he cited potential health risks, a possible increase in the number of users, and Canada's obligations under the Single Convention on Narcotic Drugs. Munro also alluded to the possibility of 'international repercussions, especially from the United States.' Despite the objections to legalization, legislative change to reduce the penalties attached to conviction was forthcoming. This time, Minister Munro overcame opposition: the decision to place cannabis and all offences (possession, possession for trafficking, trafficking, importing and exporting, and cultivation) under the Food and Drugs Act or a new legislation was endorsed by Cabinet.[98]

At the end of July 1972 John Munro informed Canadians about the government policy on cannabis. The government had rejected legalization but would transfer cannabis from the Narcotic Control Act to the Food and Drugs Act or another piece of legislation, since it felt under the obligation 'to reduce the impact of the criminal law on the young offender involved with mere possession of the drug.' Yet this leniency would not apply to other cannabis offences. In his statement, Munro reassured Canadians that this transfer did not constitute a major departure from current practice. Since 1969, as the amendment of the Narcotic Control Act illustrated, the government had intended to reduce penalties for simple possession. The proposed change would simply continue this course of action.[99]

Many daily newspapers supported Munro's announcement. For the *Toronto Star*, the uncertainties over the long-term marijuana health effects required a cautious approach, as reflected in Munro's choice of policy.[100] The Vancouver *Sun* justified its support because Munro's policy did not mean real change; it reflected what was going on in the courts.[101] For the *Winnipeg Free Press* and the *Halifax Chronicle-Herald*, Munro's announcement meant the rejection of legalization, which reflected the views of a majority of Canadians. For that, these newspapers supported the minister.[102] However, there were some dissenting voices. The *Ottawa Citizen* and the *Montreal Gazette* found Munro's announcement very timid.[103] *Le Devoir*, *La Presse*, and the *Globe and Mail* did not cheer, since Munro's choice demonstrated a lack of leadership and his indecision.[104] The *Globe and Mail* editorial stressed the fact that 'the government lack the guts to face the issue squarely and come to a clear-cut decision that will not do violence to the integrity of the law and its administration.'[105]

A Choice Not Implemented

When Munro announced the government policy on cannabis in July 1972, he mentioned that a bill would be introduced in the fall or, if possible, before the federal election. However, the October 1972 election results dictated the legislative calendar of the Liberals, who formed a minority government for the next few months. And so the bill, promised for the fall by Munro, was put on the back burner to avoid unnecessarily provoking interest groups and, thereby, making the situation of the minority government even more precarious. For the new minister of national health and welfare, Marc Lalonde, the cannabis question was a 'contentious issue that a government in a minority position is not anxious to tackle at this time' and that could threaten 'the minority government's power.'[106] In addition to the arrival of Marc Lalonde, the delay of the Le Dain Commission in submitting its final report became a useful excuse to explain the hesitation of the government to act. The final report was submitted at the end of 1973, which according to Lalonde prevented the government from acting on the file, because after all, the government did not want to finalize the issue before the Commission released its conclusions.[107] In 1974, furthermore, another interdepartmental committee was set up to study the final report. Although committee members were informed by R.A. Draper, the director-general of the Non-Medical Use and Drugs Directorate and chair of the committee, that they should not deal with cannabis, the committee's would delay further any policy announcement on marijuana.[108]

The 1974 election allowed the Liberals to remain in power and form a majority government. For a time, the minister of national health and welfare entertained the idea of introducing a new law, the Dangerous Drugs Act, as suggested by the 1974 interdepartmental committee.[109] However, the idea was abandoned, not only because of the complexity of introducing a new bill, but especially because the government had once again decided 'to take one step at a time.'[110] Bill S-19, which saw the transfer of marijuana from the Narcotic Control Act to the Food and Drugs Act, was submitted to the Senate in November 1974. The government used the pretext of the 'heavy legislative workload' of the House of Commons to justify its decision to proceed this way.[111]

In introducing its bill, the government was aware that it was walking a fine line. On the one hand, it had to reiterate that marijuana represented a danger to users in order to justify its rejection of the legalization option. On the other hand, Ottawa had to justify the reduction of penalties. Although youth were not explicitly identified when the national health and welfare minister met senators in 1975, Lalonde's strategy was to associate convictions for marijuana use with young people. Under the Narcotic Control Act, Lalonde argued, in certain cases bad decisions made by young people were punished too harshly.

Officials from the Department of National Health and Welfare emphasized the continued necessity of discouraging marijuana use in order to reassure what they called 'the public'; at the same time, the government needed to reduce what was called the 'social cost' for

'This year, next year, sometime, never, this year, next year ...'
Source: *The Journal* 3:12 (December 1974), 6; © 2004 Centre for Addiction and Mental Health

youth. Why? Jail terms were an excessive form of punishment for the crime of possession. Furthermore, the enforcement of the Narcotic Control Act entailed economic costs, since police forces and prison guards were assigned to its enforcement. Under Bill S-19, fines, instead of jail terms, would be the punishment for first and second offences in cases of possession. Consequently, it was important to constantly repeat to the public that Bill S-19 did not legalize marijuana. Marijuana remained an illegal substance, but it was crucial to reduce the 'social costs' for youth who decided to try marijuana and had to deal with the justice system because of their actions. Consequently, the solution was to reduce these 'social costs' by eliminating a jail term as a punishment for simple possession of marijuana, except for those who could not pay the fine. At the same time, penalties for cultivation and importing or exporting were increased.[112]

Another argument was used to justify the legislative change: the government was giving official sanction to court practices that had recently developed. In 1972 criminal prosecutors received instructions that people with no prior criminal records arrested for possession of marijuana should receive an 'absolute and conditional discharge.' In his letter to senators, the national health and welfare minister wrote that of the 18,603 individuals convicted for possession of marijuana in 1973, 17,733 did not receive a jail sentence.[113]

In order to counter potential opponents and the perception that the government was setting the course towards decriminalization and eventual legalization, the minister of national health and welfare argued before the Senate Committee on Legal and Constitutional Affairs that Bill S-19 did not decriminalize the possession of marijuana. Offenders would still receive criminal records on conviction, which could be dropped if the convicted applied for a pardon. Although cannabis was not a harmless drug, research had produced, so far, contradictory conclusions. And despite the health dangers, the transfer was required because 'in terms of pharmacology' *cannabis sativa* was not a narcotic.[114]

Senators raised the profile of their study of the bill by authorizing the presence of television cameras at the hearings of the Committee on Legal and Constitutional Affairs. However, few organizations, interest groups, and individuals were invited; indeed, several groups, including student associations and church groups, were noticeably absent.

Among the health organizations that intervened, the CMA sowed confusion among opponents of the liberalization of marijuana laws. This controversy was by no means a result of the CMA's position on

Source: *The Journal* 4:3 (March 1974), 6; © 2004 Centre for Addiction and
Mental Health

the federal bill; after all, the CMA had proposed such a transfer since
the end of the sixties. Furthermore, CMA representatives asserted, as
did federal civil servants, that cannabis was not a narcotic in terms of
pharmacology. The controversy resulted rather from a recommendation of the CMA–Canadian Bar Association Joint Committee (formed
to study the marijuana issue) to partially decriminalize cannabis. In

fact, the CMA recommended the elimination of a criminal record for the offence of possession of cannabis for personal use. Furthermore, it recommended that 'provisions be made for the automatic erasure of the criminal record for those found guilty of simple possession for personal use following a two or three year "charge free" probationary period.'[115]

How is one to reconcile the CMA's position with the fact that its delegation to the hearings stated that there were still some health dangers for users, such as brain and chromosomal damages and damage to the respiratory system, although the risks varied according to the dose, frequency, and characteristics of the users? In their attempt to overcome this apparent contradiction, CMA representatives stressed the fact that marijuana use was a medical problem. Accordingly, the medical profession had taken charge of it by pursuing research and by informing the population about the dangers of this drug. Although research conclusions were often contradictory, the CMA had decided to adopt a cautionary approach. Furthermore, marijuana use was a legal problem. The CMA was of the opinion that the punishment for someone convicted for simple possession of marijuana exceeded the crime; it was therefore necessary to amend the Narcotic Control Act. Moreover, supporting the reduction of penalties for cannabis use reflected a trend among governmental commissions appointed by the American and Canadian governments. The CMA delegation reminded senators and opponents of Bill S-19 that 'criminalization frequently produces far more serious, deleterious effects on the user than does the use of cannabis.'[116]

Health professionals, among them Schwarz and Lundell, denounced the CMA position because it did not reflect the views of the members of organization.[117] Before the Senate committee, Dr Patrick McGeer, British Columbia MLA and member of the Faculty of Medicine of the University of British Columbia, and Dr Andrew Malcolm, a psychiatrist at the ARF, denounced the CMA brief and presentation on Bill S-19 and especially the way the CMA treated the health issue involved in any discussion of marijuana. Although Malcolm was not a strong opponent of Bill S-19, he emphasized the health risks (most notably to brain functions) associated with marijuana use. These risks justified the launch of a far-reaching education campaign by the federal government.[118] At the 1975 CMA annual meeting, members approved the CMA brief on Bill S-19, which constituted a victory for the Subcommittee on the Non-Medical Use of Drugs, chaired by Solursh.[119]

The only health-related organization opposed to Bill S-19 was CODA. Its youth consultant, Norman Panzica, declared the bill too lenient. Although Panzica approved the transfer of cannabis, he judged that the new schedule for cannabis in the Food and Drugs Act rendered marijuana less dangerous than LSD. In fact, Panzica recommended that cannabis should be in the same schedule as LSD in the Food and Drugs Act and that the penalties, notably for possession, should be stiffened.[120]

Police forces made their voice heard and shared some of the concerns expressed by CODA. The CACP repeated familiar arguments used by opponents of softening penalties for marijuana use. They cited health dangers and the necessity to maintain the repressive approach in order to deter people, in particular youth, from using marijuana and other illegal drugs. In its current form, Bill S-19 would incite the population to believe that the government would go on to soften penalties for other drugs, or even worse, it could vindicate the pro-marijuana lobby. The CACP argued that 'any leniency in present legislation even though this legislation intrinsically may be acceptable and operable will have this side effect of conditioning youth to recognize such practices as acceptable particularly in the light of relatively harmless sentences or legal sanctions.'[121] Hoping that senators could amend the bill in order to reflect the organization's concerns, the CACP reiterated its belief in the theory that marijuana was a stepping-stone drug: 'the majority of heroin users start with soft drugs, generally cannabis.'[122]

For its part, the RCMP thought that drug policy had become very lenient. Although the Mounties did not reject Bill S-19, they wanted to prevent any change that would further relax drug legislation. This meant that the legalization of cannabis had to be prevented by reminding senators of the health dangers associated with cannabis use. Furthermore, RCMP Deputy Commissioner J. Ross reminded senators that cannabis incited its users to experiment with other drugs and that legalization would create serious problems within the international community, since Canada would become a 'transportation centre.' Ross rejected the CMA recommendation because the possession charge was necessary to control the availability of drugs. It was imperative to keep a deterrent aspect in the drug legislation to make sure that offenders continued 'to suffer the stigma attached, if they were apprehended, that they have a criminal record for a period of time, and that every police officer therefore is a threat to them if they do [possess marijuana].' Furthermore, 'if you have a control mechanism operating whereby people are forced to be discreet in their indulgence and use of the drug, you also, at the same time, keep down the spread of the drug, and it is not that freely available for everyone to indulge in.'[123] In its brief, the RCMP insisted on the changing nature of the illicit traffic. It stated that young people were involved in cannabis traffic during the sixties, but it was now organized crime groups that controlled it. Because of that, legalization and decriminalization were out of the question, since cannabis traffic was a 'multi-billion dollar business.' The RCMP also attempted to convince senators that the 'one ounce law' of the state of Oregon was not a model of action. Since 1973 the Oregon State Legislative Assembly defined possession of less than one ounce of marijuana as a violation, punishable by a maximum $100 fine. Because of this legislative change, the number of court cases for simple possession decreased. Furthermore, the offender did not receive a criminal record. Despite these positive aspects, which were cited by proponents of marijuana, the RCMP reminded senators that law-enforcement officers in the State of Oregon opposed the law because marijuana was defined as 'detrimental to society's well-being.'[124]

Except for the PEI Department of Education and the Quebec Department of Justice, no provincial governments appeared before the Senate committee. The PEI Department of Education forced senators to invite Cowan to express the views of the PEI government. Contrary to the Quebec Department of Justice, which supported Bill S-19, Cowan used the Senate committee to denounce, once again, the pro-marijuana lobby that tried to force its agenda upon legislators in Canada and in the United States. In his presentation Cowan underlined the importance of launching a strong educational campaign that would acquaint Canadians with the dangers of marijuana use. That was necessary to fight the impression that marijuana was harmless; such a campaign should be launched before the enactment of Bill S-19. Concerning the bill itself, Cowan recommended that every offender convicted for possession of marijuana should attend a compulsory course on the dangers of marijuana use. Furthermore, possession of marijuana should remain an offence. Finally, a criminal record could be dropped, as current legislation allows, if offenders applied for a pardon. Cowan disagreed with the proposal that criminal records be automatically dropped after one or two years.[125]

In terms of provincial drug research organizations, the Alberta Alcoholism and Drug Abuse Commission and the Alcohol and the Drug Commission of British Columbia appeared before the Senate. The

Alberta commission recommended that cannabis offenders be forced to take a compulsory drug-education course similar to the one imposed, since 1970, on convicted impaired drivers in the province. For its part, the British Columbia commission, through its president, former Le Dain commissioner J. Peter Stein, insisted that any efforts to reduce penalties would help in the control of cannabis use and abuse.[126] Although OPTAT supported Bill S-19, it did not appear before the Senate.[127] ARF also did not appear, although some of its staff made personal statements.

Before and after the hearings, the senators' debate on the marijuana issue often cut across party lines. Proponents of the bill judged that it offered much needed change in controlling drug availability through law enforcement. Frederick William Rowe justified his stand by reminding his fellow senators that Canada's approach 'to marijuana is unjust, discriminatory, irrational, and ... because of it we have not been able to deal effectively with other more serious drug problems afflicting our society.'[128] Opponents denounced the moral dangers that Bill S-19 represented for a society that was already under threat. According to Senator Sullivan, 'this is the age of permissiveness. In the name of freedom, people, including children, are allowed to be lazy, dirty, foulmouthed, disgusting and violent. Abnormality is equated with normality: lawlessness with justice.'[129] This moral permissiveness nurtured the emergence of a society that did not reflect the values that Senator Sullivan espoused. Despite reassurances provided by proponents of the bill[130] that it was not an attempt to legalize marijuana, Sullivan believed that the bill marked the abandonment of the repressive approach. For opponents, it was imperative to draw a line in order to prevent the further disintegration of moral values in a society that was riven by a generational conflict.[131]

Senators were divided over the argument that marijuana was a stepping-stone drug. Opponents of the bill believed that marijuana led to the use of hard drugs. For Ernest C. Manning, the former Alberta premier, there was plenty of evidence that pointed in that direction. Even though medical experts were divided on this question, Manning sided with those who shared his convictions on the stepping-stone theory: '[T]he use of marijuana inevitably leads to the use of more serious drugs, it is a door, perhaps the principal door, most frequently used by young people for their entrance to the drug subculture of our times.'[132]

However, the role of medical expertise marks an important difference between this debate and the one that took place in 1967. Medical evidence became politicized because opponents of the bill used it to instil fear by emphasizing the negative health effects of marijuana use. Dr Joseph A. Sullivan, who had become a senator, stated that 'marijuana smoking interferes with reproduction, disease resistance and basic biologic processes.'[133] For his part, Edward M. Lawson asserted that marijuana use created a vegetative state: '[I]f [senators] visited [Vancouver], they would see young people ranging from 12 to 16 years of age virtually mindless vegetables as a result of using this drug.'[134] According to Senator Fred A. McGrand, marijuana 'can produce sharp personality changes,' 'can lead to mutation of certain cells,' and 'may effect a change in the chromosomes.' Young people ran serious risks when they consumed marijuana, among which were difficulties in 'acquiring knowledge, developing skills and absorbing the countless facts that shape future personalities and abilities.'[135]

Proponents of Bill S-19 pointed out that the medical community was divided over this issue. As Martial Asselin, Frederick William Rowe, and Henry D. Hicks stated, medical expertise should therefore be taken cautiously. Although Senator Sullivan had enjoyed the moral authority conferred by his professional status during the debate over LSD use in 1967, this was no longer the case during the discussion of Bill S-19. Senator Rowe stated: 'I got the impression that he feels that unless you are a medical doctor you have no business to be saying too much about this business of drugs.'[136] Rowe rejected this argument of authority by insisting that the drug problem was not exclusively a medical problem. The drug problem, Rowe argued, 'is too important a matter to be left to the doctors.' Why? Because the medical profession 'has been wrong more often than it has been right' in assessing the health implication of drugs.[137]

Following the hearings, senators adopted in May 1975 a series of amendments to the bill. The amendments, which reflected suggestions made by the CMA, ensured that all first-time offenders for possession of cannabis should be given an absolute or conditional discharge and granted a pardon. Furthermore, there would be no minimum sentence for exporting or importing and the maximum sentence for trafficking and possession for the purpose of trafficking would be fourteen years less one day, instead of ten years.[138]

The bill was introduced in the House of Commons but was not approved because the priorities of the government, at the end of 1975, were the economy and fighting inflation. Consequently, the cannabis bill was put on hold.[139] Although the Department of National Health and Welfare deemed the amended bill acceptable, it seemed that the opposition it generated during the Senate hearings gave the federal government cold feet.[140] Not only did the Department of National Health and Welfare monitor the debate in the Senate very closely, it also paid attention to views expressed outside the Senate. Of the 116 letters Lalonde's department received by February 1975, 105 were opposed to Bill S-19. Many of the opponents were from British Columbia; officials from the department attributed this to the fact that a Vancouver radio commentator was outspoken about drug issues, and this 'may have had a bearing on the number of letters received from British Columbia.'[141]

Although the transfer of marijuana from the Narcotic Control Act to the Food and Drugs Act never took place, in 1969 a most important change occurred: penalties were reduced. When Bill S-15 was finally adopted, it contained an amendment to the Narcotic Control Act. Crown prosecutors and judges now had a choice on how to proceed and the types of penalties to impose, but the Department of Justice issued instructions that suggested that for a first or second offence for cannabis possession the Crown should proceed by summary conviction. For subsequent offences, it should proceed by indictment.[142] Although not the solution favoured by Department of National Health and Welfare officials, this new procedure did offer the flexibility they sought. As a result, 95 per cent of individuals convicted for simple possession of marijuana in 1972 were not sent to jail.[143] With the Criminal Law Amendments Act, which came into force in July 1972, judges could discharge a first offender. For its part, the justice department instructed its crown attorneys to ask courts for absolute or conditional discharges for cases of simple possession of cannabis in which there was no criminal record and no other conviction.[144] However these instructions meant that there would be disparities in sentencing, since judges did not have to comply, as pointed out by senators who studied Bill S-19.[145] For instance, no more than 10 per cent of those charged for cannabis possession received absolute discharges from 1973 to 1977.[146]

By reducing the penalties for narcotics possession in the Narcotic Control Act, which included marijuana, the government believed that it was adapting the legislation to new circumstances arising out of the burgeoning drug culture. In 1969 the action was perceived as the first step towards the transfer of marijuana from the Narcotic Control Act to the Food and Drugs Act. But further change became impossible due to divisions in society, among interest groups, the cabinet, and the continental and international context. Thus, this first step, the reduction of penalties, was in fact the last.

Although the transfer of marijuana from the Narcotic Control Act to the Food and Drugs Act generated discussions and exposed divisions within the cabinet and federal bureaucracy, it did not prevent the federal government from implementing programs. Created in 1971, the Non-Medical Use of Drugs Directorate was the governmental response to the drug discussion in the public domain and to the Le Dain interim report. Under the control of the Department of National Health and Welfare (Health Protection Branch), this directorate, assisted by five regional offices, directed research on drugs and drug users, analysed for physicians drugs available on the street, and assisted in the delivery of treatment and rehabilitation services through its Innovative Services Grants Program. This program was designed to assist financially crisis centres, drop-in centres, short-term treatment programs, and so forth. With assistance from ARF, the directorate also orchestrated drug information campaigns. These campaigns were directed at various groups such as children, youth, parents, and educators and distributed information about drugs that was free of moralizing attitudes. Quebec was sometimes unreceptive to federal initiatives, especially when they dealt with education and treatment, but federal bureaucrats emphasized the need to work with provinces.[147]

The directorate's definition of drugs was restricted to those that were not supervised by the medical professional. In other words, the term 'misuse' applied to all drugs (and this would come to include alcohol and cigarettes) taken with no proper medical supervision. As the directorate stated in 1973, its overall objective was 'to eliminate physical, mental and social health problems among Canadians associated with the non-medical use of mood-altering substances.' How? Through prevention campaigns and support of research, treatment, and rehabilitation centres and initiatives, and by encouraging 'lifestyle conditions consistent with physical, mental and social health.'[148]

Although the RCMP was able to prevent the transfer of marijuana to the Food and Drugs Act, it nevertheless had to readjust some of its drug-enforcement practices. For instance, before the members of the Quebec Interministerial Committee on illicit drug use, RCMP officials admitted that their agents no longer conducted investigations in Quebec schools. Instead they preferred to use informants. In the case of CEGEPs, they were very cautious, since a police presence could be perceived as an attempt to infiltrate the school instead of carrying out drug-law enforcement. In fact, the RCMP drug squads were more concerned with national and international drug traffickers and organized crime. This change of policy was partly due to the fact that municipal and provincial drug squads had been formed and were the ones who cracked down on small pushers and individuals.[149]

Conclusion

The choice made by the Canadian government concerning LSD and marijuana reflected positions expressed by individuals and social actors and discussions within the federal bureaucracy. It reflected as well the consideration of the constraints put on Canadian sovereignty. By signing the 1961 Single Convention on Narcotic Drugs, the federal government agreed to see its ability to define its drug policy constrained by its international obligations. Ottawa's choice, reducing penalties for cannabis, also recognized the fact that Canada shared its borders with one of the most powerful nations in the world, the United States, which in the Cold War context was the leader of the Western camp. With the arrival of the Nixon administration in 1969 and its new domestic and international activism on the drug issue, Canada had to take events south of the border into consideration. Since Canada had played a role in convincing sovereign states to adopt international agreements in order to bring the drug trade under control, any move by Canada on the drug front had to take into account the international community. In the end, economic priorities, new concerns for alcohol use and not recreational drug use, divisions in society and the medical community, as well as resistance from law-enforcement agencies convinced the government to let Bill S-19 die.

Conclusion

Years of debate resulted in few changes to the legal status of marijuana. The drug remained under the Narcotic Control Act, and it retained its symbolic place as a criminal substance. Put in these terms, the only outcome of this episode of public discussion about recreational marijuana use was the preservation of the status quo. Not only did possession, possession for trafficking, trafficking, importation and exportation, and cultivation of marijuana remain criminal offences, but proponents of decriminalization – one solution which appeared during the course of the debate – failed to convince the federal government of the merits of this solution. It could be argued that the marijuana issue was a textbook case of the theory of moral panic: the status quo was maintained in law and law enforcement received more human and financial resources. Some cities, aware that they lacked the means to repress illegal drug use, created drug squads. In reaction to concerns expressed by parents and teachers, many schools created drug-prevention programs, and some even hired security personnel as part of their anti-drug-use programs. This was the case in some Montreal Catholic School Board schools.

Nevertheless, change did occur as a result of pressure by print media, individuals, social actors, bureaucrats, and politicians. While possession, possession for trafficking, and trafficking of LSD became criminal offences with amendments to the Narcotic Control Act in 1969, those charged with the offence of possession of a narcotic could be prosecuted either by summary conviction or by indictment. In 1972 the Department of Justice instructed its crown attorneys to ask courts for absolute or conditional discharges in cases of simple possession of cannabis. Naturally, more latitude meant disparities in how these instructions were carried out.

In his book on 'bad habits,' such as gambling and drug use, John C. Burnham[1] notes that the status quo also prevailed in the United States, but that it should not be interpreted as a sign of weakness on the part of those who pushed for change either through legalization or the reduction of penalties. The conclusion of Burnham's study is applicable to the situation in Canada. Interest groups, such as university student associations, the Canadian Medical Association, ARF, and OPTAT, and individuals (such as Le Dain commissioner Marie-Andrée Bertrand and psychiatrist Lionel Solursh, did not succeed in changing public policy on drugs. But as Burnham argues, we should examine 'the strengths of the forces' with which these groups and individuals 'contended.' In short, newspapers (although they were not unanimous in their opposition to change), organizations such as CODA, police forces, provinces (PEI), instruments of state apparatus such as the RCMP and the NAFBC, and individuals, such as G.K. Cowan, C.J. Schwarz, and F.W. Lundell, opposed change, and repression of marijuana remained a feature of Canada's public drug policy. For these groups and individuals, the status quo was a preferable option to legalization and a reduction of penalties. In addition, changes introduced by the government were more acceptable than the solutions proposed by other groups.

The cluster of groups and individuals that pleaded for change not only had to compete against a coalition of opponents to legalization and reduction of penalties, but they also had to deal with their own internal divisions. For instance, high school and university students triggered the debate by using drugs for recreational purposes, but to achieve a common pro-marijuana front, university student associations needed to form alliances with like-minded groups. This never happened because students considered other groups to be part of the establishment that they denounced. Furthermore, the constant change of student leadership made it impossible to sustain a campaign over time. Finally, the student lobby suffered because they were not present in force at the forum offered by the Le Dain Commission. The fact that no representatives of the student movement attended the Senate hearings on Bill S-19 in 1975 is telling.

Those who promoted decriminalization or the reduction of legal penalties for marijuana users also had to deal with dissent within their ranks. Through its national organization, the Canadian Medical Association, the medical community had access to the centres of decision-making, but physicians themselves were divided on the marijuana issue. What could be said about marijuana when there were so many unknowns about its health effects? Should physicians promote marijuana use despite the fact that it entailed health risks? For some, the answer was 'yes' since society had come to rely more and more on drugs to cure its physical and mental illnesses. Marijuana was a drug like many others and should be classified according to its dangers to health and not according to the moral views held by some. Thus, some members of the CMA, ARF, and OPTAT sought a redefinition of drug abuse. As the hearings of the Le Dain Commission revealed, all drugs, including those prescribed by physicians and sold by pharmacists, could potentially be abused or misused. This standpoint was based on a medical approach to addiction which argued for increased control by physicians over drugs. However, this line of reasoning was not shared by everyone within the medical community, as the CMA annual meetings illustrated.

The medical community's ability to develop a powerful lobby was weakened by its divisions. Physicians, such as Schwarz and Lundell, who believed that marijuana use constituted a serious health risk made their positions known within and outside the CMA. By doing so, Schwarz and Lundell provided legitimacy to groups opposed to the legalization of marijuana, as seen during the Le Dain Commission hearings. But they also demonstrated to the pro-marijuana lobby that research on marijuana was sometimes tainted by moral and political bias, a fact that senators noted during the 1975 debate over the transfer of marijuana from the Narcotic Control Act to the Food and Drugs Act.

Not only did physicians disagree among themselves, but their potential allies, such as pharmacists and the pharmaceutical industry, threw their support behind those who opposed a redefinition of drug abuse that would include every drug, even socially accepted drugs. In fact, the pharmaceutical industry and CODA pleaded for the status quo. This meant that state control continued to apply to illicit substances and at the same time no further state intrusion was encouraged. In short, the pharmaceutical sector believed that it was in the best position to discipline itself and to prevent abuse of manufactured drugs, if such cases occurred.

These internal rifts only helped groups that supported the status quo, which meant that law enforcement was still required to control the drug supply. For police forces and, in particular, the RCMP, divisions within the medical community offered proof that a cautious approach was required to tackle the drug problem, in general, and marijuana, in particular. Feeling besieged and fearing the worst in the event of legalization, police forces advanced a clear agenda in favour of the status quo in order to prevent the collapse of social values. Throughout the debate, law-enforcement organizations relied on allies such as the NAFBC, CODA, some physicians, women's groups, church groups, and international organizations such as Interpol.

When the federal government dealt with the marijuana issue, it took into account the views expressed by interest groups, the differences of opinion among provinces, and the continental and international context. A clear focus was needed for any initiative on the drug front. In this regard, National Health and Welfare officials tried to change the construction of the drug-use problem. They wanted it to become a health issue, with a focus on engendering greater access to treatment facilities and better education programs. On the other hand, Department of Justice and RCMP officials perceived the repression of marijuana as a key component of the overall anti-drug strategy, and enforcement of marijuana laws as the best deterrent against experimentation by young people with other drugs.

It was also true that any drug initiative required a certain level of federal-provincial cooperation. In this regard, however, provinces held divergent views: Quebec was anxious to protect its jurisdiction; Ontario saw itself as best able to play a leading role in any national initiative; British Columbia pleaded for a reclassification of drugs according to their dangers; and PEI, while not challenging federal authority over any drug initiative, was clearly concerned about the message that might be delivered. Starting in 1971, the Department of National Health and Welfare launched a series of drug-related initiatives. While these caused some tensions with Quebec, the other provinces felt that this area was a responsibility to be assumed by the federal government.

Drugs also have an international dimension. Indeed, Canada had actively participated in the creation of an international drug control system throughout the twentieth century. When revising its drug legislation in the sixties, the federal government had to take into account its international obligations resulting from the 1961 Single Convention on Narcotic Drugs, under which marijuana was defined as a criminal substance by virtue of the fact it had no proven medical purpose. Any attempt by Ottawa to amend drug policy had to consider Canada's relations with international organizations, which followed closely how Europe and North America handled calls to legalize marijuana. With the exception of the Netherlands, legalization was eventually rejected by almost all Western states.

Canada also had to take into account how the American government approached the drug issue, since both countries had a long history of bilateral relations and cooperation at the international level. As part of North America, Canada was obliged to consider not only public policies designed by the American government, but also those supported by Mexico. Ultimately, the drug debates would lead to a greater degree of cooperation between the United States, Mexico, and Canada. By agreeing to North American cooperation on drugs, Canada also lent support to Mexico in its overall objective to receive more economic aid in return for increased drug repression. Finally, the nature of drug trafficking itself was changing. Greater cooperation between states was required to curtail or limit the expansion of the role of organized crime in the international drug trade. Although legalization was out of the question, the option of reducing penalties was still within the range of possibilities. In the end, the convergence of political realities and a shift in public interest from marijuana to alcohol led to a political cul-de-sac, where no decision on marijuana was forthcoming.

The marijuana issue has recently resurfaced because of stories about the health benefits of marijuana. For instance, a woman who suffers from multiple sclerosis has been smoking marijuana for more than twenty years and has noticed some improvement in her condition. Furthermore, smoking pot on a daily basis has helped to alleviate her pain. Some AIDS patients who take several drugs to fight their illness, and consequently lose their appetite, smoke marijuana in order to regain it. For their part, some physicians argue for more research on the health benefits of marijuana use. They have observed that there are cells with cannabinoid receptors in the human body. Some of these receptors are located in the human brain, and the psychoactive chemical Delta-9-tetrahydrocannabinol or THC, present in marijuana, binds with them. Because THC binds with the cannabinoid receptors located in a part of the brain that controls pain transmission, THC has some medical benefits.[2]

In 1999 the Department of National Health announced that Canadians could get a special exemption under the Controlled Drugs and Substances Act in order to smoke marijuana because they were critically ill. However, patients had to be under the supervision of a physician.[3] The difficulties in qualifying for this new program encouraged many to question the true motives of the federal government. Was there a real willingness on the part of the department to allow Canadians to use marijuana because their critical medical condition required it? Furthermore, there was the crucial issue of having access to a safe supply without having to commit a crime, since cultivation of cannabis remained illegal.

Individual activism through the court system forced society, in general, and the state, in particular, to revisit the marijuana issue. Some Canadians, such as Terrance Parker, got from the courts the right to smoke marijuana for health reasons. In July 2000 the Ontario Court of Appeal declared the federal law prohibiting possession of cannabis unconstitutional since the legislator had not considered that marijuana could be used for medical purposes, notably for those who suffer from chronic illnesses. It gave the federal government twelve months to amend its drug legislation or it would be struck down.[4] With this court decision, the cannabis issue has again been placed in the hands of the federal government.

This court victory forced the Department of Health to issue the Marijuana Medical Access Regulations that took effect a year later. Critically ill patients and those who have chronic medical conditions would have access to marijuana if two physicians agreed to it. In the case of individuals with a terminal disease, they needed the approval of only one physician. Furthermore, those who qualify for medicinal marijuana could grow their own crop, ask someone to do it for them, or receive their supply from the government-approved marijuana growing centre, located in Flin Flon, Manitoba.[5]

The health department backed away from its original plan to supply marijuana. At the annual meeting of the Canadian Medical Association in August 2002, the minister of health, Anne McLellan, admitted that she was 'uncomfortable with the idea of people smoking pot to relieve pain.' Consequently, the health department would not 'distribute marijuana for medicinal purposes until clinical trials' were done.[6] This decision meant that the 747 Canadians who got permission to use marijuana had to find supplies on their own. Forced by an Ontario Court of Appeal decision in October 2003, the health department distributed the drug to those who had registered. However, many patients complained about the poor quality of the substance.[7]

The new marijuana debate created a window of opportunity in favour of decriminalization. Several voices such as the *Globe and Mail*[8] and the Canadian Medical Association supported this option.[9]

Although the Canadian Association of Chiefs of Police was opposed, some of its members supported it.[10] Among them, Toronto Chief of Police Julian Fantino supported the decriminalization of marijuana for anyone in possession of a small quantity. Fantino argued: 'I don't think every case involving a minute amount of marijuana needs to go through the criminal-justice system. However, I'm not prepared to sanction marijuana smoking until the law's changed.'[11] These groups hoped to influence public opinion, which was divided on the issue,[12] and in particular politicians and those close to the decision-making centres.

Among politicians, it became fashionable to acknowledge drug use. Following the acknowledgment by former American president Bill Clinton that he smoked but did not inhale marijuana, some Canadian politicians, such as the former leader of the defunct Canadian Alliance, Stockwell Day,[13] have acknowledged using drugs in the past. Even Prime Minister Paul Martin has admitted that he had not smoked marijuana, but his wife might have once put some in his brownies.[14] For their part, proponents of legalization had a political voice on the federal scene with the foundation of the Marijuana Party in 1999. During the 2000 federal election it captured 2 per cent of the vote in 73 ridings.[15]

In reaction to individual activism, pressure from lobby groups, and court decisions, the legislative branch of government became active. The Senate Special Committee on Illegal Drugs, created in 2000 and chaired by Senator Pierre Claude Nolin, and the House of Commons Special Committee on Non-Medical Use of Drugs, appointed in 2001, examined the issues of marijuana use and public policy.

In September 2002 the Senate committee recommended the legalization of 'pot,' since senators concluded that cannabis 'used in moderation ... pose[d] very little danger to users and to society as a whole.' Furthermore, marijuana distribution would become a state monopoly, and an amnesty for any Canadian convicted of marijuana possession would be granted.[16] Three months later, the House of Commons committee did not go that far, but recommended decriminalization for possession and cultivation of marijuana in amounts of less than 30 grams. However the Alliance MPs on the committee recommended setting the limit to 6 grams.[17]

Both committees agreed that the war on drugs was costly and ineffective, that marijuana convictions had social consequences 'disproportionate to the potential harm associated with' its use,[18] and that drug policy did not lead to a significant decrease of marijuana consumption.[19] In fact, financial and human resources should be allocated to the implementation of harm-reduction policies and addiction treatments. Furthermore, law enforcement should be directed towards the repression of large-scale growers and dealers, drug importers, and manufacturers.[20]

The legalization option was not a possibility, since it would violate the 1988 United Nations Convention against Illicit Traffic in Narcotic Drugs and Psychotropic Substances and the 1961 Single Convention on Narcotic Drugs. Decriminalization sat well with the Chrétien government, since the minister of justice, Martin Cauchon, announced in July 2002 that a bill to decriminalize the possession of less than 15 grams of marijuana would be introduced, which was done in May 2003. Although marijuana remained illegal, the penalty for the offender was a fine. Canadians who had a criminal record because they were found guilty of possessing this substance could apply for a pardon. However, the trafficking and cultivation of marijuana would remain criminal offences. In order to reassure opponents of decriminalization, a five-year educational campaign with a budget of $240 million on the dangers of smoking marijuana would be launched by the health department.[21]

Opponents were vocal during these years. Besides the warning signals sent by physicians about the health dangers of smoking marijuana and its effects on the respiratory system, the opposition of the Canadian Association of Chiefs of Police was made public. For instance, following the release of the Senate committee's report, David Griffin, executive officer for the CACP, denounced it because 'it ignores countless studies about the harmful effects of marijuana.'[22]

As well, strong opposition signals were sent by various American elected officials and departments. In 1999 the Narcotics and Law Enforcement Division of the State Department considered the possibility of recommending that Canada 'be added to the annual list of major drug-producing and trafficking countries.' Such a possibility was considered because Canada was seen to be too soft on drug repression.[23] In an interview with the Globe and Mail, Republican Congressman Mark Souder, chairman of the Committee on Drug Policy, warned Canadians that the decriminalization of marijuana would have dire consequences: 'Proceed and we'll crack down even more on your borders.' Since many marijuana growers operated in British Columbia, Congressman Souder added that BC marijuana pot was 'as dangerous as cocaine.'[24] Similar discomfort about how Canada handled drug repression was expressed by various branches of the American government. Following the recommendation of legalization by the Senate Committee in September 2002, the director of the US National Drug Control Policy, John Walters, expressed his strong disappointment. He rejected the statement that marijuana was not harmful. 'We know that marijuana is a harmful drug, particularly for young people.'[25] Speaking at a Detroit news conference, Walters argued that 'the claim that medical marijuana is an efficacious medicine is a lie.'[26] Commenting on the House of Commons committee's recommendation of decriminalization in December 2002, Walters qualified this alternative as a 'dangerous threat' to the United States. 'We have,' argued Walters, 'to make security at the border tougher because this is a dangerous threat to our young people and it makes the problem of patrolling the border more difficult.' Basically, warned the American bureaucrat, and later the American ambassador to Canada, Paul Cellucci, there would be longer waits for Canadians at the U.S. border.[27] In August 2003 Walters blamed Canadian political leaders for not doing enough to crack down on the marijuana industry in British Columbia. Instead, they preferred, complained the American bureaucrat, to deal with decriminalization.[28] In the context of tensions in US–Canada relations over several issues (the war in Iraq and the refusal of Canada to participate, and softwood lumber), American views on the marijuana issue were taken seriously by Canadian opponents to the campaign for its decriminalization.

Opposition to decriminalization, divisions within the Liberal caucus on the issue, and the Liberal leadership race that crowned Paul Martin at the end of 2003 contributed to the death of the bill.[29] Furthermore, those who thought that the courts would rule cannabis laws unconstitutional lost their case in December 2003. The Supreme Court of Canada ruled that there was 'no free-standing constitutional right to smoke "pot" for recreationa purposes.'[30] Basically, Supreme Court judges stated that the marijuana debate was a political issue and Parliament had the authority to amend its drug legislation if it chose to do so. The Liberals, who formed a minority government following the 2004 federal election, reintroduced a bill to decriminalize marijuana possession. However, the bill's future remains unclear.

If I venture to compare the current debate with the one that took place thirty years ago, what can be said? Although the argument that marijuana use had some health benefits barely surfaced between 1961 and 1975, the current debate does feature some similarities with that of a generation ago: opposition from police forces despite any dissenting voices from within; divisions among Canadians on how to handle marijuana use, in the medical community over the issue of how to balance health benefits and dangers, and among federal bureaucrats (Justice versus Health); opposition from American bureaucrats and officials; and a federal government handling the issue cautiously.

However, in the current debate, the courts have forced the legislative branch to act. It also reminded everyone that the drug issue is a social and political debate, as those who pushed for change in the sixties reminded society and politicians. Since the marijuana issue is framed in moral terms (what constitutes proper social behaviour, what circumstances allow for marijuana use, how chronic pain may modify attitudes to drug use), it has encouraged several social actors to intervene in order to shape the debate and influence centres of decision-making. Although those who oppose marijuana use believe that drugs, unless prescribed by physicians, are an unacceptable way of coping with life, proponents use the issue to demonstrate that public policies, based on moral views, are inefficient, since they fail to change individual behaviour and constitute a waste of money and human resources.

Drugs, like gambling and alcohol use, came onto the radar screen of many individuals and interest groups who wanted to restrict their use because of their values. They pressed the state to adopt regulatory mechanisms for controlling behaviours. At the beginning of the twentieth century, they succeeded in imposing their views, since state policy was based on severe restriction and prohibition. In the 1920s, prohibition of alcohol was replaced by new regulatory mechanisms to control access: state monopoly of the sale of alcohol. In the sixties, states revisited the gambling issue: lotteries are now operated by the provinces and constitute a lucrative source of revenue. Despite changes to how the drug policy has been implemented, marijuana remains an illegal substance.

The marijuana issue forces us to question the autonomy of the state. Constraints imposed by international treaties still circumscribe Canada's ability to design its own drug policy. In the sixties, the federal government had to take into consideration the 1961 Single Convention on Narcotics. In the 1990s, Canada was a signatory of the 1988 United Nations Convention against Illicit Traffic in Narcotic Drugs. Also, the marijuana issue raises important questions about the public-policy process. It demonstrates the unequal distribution of power, influence, and resources among individuals, experts, social actors, and interest groups in their ability to shape the public debate and to impose their choice of policy. Provincial and federal bureaucrats interfere in the process and use, among other things, their networking abilities. The marijuana issue reveals the complexity of the public-policy process, since opposite agendas (legalization, liberalization, keeping the status quo) put forward by various participants collide and the continental and international context circumscribes state sovereignty.

Notes

Introduction

1 *Toronto Daily Star*, 29 January 1970, 1.
2 Commission of Inquiry into the Non-Medical Use of Drugs, *Interim Report* (Ottawa: Information Canada, 1970), Appendix B3, 5.
3 See Timothy Miller's interesting analysis in *The Hippies and American Values* (Knoxville: University of Tennessee Press, 1991).
4 François Ricard, *The Lyric Generation: The Life and Times of the Baby Boomers* (Toronto: Stoddart Publishing Co., 1994); Douglas Owram, *Born at the Right Time: A History of the Baby Boom Generation* (Toronto: University of Toronto Press, 1996).
5 Theodore Roszak, *The Making of a Counter Culture: Reflections on the Technocratic Society and Its Youthful Opposition* (Garden City, NY: Doubleday, 1969), 42–83.
6 Ricard, *The Lyric Generation*, 107.
7 'High Priest Points Ahead to Happy Era,' *Berkeley Barb*, 14–21 February 1969, quoted in Timothy Miller, *The Hippies and American Values*, 119.
8 Quoted in Roszak, *The Making of a Counter Culture*, 67.
9 Howard Adelman, 'A Postscript: Reflections on Rochdale' and 'A Post Postscript: Roots of Rochdale,' in *The Beds of Academe: A Study of the Relation of Student Residences and the University* (Toronto: Praxis Press, 1969), 187–98, 252–9; Henry Mietkiewicz, *Dream Tower: The Life and Legacy of Rochdale College* (Toronto: McGraw-Hill Ryerson, 1988).
10 See Bryan D. Palmer, *Working-Class Experience: Rethinking the History of Canadian Labour, 1800–1991*, 2nd ed. (Toronto: McClelland & Stewart, 1992), 313–33.
11 Arthur Marwick, *The Sixties: Cultural Revolution in Britain, France, Italy, and*

the United States, 1958–1974 (Oxford: Oxford University Press, 1998), 16–19. The notion that baby boomers shaped the sixties influences how this period has been analysed. Ron Verzuh's *Underground Times: Canada's Flower-Child Revolutionaries* (Toronto: Deneau, 1989) is a good example. See also Myrna Kostash, *Long Way from Home: The Story of the Sixties Generation in Canada* (Toronto: James Lorimer, 1980).

12 Catherine Carstairs, 'Innocent Addicts, Dope Fiends and Nefarious Traffickers: Illegal Drug Use in 1920s English Canada,' *Journal of Canadian Studies* 33:3 (Fall 1998), 145–62; Catherine Carstairs, 'Deporting "Ah Sin" to Save the White Race: Moral Panic, Racialization, and the Extension of Canadian Drug Laws in the 1920s,' *Canadian Bulletin of Medical History* 16:1 (1999), 65–88; Stanley Cohen, *Folk Devils and Moral Panics: The Creation of the Mods and Rockers* (London: MacGibbon & Kee, 1972); Elizabeth A. Comack, 'The Origins of Canadian Drug Legislation: Labelling versus Class Analysis,' in T. Fleming, ed., *The New Criminologies in Canada: Crime, State and Control* (Toronto: Oxford University Press, 1985), 65–85; Shirley J. Cook, 'Canadian Narcotics Legislation, 1908–1923: A Conflict Model Interpretation,' *Canadian Review of Sociology and Anthropology* 6:1 (1969), 36–46; Erich Goode and Nachman Ben-Yehuda, *Moral Panics: The Social Construction of Deviance* (Oxford: Blackwell, 1994); Stuart Hall et al., *Policing the Crisis: Mugging, the State, and Law and Order* (London: Macmillan, 1978); Colin Hay, 'Mobilization Through Interpellation: James Bulger, Juvenile Crime and the Construction of a Moral Panic,' *Social and Legal Studies* 4 (1995), 197–223; Philip Jenkins, *Synthetic Panics: The Symbolic Politics of Designer Drugs* (New York and London: New York University Press, 1999); Glenn F. Murray, 'Cocaine Use in the Era of Social Reform: The Natural History of a Social Problem in Canada, 1880–1911,' *Canadian Journal of Law and Society* 2 (1987), 29–43; Kenneth Thompson, *Moral Panics* (London: Routledge, 1998).

13 Graham E. Parker, 'High Sentences,' *Canadian Forum*, June 1969, 56.

14 Neil Boyd, 'The Origins of Canadian Narcotics Legislation: The Process of Criminalization in Historical Context,' *Dalhousie Law Journal* 8:1 (January 1984), 102–36; Carstairs, 'Innocent Addicts, Dope Fiends and Nefarious Traffickers' and 'Deporting "Ah Sin" to Save the White Race,' '"Hop Heads" and "Hypes": Drug Use, Regulation and Resistance in Canada, 1920–1961,' Doctoral dissertation, University of Toronto, 2000; Cook, 'Canadian Narcotics Legislation'; Comack, 'The Origins of Canadian Drug Legislation'; P.J. Giffen, S. Endicott, and S. Lambert, *Panic and Indifference: The Politics of Canada's Drug Laws* (Ottawa: Canadian Centre on Substance Abuse, 1991); J. Giffen and S. Lambert, 'What Happened on the Way to Law Reform?' in J.C. Blackwell and P.G. Erickson, eds., *Illicit Drugs in Canada: A*

Risky Business (Scarborough: Nelson Canada, 1988), 345–69; Daniel J. Mal-
leck, '"Its Baneful Influences Are Too Well Known": Debates over Drug Use
in Canada, 1867–1908,' *Canadian Bulletin of Medical History* 14 (1997), 263–88;
Murray, 'Cocaine Use in the Era of Social Reform'; R. Solomon and M.
Green, 'The First Century: The History of Non-Medical Opiate Use and
Control Policies in Canada, 1870–1970,' in Blackwell and Erickson, eds.,
Illicit Drugs in Canada, 88–116.
15 The exception is Catherine Carstairs. Her book, *Jailed for Possession: Illegal
Drug Use, Regulation, and Power in Canada, 1920–1961* (Toronto: University
of Toronto Press, 2005) looks at the drug issue from 1920 to 1961. Her study
of the drug scene includes an analysis of the role of social actors, such as
police officers, physicians, and social workers. My book picks up more or
less where Dr Carstairs left off.
16 See Léandre Bilodeau, *Drug Use among the Students in the Secondary Schools
and Cegep's on Montreal Island in 1969 and 1971* (Quebec: Office for the Prevention and Treatment of Alcoholism and the Other Toxicomanias, 1971);
John Russell, *Survey of Drug Use in Selected British Columbia Schools* (Vancouver: Narcotic Addiction Foundation of British Columbia, 1970); John Russell, *Drug Use among Vancouver Secondary Students* (Vancouver: NAFBC,
1971); John S. Russell and Marcus J. Hollander, *Drug Use among Vancouver
Secondary School Students: 1970 and 1974* (Vancouver: NAFBC, 1974); Reginald G. Smart, Dianne Fejer, and Jim White, *The Extent of Drug Use in Metropolitan Toronto Schools: A Study of Changes from 1968 to 1970* (Toronto:
Addiction Research Foundation, 1970); Reginald G. Smart and Dianne
Fejer, *Changes in Drug Use in Toronto High School Students between 1972 and
1974* (Toronto: ARF, 1974); and Paul C. Whitehead, Carl F. Grindstaff, and
Craig L. Boydell, eds., *Alcohol and Other Drugs: Perspectives on Use, Abuse,
Treatment, and Prevention* (Toronto: Holt, Rinehart and Winston of Canada,
1973).
17 Line Beauchesne, *Les drogues: Les coûts cachés de la prohibition* (Montreal:
Lanctôt Éditeur, 2003); Sheila Gormely, *Drugs and the Canadian Scene*
(Toronto: Pagurian Press, 1970); Reginald Whitaker, *Drugs and the Law: The
Canadian Scene* (Toronto: Methuen, 1969).
18 John W. Kingdon, *Agendas, Alternatives and Public Policies* (Boston: Little,
Brown and Co., 1984; New York: Harper Collins, 1995); Vincent Lemieux,
Les cheminements de l'influence: Systèmes, stratégies et structures du politique
(Quebec: Les Presses de l'Université Laval, 1979); Vincent Lemieux, *L'étude
des politiques publiques: Les acteurs et leur pouvoir,* 2nd ed. (Quebec: Les
Presses de l'Université Laval, 2002); Kenneth J. Meier, *The Politics of Sin:
Drugs, Alcohol and Public Policy* (Armonk, NY: M.E. Sharpe, 1994).

1. 'A Growing Problem'

1 Lois Light, 'They Jailed My Son for Smoking Marijuana,' *Chatelaine* 41:9 (September 1968), 38, 107.
2 Thompson, *Moral Panics*, 8.
3 Carstairs, 'Deporting "Ah Sin" to Save the White Race'; Hall et al., *Policing the Crisis*; Jenkins, *Synthetic Panics*.
4 Goode and Ben-Yehuda, *Moral Panics*, 229.
5 Claude Hénault, 'Survey of Newspapers and Magazines for the Le Dain Commission,' 21 May 1971, Commission Research Paper, Project no. 81, 180, 182, 183, 197, National Archives of Canada (NAC), R 923, vol. 20, file 20–9.
6 Hay, 'Mobilization Through Interpellation,' 204.
7 Blackwell and Erickson, eds., *Illicit Drugs in Canada*; Boyd, 'The Origins of Canadian Narcotics Legislation'; Carstairs, 'Deporting "Ah Sin" to Save the White Race'; Cook, 'Canadian Narcotics Legislation, 1908–1923'; Comack, 'The Origins of Canadian Drug Legislation'; Giffen, Endicott, and Lambert, *Panic and Indifference*; Malleck, '"Its Baneful Influences Are Too Well Known"'; Murray, 'Cocaine Use in the Era of Social Reform.'
8 *Toronto Telegram*, 20 March 1967, 1; 21 March 1967, 1; *Globe and Mail*, 21 March 1967, 1; *Toronto Daily Star*, 20 March 1967, 1; *La Presse* (Montreal), 21 March 1967, 6.
9 There are two other examples of stories published in newspapers: On 13 August 1968, the *Globe and Mail* told of a young man who took LSD, went to Toronto's Islands and jumped into Lake Ontario. 'His body was recovered a short time later in 15 feet of ... water.' On 5 August 1969, the *Toronto Daily Star* published a short story about three youth who were admitted to hospital 'with lacerations and two others were treated and released following a fight on a farm.' They told the police they had taken LSD.
10 *Toronto Daily Star*, 3 February 1970, 1.
11 'Survey of Newspapers and Magazines for the Le Dain Commission,' 153e.
12 'New Research Findings Compel the Prince Edward Island Government to Oppose Legalization of Marijuana' brief presented to the (Le Dain Commission), 21 February 1970, Prince Edward Island Public Archives and Records Office (PEIPARO), RG 22, series 8, sub-series 2, file 38.
13 Gormely, *Drugs and the Canadian Scene*, 22.
14 Ibid., 23.
15 Ibid., 125.
16 Commission of Inquiry, *Interim Report*, 146.

17 Pierre Berton, *The Smug Minority* (Toronto: McClelland and Stewart, 1968), 33.

18 Whitaker, *Drugs and the Law,* 147.

19 Larry Sloman, *Reefer Madness: The History of Marijuana in America* (Indianapolis: Bobbs-Merrill Co., 1979), 243.

20 'Survey of Newspapers and Magazines,' 80, 81, 82.

21 Ibid., 121, 122. This part of the study is based on 48 daily newspapers from the following provinces: 5 from Alberta, 7 from British Columbia, 2 from Manitoba, 1 from New Brunswick, 2 from Newfoundland, 2 from Nova Scotia, 19 from Ontario (1 French-language), 1 from Prince Edward Island, 7 from Quebec (5 French-language), and 2 from Saskatchewan.

22 Ibid., 83, and 84.

23 Ibid., 135b. The author of the study considered only editorials submitted by newspapers. The *Globe and Mail* and the *Vancouver Province,* as opposed to the other newspapers, submitted almost all their editorials on the drug issue.

24 Ibid, 142d.

25 Ibid., 142a, 142b.

26 Ibid., 142b.

27 Ibid., 142b.

28 Ibid., 137a.

29 Ibid., 136a. For this newspaper, the analysis of editorials covers the 1964–71 period.

30 Ibid., 153a.

31 Ibid., 148b.

32 Ibid., 148a.

33 Ibid., 150a.

34 Ibid., 167a, 167b.

35 Ibid., 200.

36 Ibid., 142c.

37 Ibid., 142c.

38 It seems that this trend is similar to the one observed by John C. Burnham, *Bad Habits: Drinking, Smoking, Taking Drugs, Gambling, Sexual Misbehavior, and Swearing in American History* (New York: New York University Press, 1993), who argues that more and more American newspapers came to denounce the harsh penalties associated with marijuana use.

39 Senate Debates, 25 April 1967, 1830.

40 Presentation to Senate Committee Hearings, 'Placing Marihuana under the Food and Drugs Act. Cannabis. The Dangerous Communications Gap,' by G.K. Cowan, Consultant to Department of Education (PEI), Member of the

PEI Drug Education Committee, 18 February 1975, NAC, MG 32 C 55, vol. 5, file 5/5 Drugs – Documents.

41 Author's translation: 'On a vu en première page de tous nos journaux la photo d'un hippie qui s'était présenté au Sénat américain en fumant une cigarette de marihuana. En période d'agitation, on interviewera facilement les chefs agitateurs, étant heureux si ces derniers accentuent la contestation. Il s'agit de contester pour avoir une tribune. Bien plus, les médias d'information, en transportant la nouvelle, en exagéreront les traits, la caricatureront afin de la rendre plus insolite.' Rapport à la [Commission Le Dain] de l'[OPTAT], Novembre 1969, NAC, RG 33/101, vol. 14, file 1676.

42 Martin Goldfarb Consultants, *The Media and the People: A Report*, Report of the Special Senate Committee on Mass Media, vol. 3 (Ottawa, 1970), 63.

43 Ibid., 65.

44 Author's translation: 'stimule l'intérêt des étudiants, souvent en leur laissant croire que l'usage des hallucinogènes n'a pas de conséquence grave, qu'un grand nombre d'étudiants l'utilisent et qu'il est facile de s'en procurer.' Réunion des ministres provinciaux de la Santé, 21 et 22 octobre 1968, ANQ-Q, E8, 1960-01-580/149, file 1968 – Septembre à Décembre inclus, Ministère de la Santé (Dossier général), Québec.

45 See Mary Louise Adams, *The Trouble with Normal: Postwar Youth and the Making of Heterosexuality* (Toronto: University of Toronto Press, 1997); Ricard, *The Lyric Generation*; Owram, *Born at the Right Time*.

46 Letter to Matthew B. Dymond, MD, Minister of Health, from H. David Archibald, Executive Director, ARF, 2 December 1966, PAO, RG 10, file 1-1-1-13.

47 Reginald G. Smart and Dianne Fejer, 'The Extent of Illicit Drug Use in Canada: A Review of Current Epidemiology,' in C. Boydell, C.F. Grindstaff and P.C. Whitehead, eds., *Critical Issues in Canadian Society* (Toronto: Holt, Rinehart and Winston of Canada, 1971), 508–20.

48 Archibald, *The Addiction Research Foundation: A Voyage of Discovery* (Toronto: ARF, 1990), 95.

49 Dianne Fejer, Reginald G. Smart, and Paul C. Whitehead, 'Changes in the Patterns of Drug Use in Two Canadian Cities: Toronto and Halifax,' in Whitehead, Grindstaff, and Boydell, eds., *Alcohol and Other Drugs*, 158.

50 Smart and Fejer, 'The Extent of Illicit Drug Use in Canada,' 509.

51 Ibid.

52 Ibid., 511; Bilodeau, *Drug Use among the Students in the Secondary Schools and Cegep's on Montreal Island in 1969 and 1971*, 29.

53 Bilodeau, *Drug Use Among the Students in the Secondary Schools and Cegep's on Montreal Island*, 109; Lucien Laforest, *La consommation de drogues chez les*

étudiants du secondaire et du collégial de l'île de Montréal (Quebec: OPTAT, 1969).

54 Smart and Fejer, 'The Extent of Illicit Drug Use in Canada,' 514.

55 Ingeborg Paulus, *Psychedelic Drug Use in Vancouver: Notes on the New Drug Scene* (Vancouver: Narcotic Addiction Foundation of British Columbia, 1967), 32.

56 Russell, *Survey of Drug Use in Selected British Columbia Schools*, 39.

57 Russell and Hollander, *Drug Use among Vancouver Secondary School Students: 1970 and 1974*, 75.

58 Smart, Fejer, and White, *The Extent of Drug Use in Metropolitan Toronto Schools*, 18; Bilodeau, *Drug Use among the Students in the Secondary Schools and Cegep's*, 66; Paul C. Whitehead, 'The Epidemiology of Drug Use in a Canadian City at Two Points in Time: Halifax, 1969–1970,' in Boyell, Grindstaff, and Whitehead, *Critical Issues in Canadian Society*, eds., 520–33; Russell and Hollander, *Drug Use among Vancouver Secondary School Students: 1970 and 1974*, 31.

59 Smart, Fejer, and White, *The Extent of Drug Use in Metropolitan Toronto Schools*, 18; Bilodeau, *Drug Use among the Students in the Secondary Schools and Cegep's*, 66; Reginald G. Smart, Dianne Fejer, and Eileen Alexander, *Drug Use among High School Students and Their Parents in Lincoln and Welland Counties* (Toronto: Addiction Research Foundation, 1970).

60 Russell and Hollander, *Drug Use among Vancouver Secondary School Students: 1970 and 1974*, 75.

61 Smart, Fejer, and White, *The Extent of Drug Use in Metropolitan Toronto Schools*, 16.

62 Smart, Fejer, and Alexander, *Drug Use among High School Students and Their Parents*, 37.

63 In 1968, 6.7% of Toronto students had used marijuana in the previous six months. In 1970, it was 18.3%. For LSD, it was 2.6% (1968) and 8.5% (1970). Smart, Fejer, and White, *The Extent of Drug Use in Metropolitan Toronto Schools*, 8; Léandre Bilodeau et André Jacob, *La prévalence de l'usage des drogues de 1969 à 1971, chez les étudiants du secondaire et du collégial de l'Île de Montréal, Quelques résultats généraux*, OPTAT, juin 1971, ANQ-Q, E8, 1984-05-001/7.

64 Smart, Fejer, and White, *The Extent of Drug Use in Metropolitan Toronto Schools*, 47.

65 Whitehead, 'The Epidemiology of Drug Use in a Canadian City at Two Points in Time,' in Boyell, Grindstaff, and Whitehead, eds., *Critical Issues in Canadian Society*, 530.

66 The gender gap did not disappear in Halifax. On the contrary, it remained a

characteristic of drug use. In their attempt to explain it, the authors attributed it to an 'element of local cultural traditions.' Fejer, Smart, and Whitehead (see n. 49), 163.

67 Smart and Fejer, *Changes in Drug Use in Toronto High School Students between 1972 and 1974*, 16.

68 Ibid., 9.

69 Ibid.; Smart, Fejer, and White, *The Extent of Drug Use in Metropolitan Toronto Schools*, 17.

70 Ruth Cooperstock, 'Sex Differences in the Use of Mood-Modifying Drugs: An Explanatory Model,' in Whitehead, Grindstaff, and Boydell, eds., *Alcohol and Other Drugs*, 177.

71 Bilodeau, *Drug Use among the Students in the Secondary Schools and Cegep's*, 78.

72 Smart, Fejer, and White, *The Extent of Drug Use in Metropolitan Toronto Schools*, 24; Reginald G. Smart, Dianne Fejer, and Jim White, *Drug Use Trends among Metropolitan Toronto Students: A Study of Changes from 1968 to 1972* (Toronto: Addiction Research Foundation, 1972), 22; Smart and Fejer, *Changes in Drug Use in Toronto High School Students between 1972 and 1974*, 12; Dianne Fejer, *Drug Use and Psychological Problems among Adolescents in a Semi-Rural Area of Ontario: Haldimand County* (Toronto: Addiction Research Foundation, 1971), 8–9.

73 Russell, *Survey of Drug Use in Selected British Columbia Schools*, 49; Bilodeau, *Drug Use among the Students in the Secondary Schools and Cegep's*, 87.

74 Lucien Laforest, 'L'appartenance religieuse des usagers de drogues parmi les étudiants montréalais,' article prepared for *L'information psychiatrique*, April 1970, ANQ-Q, E8, 1984-05-001/5, file 5.2.17.

75 Bilodeau, *Drug Use among the Students in the Secondary Schools and Cegep's*, 81.

76 Russell, *Survey of Drug Use in Selected British Columbia Schools*.

77 Smart, Fejer, and White, *The Extent of Drug Use in Metropolitan Toronto Schools*, 27; Smart, Fejer, and Alexander, *Drug Use among High School Students and Their Parents*, 15; David H. Archibald, 'Where We Are At ... A Time of Assessment' (Presentation to Staff Conference, Geneva Park, 1971); David H. Archibald, 'Action communautaire face à l'alcool et aux drogues,' *Information sur l'alcoolisme et les autres toxicomanies* 7:2 (March–April 1971), 3–8.

78 Bilodeau, *Drug Use among the Students in the Secondary Schools and Cegep's*, 98.

79 Russell, *Survey of Drug Use in Selected British Columbia Schools*, 63.

80 Bilodeau, *Drug Use among the Students in the Secondary Schools and Cegep's*, 83.

81 Russell, *Survey of Drug Use in Selected British Columbia Schools*, 55; Bilodeau, *Drug Use among the Students in the Secondary Schools and Cegep's*, 112.

82 Russell, *Survey of Drug Use in Selected British Columbia Schools*; Russell, *Drug Use among Vancouver Secondary Students*; Paul C. Whitehead, Reginald G. Smart, and Lucien Laforest, 'La consommation d'autres drogues chez les fumeurs de marijuana de l'Est du Canada,' *Toxicomanies* 3:1 (January–April 1970), 49–63.

83 Smart, Fejer, and White, *The Extent of Drug Use in Metropolitan Toronto Schools*; Smart, Fejer, and White, *Drug Use Trends among Metropolitan Toronto Students*.

84 Russell and Hollander, *Drug Use among Vancouver Secondary School Students: 1970 and 1974*, 111; Russell, *Survey of Drug Use in Selected British Columbia Schools*; Russell, *Drug Use among Vancouver Secondary Students*; Bilodeau, *Drug Use among the Students in the Secondary Schools and Cegep's*.

85 Simone Radouco-Thomas et al., 'Enquête sur l'usage des psychodysleptiques (hallucinogènes) dans les collèges et universités de la province de Québec. Partie II: Méthodologie et résultats préliminaires,' *Laval Médical* 40 (January 1969), 105–6.

86 Daniel Monnier, *Les étudiants du Québec et les drogues hallucinogènes* (Quebec: Direction générale de la planification, Ministère de l'Éducation, 1970), 1.

87 Smart and Fejer, 'The Extent of Illicit Drug Use in Canada,' 508–20.

2. 'We Can't Afford to Take a Neutral Position'

1 J.P. Mackey, 'To Serve and Protect,' *Canadian Police Chief*, January 1970.

2 Kingdon, *Agendas, Alternatives and Public Policies*, 1984 and 1995; Lemieux, *L'étude des politiques publiques. Les acteurs et leur pouvoir*.

3 William I. Jenkins, *Policy Analysis: A Political and Organizational Perspective* (London: Martin Robertson, 1978); Michael Howlett and M. Ramesh, *Studying Public Policy: Policy Cycles and Policy Subsystems* (Toronto: Oxford University Press, 1995).

4 Alan Hunt, *Governing Morals: A Social History of Moral Regulation* (Cambridge: Cambridge University Press, 1999), 9–10.

5 Michel Foucault, *The Order of Things: An Archaeology of the Human Sciences* (New York: Vintage Books, 1973); Alan Sheridan, *Michel Foucault: The Will to Truth* (London: Tavistock Publications, 1980); Michel Crozier and Erhard Friedberg, *L'acteur et le système: Les contraintes de l'action collective* (Paris: Seuil, 1977); Lemieux, *Les cheminements de l'influence*.

6 Mariana Valverde, *The Age of Light, Soap, and Water: Moral Reform in English Canada, 1885–1925* (Toronto: McClelland & Stewart, 1991), 165.

7 Burnham, *Bad Habits*, 121.
8 Report on Government-Press Communications (McToggart Report on Yorkville Hepatitis), PAO, RG 10-6, box 182, file 10-6-0-1894K.
9 Reginald G. Smart and David Jackson, *The Yorkville Sub-Culture: A Study of the Life Styles and Interactions of Hippies and Non-Hippies* (Toronto: Addiction Research Foundation, 1969).
10 Quoted in Owram, *Born at the Right Time*, 211.
11 National Film Board, *Flowers on a One-Way Street*, 1967; Owram, *Born at the Right Time*, 211–15.
12 *Toronto Daily Star*, 6 February 1967, 6.
13 *The Varsity*, 23 January 1967, 1; 10 February 1967, 1: *Canadian Forum*, March 1967, 1.
14 *The Varsity*, 9 January 1967, 1.
15 *Toronto Daily Star*, 11 February 1967, 1.
16 Gormely, *Drugs and the Canadian Scene*, 56.
17 Letter to the Canadian Union of Students Representative, York Student Federation Papers, 1974-019/006, file 130; Council of York Student Federation, 4 November 1969, York Archives, York Student Federation Papers, 1974-019/003, file 71.
18 Letter from the University Students' Council / Conseil des étudiants universitaires, University of Western Ontario, to the Minister of Health, M.B. Dymond, 5 February 1968, PAO, RG 10-1, box 35, file 35.3.
19 Letter from the Humberside Collegiate Students' Council to Premier John Robarts, March 1970, PAO, RG 3-26, box 124, file Alcoholism & Drug Addiction.
20 Letter from Christine Krawczyk, Referendum co-ordinator, University of British Columbia, to the Le Dain Commission, 13 November 1970, NAC, RG 33/101, vol. 22, file B.C. Educational.
21 *Toronto Daily Star*, 29 January 1970, 1.
22 Owram, *Born at the Right Time*, 199.
23 Gormely, *Drugs and the Canadian Scene*, 102–3.
24 Radouco-Thomas et al., 'Enquête sur l'usage des psychodysleptiques,' 107.
25 *Toronto Telegram*, 11 March 1970, 35.
26 Memorandum to Mr J.K. Crossley, Group Chairman – Arts, from G.M. Mac-Martin, Assistant Superintendent of Curriculum, 10 January 1969; To Miss D.H.M. Dunn, Group Chairman – Arts from G.M. MacMartin, Assistant Superintendent, Curriculum Branch, Statement regarding drug education in the schools, 10 May 1971, PAO, RG 2-245, access 21353, box 1, file Drug Correspondence 1968–1976; Letter from J.R. McCarthy, Deputy Minister of Education, Government of Ontario, to Dr R.D. Miller, Director of Research

(Le Dain Commission), 30 October 1970, NAC, RG 33/101, volume 21, file Ont. Government; Memorandum to Dr J.K. Reynolds, Secretary to the Cabinet from M. Collins, 28 July 1970, PAO, RG 3-26, box 125, file Alcohol and Drug Addiction, February–July 1970.

27 Ibid.

28 Memorandum from G.M. MacMartin, Assistant Superintendent, Curriculum Branch, 21 May 1971, PAO, RG 2-245, box 1, file Drug Correspondence 1968–1976.

29 Procès-verbal, 2e réunion du Comité interministériel sur le problème de la drogue dans le milieu scolaire et autres, 2 novembre 1972, ANQ-Q, E8, 84-05-001/3 file Procès-verbaux du Comité interministériel sur les toxicomanies.

30 Author's translation: 'Ce document s'inspire d'une philosophie d'éducation préventive et de sensibilisation des adultes [enseignants et parents] plutôt que d'une action directe auprès des étudiants.' CECM, *Trouver le Joint: Guide de l'éducateur sur l'usage non médical des drogues* (Montreal: Office des relations publiques de la CECM, 1973), 5.

31 Author's translation: 'Toutes les mesures qui s'imposent, dans le respect des personnes et en tenant compte de la gravité des situations,' ibid., 5.

32 Author's translation: 'L'indice ou le symptôme d'un malaise social ou individuel. La nécessité et [le] respect de la loi, à prendre une décision personnelle éclairée ... en regard [aux] drogues.' Ibid., 4; Rapport de la vingt-troisième réunion du Comité interministériel sur les toxicomanies, 28 février 1974, ANQ-Q, E8, versement 1984-05-001/3.

33 Author's translation: '[L]es drogues ne seront jamais que des béquilles. Certaines peuvent être utiles à des handicapés. Mais un homme qui sait marcher n'a pas besoin de prothèse.' Commentaires remis par Robert Trempe sur le guide de la CECM *Trouver le Joint*, DIGEC, 14 novembre 1973, ANQ-Q, E13, 1992-11-000/111, file Rapports divers toxicomanies, 72–7.

34 Procès-verbal de la 21e réunion du Comité interministériel sur les toxicomanies, 1er février 1974, ANQ-Q, E8, 1984-05-001/3, file Procès-verbaux du Comité interministériel sur les toxicomanies.

35 Rapport de la vingt-troisième réunion du Comité interministériel sur les toxicomanies, 28 février 1974, ANQ-Q, E8, versement 1984–05–001/3.

36 Author's translation: 'détérior[ait] davantage le climat et pourrait même engendrer des résultats contraires à ceux que nous tentons d'obtenir.' Lettre à Jérôme Choquette, Ministre de la Justice, d'André Boudreau, Directeur de l'OPTAT, 26 novembre 1973, ANQ-Q, E13, 1992-11-000/111, file Rapports divers toxicomanies, 72–7.

37 Author's translation: 'tant qu'il n'y a pas de victime pas d'intervention policière.'

38 Author's translation: 'Dans la mesure ou un étudiant consomme des drogues en étant conscient des dangers qu'il court et que cette décision n'implique que lui, il ne faut pas qu'il y ait d'intervention judiciaire.' Plan d'action pour le ministère de la justice et le ministère de l'éducation concernant le problème de la consommation de la drogue en milieu scolaire, par R. Trempe et P. Clermont, 26 mai 1975, ANQ-Q, E13, 1992-11-000/111, file Rapports divers toxicomanies, 72–7.

39 Rapport de la vingt-troisième réunion du Comité interministériel sur les toxicomanies, 28 février 1974, ANQ-Q, E8, versement 1984-05-001/3.

40 Gormely, *Drugs and the Canadian Scene*, 166.

41 Author's translation: 'Il y a encore beaucoup d'ignorance, d'inquiétude et de panique ... Ce programme [ne] fera [pas] de miracles. Il faudra plusieurs années avant de changer les mentalités.' Rapport de la vingt-troisième réunion du Comité interministériel sur les toxicomanies, 28 février 1974, ANQ-Q, E8, versement 1984-05-001/3.

42 Ibid.

43 *The Varsity*, 13 February 1967, 5

44 Letter from Murray Ross to John Robarts, 14 May 1969, PAO, John P. Robarts Papers (F 15), series 4–3, MU 8008, file York University Drug Use, 1969.

45 Letter from M.B. Dymond, Minister of Health, to John Robarts, 18 June 1969, ibid.

46 Author's translation: 'n'ont pas de valeur de règlement parce que non édictées par résolution du Conseil d'administration.'

47 Author's translation: 'Certains fabricants de bière donnent des trophées ou fournissent des équipements sportifs. En retour, les organisations des collèges vont offrir une 'sauterie' identifiée à une marque de bière.' Rapport de la vingt-sixième réunion du Comité interministériel sur les toxicomanies, 24 mai 1974, ANQ-Q, E8, versement 1984-05-001/3.

48 *Canadian Police Chief*, October 1972, 19.

49 *Globe and Mail*, 20 August 1968, 5; the *Vancouver Province*, 21 August 1968, 9; Whitaker, *Drugs & the Law*, 112.

50 J.P. Mackey, 'To Serve and Protect,' *Canadian Police Chief*, January 1970.

51 *Globe and Mail*, 30 April 1971, 7.

52 *Toronto Star*, 30 June 1972, 13.

53 In its reaction to the interim report of the Le Dain Commission, the government of Saskatchewan noted the very limited participation of police forces in the drug debate. Position of the Province of Saskatchewan on the Interim Report of the Le Dain Commission, PAO, RG4-2, file 446.1.

54 *Canadian Police Chief*, October 1970, October 1972; Canadian Association of

Chiefs of Police, Journal of Proceedings, 63rd Annual Conference, 1–6 September 1968, NAC, RG 33/101, vol. 16, file Royal Canadian Mounted Police.
55 *Canadian Police Chief*, October 1973.
56 Nora and William Kelly, *The Royal Canadian Mounted Police: A Century of History, 1873–1973* (Edmonton: Hurtig Publishers, 1973), 299.
57 Letter from Eric Silk, Commissioner, Ontario Provincial Police, to Allan F. Lawrence, Minister of Justice and Attorney-General, 6 April 1971, PAO, RG 4-2, file 496.2; Dahn D. Higley, *O.P.P.: The History of the Ontario Provincial Police Force* (Toronto: Queen's Printer, 1984), 493.
58 Lettre à Gerald Le Dain, président, Commission d'enquête, de Maurice St-Pierre, Directeur général, Sûreté du Québec, Montréal, 29 octobre 1969, NAC, RG 33/101, vol. 21, file Quebec Legal.
59 Canadian Association of Chiefs of Police, Minutes, 3rd Meeting, 1973–4. CACP Board of Directors, 6–7 February 1974.
60 *Canadian Police Chief*, October 1972, 19.
61 Ibid., 17.
62 Ibid., 19.
63 Ibid.
64 Ibid.
65 Greg Marquis, *Policing Canada's Century: A History of the Canadian Association of Chiefs of Police* (Toronto: University of Toronto Press, 1993), 345.
66 *Canadian Police Chief*, October 1969, April 1970.
67 Standing Committee on Justice and Legal Affairs, 1969, 868.
68 *Globe and Mail*, 30 April 1971, 7.
69 Letter from Chief of Police, Harold Adamson, Metropolitan Toronto Police, 5 May 1971, PAO, RG 4-2 file 496.2.
70 Miller, *The Hippies and American Values*, 82.
71 Quoted ibid., 76.
72 Memorandum to the Commissioner, Attn. Deputy Commissioner, Operations, from L. Gartner, Chief Superintendent (Field), 22 September 1970, PAO, RG 23-42, file 6.5.
73 Malcolm C. Courtis, assisted by Inez Dussuyer, *Attitudes to Crime and the Police in Toronto: A Report on Some Survey Findings* (Toronto: Centre of Criminology, University of Toronto, 1970), 73.
74 Study by the Vancouver Inner-City Service Project, July 1970, NAC, R923, vol. 10, file 10-3 Drug Commission.
75 Association des Chefs de Police et Pompiers de la Province de Québec, *Police-Jeunesse* (Montreal: Graph-O Pier Inc., 1970), 122.
76 Author's translation: 'important que l'image que les jeunes se font du

policier ne soit pas d'abord celle de la police matraqueuse lors d'une manifestation.' Ibid., 48.

77 Author's translation: 'En d'autres mots, il faut que le jeune [et le public] perçoive[nt] le policier comme un guide compréhensif mais ferme.' Ibid., 48.

78 Author's translation: 'des exigences souvent contradictoires [du public] vis-à-vis de la police ... Ces contacts éviteront que ne se crée, entre la police et la société ..., un fossé.' Ibid. 48–9.

79 Author's translation: 'en tant que figure d'autorité, investie d'un pouvoir particulier et dont le rôle ... est d'aider et de protéger les droits de tous.' Ibid., 94.

80 Author's translation: 'une habitude détestable et un vice qui réduit les adolescents à l'esclavage.' Ibid., 103–4.

81 Ibid., 67–8.

82 Author's translation: 'une formation adéquate et [avoir] la personnalité voulue.' Rapport de la vingt-troisième réunion du Comité interministériel sur les toxicomanies, 28 février 1974, ANQ-Q, E8, versement 1984-05-001/3.

83 Author's translation: 'Toutes les figures d'autorité ... ont tendance à être mal acceptées par les jeunes actuellement.' Ibid.

84 Rapport de la vingt-sixième réunion du Comité interministériel sur les toxicomanies, 24 mai 1974, ANQ-Q, E8, versement 1984-05-001/3.

85 Chief Constable John R. Fisk, Vancouver Police Department, 'Law and Order. Today and Tomorrow,' *RCMP Gazette: A National Police Service*, June 1971.

86 Appendix A, Local Board of Health Report No. 3 by Horace Brown, Chairman, 28 April 1970, City Council Minutes, Toronto, 1970, vol. 2, 14 May 1970 to 14 October 1970.

87 'Police Community Relations. Community Services Bureau. Community Service Officer Program,' *RCMP Gazette*, Fall 1974, 3.

88 Richard A. Weir, 'Federalism, Interest Groups, and Parliamentary Government: The Canadian Medical Association,' *Journal of Commonwealth Political Studies* 11:2 (July 1973), 168.

89 See Joan Price Boase, *Shifting Sands: Government–Group Relationships in the Health Care Sector* (Montreal and Kingston: McGill-Queen's University Press, 1994).

90 See Raymond Tatalovich, *The Politics of Abortion in the United States and Canada: A Comparative Study* (Armonk, NY: M.E. Sharpe, 1997).

91 John Sutton Bennett, *History of the Canadian Medical Association, 1954–94* (Ottawa: CMA/Association médicale canadienne, 1996).

92 Ibid., 163.

93 J. Robertson Unwin, *Review and Position Paper Re Non-Medical Use of Drugs with Particular Reference to Youth* (CMA Council on Community Heath Care Special Committee on Drug Misuse, 1969), 4.

94 Ibid., 5.

95 Ibid., 1.

96 G. Dion, 'Le rôle des intervenants du monde médical dans le contrôle des drogues au Canada au début du XXe siècle' (Montreal: École de criminologie, Université de Montréal, 1999).

97 Unwin, *Review and Position Paper Re Non-Medical Use of Drugs*, 2.

98 Canadian Medical Association, *Interim Brief Submitted by the Canadian Medical Association to the Commission of Inquiry into the Non-Medical Use of Drugs* (Ottawa: Canadian Medical Association, 1969).

99 Ibid., 38.

100 Ibid., 43.

101 Ibid., 56.

102 Ibid., 45.

103 Ibid., 56.

104 Ibid.

105 Canadian Medical Association, *Proceedings of General Council*, 1971, 67, 83.

106 CMA, *Proceedings of General Council*, 1972, 71.

107 Ibid.

108 Ibid., 72.

109 *CMA Journal*, June 1972, 1342.

110 *Globe and Mail* and *Montreal Gazette*, 16 June 1972.

111 *CMA Journal*, June 1972, 1341.

112 CMA, *Proceedings of General Council*, 1973, 96.

113 CMA, *Proceedings of General Council*, 1973.

114 CMA, *Proceedings of General Council*, 1974, 137.

115 *Globe and Mail*, 13 October 1967, 2.

116 Gormely, *Drugs and the Canadian Scene*, 101.

117 Ibid., 93.

118 *Addictions*, summer 1972, 5–6.

119 The Council on Drug Abuse, 'A Presentation to the (Le Dain Commission),' PAO, RG 3-26, box 125, file Council on Drug Abuse 1970–1971.

120 William B. McAllister, *Drug Diplomacy in the Twentieth Century: An International History* (London and New York: Routledge, 2000), 226; Burnham, *Bad Habits*; Sloman, *Reefer Madness*.

121 Letter from Frank C. Buckley, President, CODA, to J. Robarts, 16 March 1970, PAO, RG 3-26, vol. 125, file CODA; 'Some Background Information

about the Council on Drug Abuse (CODA),' PAO, RG 3-26, vol. 124, file Alcoholism and Drug addiction, June 1–30/70.

122 Council on Drug Abuse, 'A Presentation to the (Le Dain Commission),' POA, RG 3-26, box 125, file Council on Drug Abuse 1970–1971.

123 Project 70 Committee, Minutes of a meeting held 26 June, 1970 at Hincks Treatment Centre, Archives of the City of Toronto, SC40, box 65, file 11C Youth, Project 70.

124 Letter from Wells to John Robarts, 29 June 1970, PAO, RG 3-26, vol. 125, file Council on Drug Abuse.

125 Procès-verbal, 2e réunion du Comité interministériel sur le problème de la drogue dans le milieu scolaire et autres, 2 novembre 1972, ANQ-Q, E8, 84-05-001/3, file Procès-verbaux du Comité interministériel sur les toxico-manies.

126 Gormely, *Drugs and the Canadian Scene*, 165.

127 Unsigned and undated evaluation of discussion concerning drugs with Mr Panzica, East Garafraxa Township Central Public School, City of Toronto Archives, 1110222-1 series 10, Item 575; *Canadian Pharmaceutical Journal* 103:9 (September 1970), 10.

128 Council on Drug Abuse, 'Presentation to the (Le Dain Commission),' POA, RG 3-26, box 125, file Council on Drug Abuse 1970–1971.

129 *The Varsity*, 30 September 1970, 1–3.

130 J.P. Mackey, 'To Serve and Protect,' *Canadian Police Chief*, January 1970.

131 Council on Drug Abuse, 'Presentation to the (Le Dain Commission),' PAO, RG 3-26, box 125, file Council on Drug Abuse 1970–1971.

132 *Canadian Pharmaceutical Journal* 103:8 (August 1970), 23.

133 Report on CODA, NAC, RG 33/101, vol. 13, file Rittenhouse J.E.

134 *Globe and Mail*, 21 August 1970, 11; *Toronto Daily Star*, 22 August 1970, 6.

135 *Canadian Pharmaceutical Journal* 104:12 (December 1971), 24.

136 Council on Drug Abuse, 'Presentation to the (Le Dain Commission),' PAO, RG 3-26, box 125, file Council on Drug Abuse 1970–1971.

137 Ibid.

138 Project 70 Committee, Minutes of a meeting held 26 June 1970, at Hincks Treatment Centre, Archives of the City of Toronto, SC40, box 65, file 11C Youth, Project 70.

139 Letter from Thomas L. Wells to John Robarts, 29 June 1970; Letter from Wells to Robarts, 26 May 1970; Memorandum from M. Collins to Robarts, 27 May 1970; PAO, RG 3–26, vol. 125, file Council on Drug Abuse.

140 Ibid.

141 Memorandum de Maurice LeClair, M.D., Sous-ministre de la santé à Dr.

Aurèle Beaulnes, Coordonnateur des Programmes sur l'usage non-médical des drogues, 12 août 1971, NAC, RG 29, vol. 1581, file 1018-7-1 pt 1.

142 *Globe and Mail*, 28 July 1970, 10; *The Varsity*, 30 September 1970, 1.

143 Legislature of Ontario, *Debates*, 16 March 1972, 495–7; 15 May 1972, 2448–51.

144 Letter from Frank C. Buckley, President, CODA, to John Munro, 13 April 1970, NAC, RG 29, vol. 1280 file 55-10-2 pt 2; Letter from Stanley Haidasz to John Munro, Minister of National Health and Welfare, 7 June 1972, NAC, RG 29, vol. 1797, file 55-10-2 pt 1.

145 Memorandum from C.A. Pearson to Gerard Garneau, Executive Assistant to Dr LeClair, 7 July 1972, NAC, RG 29, vol. 1582, file 1018-7-1 pt 5; Memorandum from Assistant Deputy Minister, Health Protection Branch, A.B. Morrison, to Dr LeClair, Deputy Minister, National Health, 27 October 1972, NAC, RG 29, access 1985–86/235, vol. 54, file 6025-C57-1; Memorandum from A.B. Morrison, Assistant Deputy Minister, Health Protection Branch, to Maurice LeClair, Deputy Minister of National Health, 19 September 1973, NAC, RG 29, vol. 1582, file 1018-7-1 pt 3.

146 Letter from J. Dean Muncaster, Murray B. Koffler, and Frank C. Buckley to John Robarts, 24 July 1970; Letter from J. Robarts to J.D. Muncaster, 12 August 1970; Letter from William Kelly to John Robarts, 28 August 1970; Memorandum to Thomas L. Wells, Minister of Health, from John Robarts, 26 August 1970; Letter from T.L. Wells to J. Robarts, 3 September 1970, PAO, RG 3-26, box 125, file Council on Drug Abuse; Letter to Thomas L. Wells from J. Dean Muncaster, Chairman CODA Urgency Appeal, 21 September 1970; Letter from N.E. Mealing, Administrative Officer, to C.A. Westcott, Executive Assistant to the Minister of Education, 9 December 1970; Letter from Thomas L. Wells to Dr K.C. Charron, Deputy Minister of Health, 17 August 1970; Letter from H. David Archibald, Executive Director, ARF, to Thomas L. Wells, 27 October 1970, OPA, RG 10-1, file 2-54.

147 Letter to the Deputy Minister Dr K.C. Charron from N.E. Mealing, 17 November 1971; Letter from A.B.R. Lawrence, Minister, to Michael Harrison, President, CODA, 1 June 1971, OPA, RG 10-1 file 2-1155.

3. The Scientific Experts and Provincial Governments

1 *Montreal Gazette*, 22 May 1972, 6.

2 Letter from J.N. Crawford, Deputy Minister of National Health to the Minister of National Health, 15 July 1968, NAC, RG 29, vol. 1581, file C-1016-7-1A pt 1.

3 Lemieux, *L'étude des politiques publiques*, 31–4.

4 Kenneth J. Meier, *The Politics of Sin: Drugs, Alcohol and Public Policy* (Armonk, NY: M.E. Sharpe, 1994), 5.
5 Legislature of Ontario, *Debates*, 2, 6, and 12 March 1970, 158–9, 322, 511.
6 Ibid., 22 March 1967, 1645.
7 Ibid., 1647.
8 Ibid., 1630–1.
9 Ibid., 1649.
10 Ibid., 1649.
11 Ibid., 1647.
12 Ibid., 1647.
13 Ibid., 1647–51.
14 Legislature of Ontario, *Debates*, 5 June 1968, 3929.
15 Ibid., 26 November 1969, 8953–4; 28 November 1969, 9063.
16 David H. Archibald, *Alcohol and Drugs: Government Responsibility* (Melbourne, Australia: Third Leonard Ball Oration, Alcoholism Foundation of Victoria, 1970), 31.
17 Letter from H. David Archibald, Executive Director, ARF, to D. Richmond, Esq., Prime Minister's Office, 26 November 1964, PAO, RG 3-26, box 123, file Alcoholism and Drug Addiction Health Apr. 63–Dec. 65.
18 See Bruce L.R. Smith, *The Advisers: Scientists in the Policy Process* (Washington: Brookings Institution, 1992).
19 'Observations sur l' "Alcoholism and Drug Addiction Research Foundation of Ontario." Points de vue favorables à la création d'une fondation sur l'alcoolisme au Québec par L. Laforest et J.M. Bernard,' 7 janvier 1964, ANQ-Q, E8, 1984-05-001/5, file 5.1.7 (1964).
20 Memorandum to H. David Archibald from R.R. Robinson, 24 January 1964, Centre for Addiction and Mental Health Archives (CAMHA), ARF Collection, box 58-28, file Issues; 'Approach of the (ARF) to the Problem of Drug Dependence and Abuse,' by H. David Archibald, October 1968, CAMHA, ARF Collection, box 64-09, file Foundation–Federal Government Relations.
21 ARF, 'Future Management of Alcoholism in Ontario,' February 1965. A copy of the document was sent to Health Minister Matthew B. Dymond on 26 February 1965, PAO, RG 10, file 1-1-1-13.
22 'Policy and Planning for a Comprehensive Approach to Drug-Related Problems,' June 1970, CAMHA, ARF Collection, Box 08-10, file White Paper Drugs.
23 Legislature of Ontario, *Debates*, 7 June 1965, 3770; Letter from M.B. Dymond to J. Robarts, PAO, RG 3-26, vol. 123, file Alcoholism and Drug Addiction, Apr. 63–Dec. 65.
24 October draft, '1968 Constitutional Summary of the (ARF),' redrafted Octo-

ber 1968, from previous working documents and proposed to the Executive Director for submission to the Members of the Foundation for adoption as policy, CAMHA, ARF Collection, box 59-02, file Policies.

25 Letter from H. David Archibald, ARF, to Matthew B. Dymond, Minister of Health, 2 December 1966, PAO, RG 10, file 1-1-1-13.

26 Ibid.

27 'The Marihuana Problem and the Alcoholism and Drug Addiction Research Foundation,' 15 November 1966, PAO, RG 10, file 1-1-1-13. This document was attached to the letter sent by Archibald to Dymond on 2 December 1966.

28 David H. Archibald (compiled and edited by Barbara Fulton), *The Addiction Research Foundation: A Voyage of Discovery* (Toronto: ARF, 1990), 88, 91–3.

29 White Papers on Policy (on Alcoholism and Drugs), no date, no author, CAMHA, ARF Collection, box 08-09, file Policy and Planning White Paper.

30 Archibald, *The Addiction Research Foundation*, 93.

31 The CMA Council on Community Health Care's Sub-Committee on the Non-Medical Use of Drugs supported the position of the Ontario Medical Association. 'Report to C.M.A. Board of Directors from Council on Community Health Care Re Final Brief to (Le Dain Commission),' 14 March 1971, NAC, RG 33/101, vol. 18, file 3244.

32 Letter from H. David Archibald, Executive Director, ARF, to Gerald Le Dain, Chairman, Le Dain Commission, 6 February 1970, NAC, R 923, vol. 12, file 2; Letter to Dr A.B. Morrison, Assistant Deputy Minister, Food and Drug Directorate, from C.G. Miles, ARF, 26 November 1971; Letter from Morrison to Dr C.D. Webster, Research Division, ARF, 29 November 1971, NAC, RG 29, vol. 1312, file 909-7-52.

33 'Foreword to a Preliminary Report on the Marihuana Small Group Study,' ARF, 1 March 1972, CAMHA, ARF Collection, box 62-05, file Foreword to a Preliminary Report on the Marihuana.

34 October draft, '1968 Constitutional Summary of the (ARF).' CAMHA, ARF Collection, box 59-02, file Policies.

35 *A Plan For Action*, 10 September 1970, 'A Working Paper Prepared by the Youth Consultant of the Social Planning Council to Outline a Realistic and Effective Program to Lessen the Current Involvement with Illicit and Harmful Drugs by Young People in Metropolitan Toronto,' by John Fisher, Youth Consultant; Anne Smith-Bingham, Planning Assistant. Social Planning Council of Metropolitan Toronto, Archives of the City of Toronto, SC40 box 65, file 11.

36 David H. Archibald, 'Where We Are At ... A Time of Assessment,' presentation to Staff Conference, Geneva Park, 1971.

37 'Approach of the (ARF) to the Problem of Drug Dependence and Abuse by H. David Archibald,' October 1968, CAMHA, ARF Collection, Box 64-09, file Foundation–Federal Government Relations.

38 David H. Archibald, 'Perspective on Marihuana,' *Addictions* 15:2 (Summer 1968), 4.

39 'Policy and Planning for a Comprehensive Approach to Drug-Related Problems,' June 1970, CAMHA, ARF Collection, Box 08–10, file White Paper Drugs.

40 United Church of Canada, Board of Evangelism and Social Service, in collaboration with the ARF, *Handbook for Parents about Drugs* (Toronto: ARF, 1970), 14.

41 October draft, '1968 Constitutional Summary of the (ARF),' CAMHA, ARF Collection, box 59-02, file Policies; Letter from H. David Archibald, Executive Director, ARF, to Matthew B. Dymond, Minister of Health, 2 June 1969, CAMHA, ARF Collection, box 63-21, file Provincial Government: Minister of Health: 1969; Alcoholism and Drug Addiction Research Foundation, Education Division (A Review of the Education Program as of January 1967), CAMHA, ARF Collection, box 59-20, file Education Division.

42 Archibald, *The Addiction Research Foundation*, 95.

43 Ibid., 145–6.

44 Letter to Dr Stanley Haidasz, Parliamentary Secretary to Minister of Consumer and Corporate Affairs, from H. David Archibald, Executive Director, ARF, 6 May 1969, CAMHA, ARF Collection, 58-05 file Le Dain Commission Correspondence.

45 Archibald, *Alcohol and Drugs*.

46 Letter from C.E. Norris, City Clerk, City of Toronto, to A.A. Wishart, Minister of Justice and Attorney-General of Ontario, 1 February 1968; 'Background: Glue Sniffing Bothered People,' PAO, RG 10 1-1, box 34, file 34.24. The province of Ontario was not an exceptional case. In numerous letters and briefs submitted to the Le Dain Commission, individuals and groups asked for the sale of glue to be prohibited. NAC, RG 33/101, vols. 9–18.

47 Memorandum about Glue-sniffing, A.A. Wishart, Minister of Justice, to John Robarts, 5 March 1968; Letter from H. David Archibald to W.C. Bowman, Director of Public Prosecutions, Toronto, 1 March 1968, PAO, RG 3-26, vol. 125, file Alcohol and Drug Addiction, December 1967–January 1969; 'Glue-sniffing in Metropolitan Toronto, Statement from the (ARF),' by H. David Archibald, Executive Director, 8 January 1968, PAO, RG 10-1, box 39, file 34-24.

48 In his report submitted to the Housing, Fire and Legislation Committee of the City of Toronto, N.R. Speirs, Teacher Training Consultant of the ARF,

wrote that the prevalence of glue-sniffing was exaggerated. Reports of three cases at a particular school were in fact three reports about the same individual. 'At the height of the scare, when the habit was believed to be rampant, the Toronto Juvenile Court was aware of only five cases.' Speirs wrote that glue-sniffing was not significant compared with alcoholism and narcotic addiction. City Council Minutes, Toronto, 1968, vol. 1, June 1968–June 1969, App. A, Housing, Fire and Legislation Report no. 1, 207.

49 Letter from John Robarts to C. Edgar Norris, City Clerk, City of Toronto, 12 February 1968, PAO, RG 10 1-1, box 34, file 34.25.

50 Letter from George M. Foster, Metropolitan Clerk, Municipality of Metropolitan Toronto, to A.A. Wishart (December 1968); City Council, 12 March 1969; City Council Minutes, Toronto, 1969, vol. 1.

51 Legislature of Ontario, *Debates*, 25 April 1968, 2144–7.

52 *Addictions* 15:1 (Spring 1968), 3.

53 Eric Single and Norman Giesbrecht, 'Rates of Alcohol Consumption and Patterns of Drinking in Ontario, 1950–1975,' ADARF Substudy no. 961 (1978), quoted by Greg Marquis in 'Public Drunkenness and the Justice System: Canada, 1945–1980,' unpublished paper of Canadian Historical Association conference, Dalhousie University, May 2003, p. 11.

54 David H. Archibald, *A National Response to the Non-Medical Use of Drugs in Canada* (San Antonio, TX: NAAAP 21st Annual Meeting, 1970); 'Where We Are At'; 'Action communautaire face à l'alcool et aux drogues,' *Information sur l'alcoolisme et les autres toxicomanies* 7:2 (March–April 1971), 3–8; *Weighing the Alternatives* (Quebec City: Canadian Conference on Social Welfare, 1972); 'Attitude of the ARF towards the Legalization of Marijuana and Our Relations with the Le Dain Commission,' no author, no date, CAMHA, ARF Collection, box 58-05, file Le Dain Commission Correspondence.

55 Archibald, *Where We Are At*.

56 Ibid.

57 Memorandum to Thomas L. Wells, Minister of Health, from John Robarts, 26 August 1970; Letter from Wells to Robarts, 3 September 1970, PAO, RG 3-26, vol. 125, file Council on Drug Abuse.

58 Legislature of Ontario, *Debates*, 6 November 1969, 8091; 28 November 1969, 9060–1; Letters from J. Robarts, PAO, RG 3-26, box 124, files Alcoholism and Drug Addiction; Letters from Matthew B. Dymond, PAO, RG 10-1, box 35, file 35.3; Letters to and from Thomas L. Wells, PAO, RG 10-1, file 2-9.

59 *Globe and Mail*, 12 March 1970, 1.

60 *Toronto Daily Star*, 1 August 1969, 1; *Telegram* (Toronto), 30 May 1970; Gormely, *Drugs and the Canadian Scene*, 104; Letter from Dr Beatty Cotnam,

Supervising Coroner, to A.A. Wishart, Minister of Justice and Attorney-General, 11 June 1970, PAO, RG 4-2, file 445.3.

61 Réunion des ministres provinciaux de la Santé, 21 et 22 octobre 1968, ANQ-Q, E8, 1960-01-580/149, file 1968 – Septembre à Décembre inclus, Ministère de la Santé (Dossier général), Québec; Memorandum to D. Archibald, Executive Director, ARF, from M.B. Dymond, Minister of Health, 27 May 1969, Re: Submission from the Executive Director of Alcoholism Foundation in Quebec, CAMHA, ARF Collection, box 63-21, file Provincial Government, Minister of Health: 1969; Letter from M.B. Dymond, Minister of Health, Gov. of Ontario, to John Munro, Minister of National Health and Welfare, 28 May 1969, NAC, RG 33/101, vol. 21, file Ont. Government.

62 *Débats de l'Assemblée nationale*, 12 juillet 1971, 3551.

63 *Débats de l'Assemblée législative du Québec*, 10 décembre 1968, 4713.

64 Ibid.

65 Benoît Gaumer, Georges Desrosiers, and Othmar Keel, *Histoire du Service de santé de la ville de Montréal, 1865–1975* (Quebec: Les éditions de l'IQRC, 2002).

66 Lettre d'Eric-W. Kierans, Ministre de la Santé, à André Boudreau, directeur, Service médical sur l'Alcoolisme, 12 avril 1966, ANQ-Q, E8, 1977-07-000/18, file OPTAT 1968–73.

67 Author's translation: 'l'état endémique dans [les] écoles. Je crois que c'est exagéré.' *Débats de l'Assemblée législative du Québec*, 10 décembre 1968, 4719.

68 Author's translation: 'ne trouvent pas dans le monde adulte des modèles capables de nourrir leurs désirs de dépassement.' *Débats de l'Assemblée législative du Québec*, 10 décembre 1968, 4719.

69 Ibid., 4724–5.

70 Ibid., 4726–7.

71 Author's translation: 'la panique en pareille circonstance ... est mauvaise conseillère.' *Le Soleil*, 25 September 1968.

72 Au Docteur Laurent Lizotte, Sous-Ministre Adjoint, de Dominique Bédard, Directeur des Services psychiatriques, Ministère de la santé, 14 mars 1966, ANQ-Q, E8, S2, 1960-01-580/124, file Correspondance et autres documents, vol. 1.

73 Lettre à M. Claude Rioux, Sous-ministre associé à la législation, Ministère de la justice, de Jean-Paul Cloutier, Ministre de la Santé, 9 septembre 1968, ANQ-Q, E8, S2, 1960-01-580/124, file Correspondance et autres documents, vol. 2; Observations du bureau de législation à propos d'une réunion tenue le 9 juin 1970, avec l'OPTAT, à la demande de cet organisme, ANQ-Q, E8, S2, 190-01-580/125, file 1970 Comité d'étude et d'information sur l'alcoolisme; Lettre d'André Boudreau, directeur général de l'OPTAT, à Jacques

Brunet, sous-ministre, Ministère des Affaires sociales, 17 janvier 1972, ANQ-Q, E8, 1977-07-000/18, file OPTAT 1968–73.

74 Rencontre avec l'honorable Quenneville, Ministre d'état à la santé, 16 juillet 1970, ANQ-Q, E8, S2, 190-01-580/125; Lettre d'André Boudreau, directeur général de l'OPTAT, à Claude Castonguay, Ministre des Affaires sociales, 21 octobre 1971, ANQ-Q, E8, 1977-07-000/18, file OPTAT 1968–73.

75 'Observations sur l' "Alcoholism and Drug Addiction Research Foundation of Ontario"'; Lettre d'André Boudreau, directeur général de l'OPTAT, à Jacques Brunet, Sous-ministre, Ministère des Affaires sociales, 15 mars 1971; Lettre d'André Boudreau, directeur général de l'OPTAT, à Claude Castonguay, Ministre des Affaires sociales, 21 octobre 1971, ANQ-Q, E8, 1977-07-000/18 file OPTAT 1968–73; Mémoire de Gérard Frigon à M. Julien Chouinard au sujet de l'OPTAT, 9 novembre 1971, ANQ-Q, E8, 1984-05-001/4.

76 Lettre de Claude-E. Forget, Ministre, Ministère des Affaires sociales, à tout le personnel de l'OPTAT, 29 janvier 1975, ANQ-Q, E8, 84-05-001/1, file OPTAT, Intégration au M.A.S; Pierre Bergeron et France Gagnon, 'La prise en charge étatique de la santé au Québec: Émergence et transformations,' in Vincent Lemieux, Pierre Bergeron, Clermont Bégin, and Gérard Bélanger, Le système de santé au Québec: Organisations, acteurs et enjeux (Quebec: Presses de l'Université Laval, 2003), 7–33; Pierre Brisson, 'Développement du champ québécois des toxicomanies au XXe siècle,' in Pierre Brisson, ed., L'usage des drogues et la toxicomanies, vol. 3 (Montreal: Gaetan Morin Éditeur, 2000, 3–44.

77 Author's translation: 'un état pathologique lié à la consommation d'alcool et perturbant l'équilibre physique et psychique ainsi que le comportement social de celui qui en est atteint.'

78 Lois refondues du Québec, 1978: chapitre 0-2, 1.

79 'Le festival pop Manseau,' par Jean-Marc Bernard, Léandre Bilodeau et André Jacob, Service de la recherche, 28 août 1970, ANQ-Q, E8, 1984-05-001, file 6.3; Lettre d'André Boudreau, directeur général, à Jacques Brunet, sous-ministre, ministère des Affaires sociales, 12 mai 1971, ANQ-Q, E8, 1977-07-000/18, file OPTAT 1968–73.

80 Lettre d'André Boudreau, directeur général, à Jacques Brunet, sous-minis-tre, ministère des Affaires sociales, 12 mai 1971, ANQ-Q, E8, 1977-07-000/18, file OPTAT 1968–73.

81 Toxicomanies 1:1, 1.

82 Marcel Bougie, 'Méthodologie et principes de base de la prévention,' Information sur l'alcoolisme et les autres toxicomanies 5:5 (November–December 1968), 7–9; André Boudreau, 'Les toxicomanies: Causes et prévention,'

Information sur l'alcoolisme et les autres toxicomanies 5:6 (January-February 1969), 3–6; Association des Chefs de Police et Pompiers de la Province de Québec, *Police-Jeunesse*, 75–6.

83 Author's translation: 'pour les malades et que les bien-portants n'en ont aucunement besoin.' 'Quelques commentaires concernant le rapport provisoire de la Commission (Le Dain),' sans date (juillet 1970), ANQ-Q, E8, 1984-05-001/4, file Commission Le Dain.

84 Author's translation: 'qu'un palliatif, une aide temporaire.' André Boudreau, 'Le médecin face à la drogue,' *Information sur l'alcoolisme et les autres toxicomanies* 7:1 (January–February 1971), 5.

85 Author's translation: 'optimum de l'individu; éducatives, préventives et psychothérapiques.' Editorial, *Toxicomanies* 1:6 (June 1968), 3–4; Boudreau, 'Les toxicomanies.'

86 Author's translation: 'envisager des solutions qui non seulement sont de nature à contribuer à la prévention des toxicomanies, mais encore à prévenir que l'utilisation des drogues soit remplacée par autre chose qui ne serait guère mieux pour la santé de l'école et de ceux qui la fréquentent.' Lettre à Gérard Nepveu, sous-ministre adjoint, Ministère des Affaires sociales, de Roger Richard, Service de l'aide aux ressources thérapeutiques, OPTAT, 13 juillet 1972, ANQ-Q, E8, 1960-01-580/202, file Éléments d'un programme d'information sur les drogues; Rapport de la vingt-sixième réunion du Comité interministériel sur les toxicomanies tenue le 24 mai 1974, ANQ-Q, E8, 1984-05-001/3.

87 Author's translation: 'en toute connaissance de cause.' Marcel Bougie, 'Le phénomène de la drogue: Occasion de réfléchir et point de départ,' *Information sur l'alcoolisme et les autres toxicomanies* 4:3 (May–June 1968), 6; Bougie, 'Méthodologie et principes de base de la prévention,' 7.

88 *Le Soleil*, 11 juin 1969; Mémoire de Gérard Frigon à M. Julien Chouinard au sujet de l'OPTAT.

89 Service de la diffusion et de l'action communautaire, Priorités relatives à nos activités de 1973, par Marcel Bougie, directeur, 16 janvier 1973, ANQ-Q, E8, 1977-07-000/007, file Groupe de travail sur l'usage non médical; 'Publication et diffusion de l'information écrite, visuelle, parlée. Inventaire, Évaluation, Suggestions,' par Rénald Chabot, Service de Diffusion et d'Animation, OPTAT, mars 1974, ANQ-Q, E8, 84-05-001/8, file 5.2.77.

90 Lettre d'André Boudreau, Directeur général de l'OPTAT, à Paul Corbeil, Secrétaire particulier, Cabinet du Ministre, Ministère de la Santé du Québec, 21 novembre 1969, ANQ-Q, E8, 1960-01-580/156, file Septembre à Décembre 1969, Ministère de la santé nationale et du bien-être social, Ottawa.

91 Lettre de Jacques Brunet, Sous-ministre, Ministère des Affaires sociales, à Maurice LeClair, sous-ministre adjoint, Ministère de la Santé nationale et du Bien-être social, 6 juin 1972; Comité conjoint et Projets d'innovation dans le domaine de la drogue, ministère des Affaires sociales (23 mars 1972), ANQ-Q, E8, 1977-07-000/007, file Groupe de travail sur l'usage non médical; Lettre de Jacques Brunet, Sous-ministre, Affaires sociales, Québec, à Maurice LeClair, Sous-ministre de la Santé, Ministère de la Santé et du Bien-être social Canada, 23 novembre 1973, NAC, RG 29, volume 1582, file 1018-7-1 pt 3; Note aux membres du groupe de travail sur l'usage non médical des drogues provenant de Louise Garant, Direction des Programmes spéciaux, Ministère des Affaires sociales, 18 octobre 1973, ANQ-Q, E8, 1984-05-001/1, file Correspondance interne 1971–75 Jean-Claude De l'Orme, directeur.
92 Letter from André Boudreau, MD, Executive Director, OPTAT, to Graeme T. Haig, President of the Canadian Foundation on Alcoholism, 16 May 1969, CAMHA, ARF Collection, box 63-21, file Provincial Government, Minister of Health: 1969; Lettre de Mercédès C. Gauvin, ministère des Affaires intergouvernementales, à Jean-Paul Cloutier, ministre de la Santé, de la Famille et du Bien-être social, 17 juillet 1969, ANQ-Q, E8, 1984-05-001/1; Lettre d'André Boudreau, Directeur général, OPTAT, à Paul Corbeil, Secrétaire particulier, Cabinet du Ministre de la Santé, 21 novembre 1969, ANQ-Q, E8, 1960-01-580/156, file Septembre à Décembre 1969, ministère de la Santé nationale et du Bien-être social.
93 Lettre d'André Boudreau à Jean-Paul Cloutier, Ministre, Ministère de la Santé, 11 juillet 1969, ANQ-Q, E8, S2, 1960-01-580/124, file Correspondance et autres documents, vol. 3.
94 Commentaires sur le rapport de la commission Le Dain (le traitement) sans date; Quelques notes et commentaires au sujet de la commission Le Dain (rapport final) en vue de la préparation de documents à être remis au Premier ministre, sans date, ANQ-Q, E8, 84-05-001/4, file Commission Le Dain; Letter from J.N. Crawford, Deputy Minister of National Health to the Minister of National Health, 15 July 1968, NAC, RG 29, vol. 1581, file C-1016-7-1A pt 1.
95 Mémoire aux autorités du ministère des Affaires sociales présenté par l'OPTAT, 22 février 1972, ANQ-Q, E8, 1977-07-000/18, file OPTAT 1968–73.
96 B.C. *Legislative Debates*, 2 February 1972, 253.
97 Ibid., 27 January 1972, 93.
98 Ibid., 4 April 1973, 2147; 19 June 1975, 3783.
99 Ibid., 29 April 1975, 1857.

100 Ibid., 5 March 1973, 990–1; 4 April 1973, 2156–7; 14 March 1974, 1164.
101 Province of British Columbia, *Statutes*, chapter 37, 1967.
102 Ibid., chapter 21, 1967.
103 Whitaker, *Drugs and the Law*, 147.
104 *Globe and Mail*, 29 January 1970, 9.
105 *B.C. Legislative Debates*, 24 January 1972, 28–9.
106 Ibid., 25 and 26 January 1972; 1 and 2 February 1972.
107 Ibid., 1 February 1972, 223.
108 Ibid., 2 March 1973, 967.
109 Ibid., 21 February 1974, 432–34; 12 March 1974; 17 April 1975; 19 June 1975.
110 Ibid., 18 October 1973, 773–4.
111 Ibid., 3 April 1970, 783; 1 February 1972, 234–5; 4 April 1973, 2147–9;
     21 February 1974, 432–4; 19 June 1975.
112 Memorandum from Jeffrey Bishop, M.D., Director, Drug Advisory
     Bureau, to Dr R.A. Chapman, Director-General, Food and Drug Director-
     ate, 20 October 1970, NAC, RG 29, vol. 1314, file 909-7-127.
113 NAFBC, *Annual Reports*.
114 Brief to the Honourable John Munro, Minister of National Health and Wel-
     fare, 'An Assessment of the Current Drug Dependency Situation, Capabil-
     ities and Requirements,' prepared by the NAFBC, January 1969, NAC,
     R 923, vol. 18, file 18-32; 'A Suggested New Approach to the Increasing
     Problem of the Use and Abuse of Mood-Changing Drugs,' February 1968,
     NAC, MG 32 C 12, vol. 6, file Drugs. Non-medical use, 1968–1969.
115 Brief to John Munro, 'An Assessment' and 'A Suggested New Approach.'
116 NAFBC, *1969 Annual Report*, 11–19.
117 Ibid., 9.
118 Russell, *Survey of Drug Use in Selected British Columbia Schools*, 107–8.
119 Brief to John Munro, 'An Assessment' and 'A Suggested New Approach.'
120 Gormely, *Drugs and the Canadian Scene*, 66.
121 NAFBC, *1968 Annual Report*, 9.
122 Brief to John Munro, 'An Assessment' and 'A Suggested New Approach.'
123 Brief to John Munro, 'A Suggested New Approach.'
124 Ibid.
125 Brief to John Munro, 'An Assessment' and 'A Suggested New Approach.'
126 NAFBC, *1972 Annual Report*.
127 *Toronto Daily Star*, 29 January 1970, 1.
128 Ibid., 16 June 1970, 13.
129 'Year of Decision' by H.F. Hoskin, 12 May 1972, PAO, RG 4-2, file 534.2.
130 From J.A. Macauley, Insp., Assistant Officer in Charge, Criminal Investiga-
     tion Branch, to CO E Victoria, 26 August 1969; Telegram from E DIV to

COMMR OTT, 29 August (1969); Letter from J.R.R. Carriere, A/Comm'r, Director, Criminal Investigation, to CO E Victoria, 2 September 1969, NAC, RG 18, vol. 4831, file GC 310-10 (1969) pt 1; Letter for H.F. Hoskin, Executive Director (HAFBC), to The Commissioner, RCMP, attention J.R.R. Carriere, A/Comm'r, Criminal Investigation, 20 November 1969, NAC, RG 18, vol. 4831, file GC 310-10 (1970) pt 2.

131 ARF, *The Journal*, 1 February 1976, 1.

132 Réunion des ministres provinciaux de la Santé, 21 et 22 octobre 1968, ANQ-Q, E8, 1960-01-580/149, file 1968 – Septembre à Décembre inclus, Ministère de la Santé (Dossier général), Québec.

133 Memorandum to Dr J.H. Maloney, Minister of Health, and to Gordon L. Bennett, Minister of Education and Justice, from G.K. Cowan, 28 January 1971, PEIPARO, RG 22, series 8, sub-series 2, file 38.

134 Presentation to Senate Committee Hearings Placing Marihuana under the Food and Drugs Act, 'Cannabis: The Dangerous Communications Gap,' by G.K. Cowan, Consultant to Department of Education, PEI, Member of the PEI Drug Education Committee, 18 February 1975, NAC, MG 32 C 55, vol. 5, file 5/5 Drugs – Documents. These arguments were included in the first brief submitted to the Le Dain Commission in February 1970. PEIPURO, RG 22, series 8, sub-series 2, file 38.

135 *Montreal Gazette*, 8 September 1971.

136 Letter to Carl Goldenberg, Chairman, Senate Legal and Constitutional Affairs, Committee re Food and Drug Act Hearings, from W. Bennett Campbell, Minister of Education, 5 February 1975, NAC, MG 32 C-55, vol. 4, file Drugs – Correspondence from Eastern provinces and Quebec.

137 Presentation to Senate Committee, 'Cannabis.'

138 Ibid.

139 'New Research Findings Compel the (P.E.I.) Government to Oppose Legalization of Marijuana,' Brief presented to the (Le Dain Commission), by J. Elmer Blanchard, Attorney-General, 21 February 1970, PEIPARO, RG 22, series 8, sub-series 2, file 38.

140 Letter from J.E. Blanchard to John Munro, Minister of National Health and Welfare, 4 March 1970, NAC, RG 29, vol. 1280, file 55-10-2 pt 2.

141 Ibid.

142 Ibid.

143 Letter from J. Elmer Blanchard, Attorney-General, P.E.I., to Arthur A. Wishart, Attorney-General, Ontario, 26 March 1970, PAO, RG 10-1 file 2-55.

144 'A Drug Is Guilty until Proven Innocent,' Statement directed by the late Honourable J. Elmer Blanchard, Attorney-General and by the Honourable

Gordon Bennett, Minister of Education and Justice (P.E.I.), 6 November 1970, NAC, RG33/101, vol. 9, file 277.

145 Ibid.

146 Letter to Thomas Wells, Minister of Health, from Gordon L. Bennett, Minister of Justice and Attorney-General, Minister of Education, P.E.I., 12 January 1971, PAO, RG 10-1, file 2-544; Letter from John N. Turner, Minister of Justice and Attorney-General of Canada, to Gordon L. Bennett, 8 February 1971, PEIPARO, RG 22, series 8, sub-series 2, file 38.

147 Letter from Edgar H. Gerhart, Attorney-General, Province of Alberta, to Gordon L. Bennett, Minister of Justice and Attorney-General, P.E.I., 4 February 1971; Letter from L.R. Peterson, Attorney-General, Province of British Columbia, to Gordon L. Bennett, 12 February 1971, PEIPARO, RG 22, series 8, sub-series 2, file 38.

148 Author's translation: 'le manque d'objectivité flagrant,' 'mentalité insulaire,' 'éviter la contamination du phénomène de l'usage de la marijuana.' Commentaires relatifs au mémoire présenté par l'Honorable J. Elmer Blanchard, à la Commission (Le Dain) (avril 1970), ANQ-Q, E8, 84-05-001/4, file Commission Le Dain.

149 Letter from H. David Archibald, Executive Director, to Thomas Wells, Minister of Health, 15 April 1970, PAO, RG 10-1, file 2-8.

150 Letter to Marc Lalonde, Minister of Health, from Bruce L. Stewart, Acting Minister of Health, P.E.I., 10 July 1974, NAC, RG 29, vol. 1582, file 1018-7-1 pt 3; Memorandum to Mr Paul Woodstock from R.A. Draper, 6 November 1973, NAC, RG 29, volume 1582, file 1018-7-1 pt 5; Presentation to Senate Committee, 'Cannabis.'

151 Memorandum to the Commanding Officer, H Division, from J. Mudge, Supt., Criminal Investigation Branch, 21 July 1970, NAC, RG 18, vol. 4831, file GC 310-10 (1970), pt 5.

152 Craig Heron, *Booze: A Distilled History* (Toronto: Between the Lines, 2003).

153 Suzanne Morton, *At Odds: Gambling and Canadians 1919–1969* (Toronto: University of Toronto Press, 2003), 187.

154 Morton writes that 'gambling became not a vice or a moral weakness, but a potentially addictive activity for certain vulnerable individuals' (ibid., 178).

4. Debating Marijuana Use

1 *House of Commons Debates*, 1 May 1969, 8203.

2 *House of Commons, Standing Committee on Justice and Legal Affairs*, 31 October 1967, 42–3.

3 Memorandum to the Deputy Minister of National Health and Deputy Minister of National Welfare from Director, Personnel Administration, 25 April 1969, NAC, RG 29, vol. 1602, file 2 pt 1.

4 To Solicitor General from Deputy Solicitor General, Re: Committee of Inquiry RE Drugs, 18 March 1969, NAC, RG 18, vol. 4831, file GC 310-10 (1969) pt 1.

5 Memorandum, Inquiry into the Non-Medical Use of Drugs, 31 March 1969, NAC, RG 18, vol. 4831, file GC 310-10 (1969) pt 1.

6 Memorandum to the Cabinet, 25 March 1969, NAC, RG 29, vol. 1602, file 2, pt 1.

7 Ibid.; Memorandum to the Cabinet, 20 May 1969, NAC, RG 29, access 1985–86/235, box 57, file 6027-3-6 pt 1; Letter from Gerald Le Dain to John Munro, 5 August 1969; Letter from John Munro to George McIlraith, Solicitor General, and John Turner, Minister of Justice, 7 October 1969, NAC, RG 29, vol. 1280, file 55-10-2 pt 1.

8 Memorandum to the Minister from the Deputy Minister of National Welfare, Joseph W. Willard, 1 April 1969, NAC, RG 29, vol. 1602, file 2 pt 1.

9 *Globe and Mail*, 3 May 1969. See also *La Presse*, 2 May 1969, 13; *Le Devoir*, 2 May 1969, 1; *Toronto Star*, 2 May 1969, 4; and *Winnipeg Free Press*, 2 May 1969, 1.

10 Gerald Le Dain, 'The Canadian Commission of Inquiry into Non-Medical Use of Drugs,' in A.S. Treback and K.B. Zeese, eds., *The Great Issues of Drug Policy* (Washington: Drug Policy Foundation, 1990), 2; P.G. Erickson and R.G. Smart, 'Canada,' in Stanley Einstein, ed., *The Community's Response to Drug Use* (New York: Pergamon Press, 1980), 102–3.

11 Statement by Gerald Le Dain, Chairman (Le Dain Commission), at the First Public Hearing in Winnipeg, 13 November 1969, NAC, RG 25, vol. 10485, file 45-CDA-9-1.

12 Opinions and Recommendations Regarding the Law, as Found in the Public Hearings, 29 June 1971, NAC, R 923, vol. 26, file 26-14.

13 Preliminary Submission subject to Later Consideration, the Canadian Psychiatric Association, (Le Dain Commission), January 1970, NAC, RG 33/101, vol. 10, file 968.

14 Ibid.

15 Ibid.

16 Submission by the Canadian Psychiatric Association to the (Le Dain Commission), 19 February 1971, NAC, RG 33/101, vol. 17, file 2534.

17 Gormely, *Drugs and the Canadian Scene*, 96.

18 Brief submission to the (Le Dain Commission) by the Canadian Pharmaceutical Association, March 1970, NAC, RG 33/101, vol. 11, file 1087.

19 Ibid.
20 Ibid.
21 Brief by the Pharmaceutical Association of the Province of British Columbia, 30 October 1969, NAC, RG 33/101, vol. 16, file 1738; Brief to the (Le
Dain Commission) by the Alberta Pharmaceutical Association, 17 April
1970, ibid., vol. 12, file 1180.
22 Mémoire présenté à la (Commission Le Dain) par le Collège des pharmaciens du Québec, 7 Novembre 1969, NAC, RG 33/101, vol. 14, file 1681.
23 Brief by the Pharmaceutical Manufacturers Association of Canada, 15 May
1970, NAC, RG 33/101, vol. 12, file 1274.
24 A Submission to the (Le Dain Commission) by the Canadian Mental Health
Association, February 1971, NAC, RG 33/101, vol. 17, file 2535.
25 'More study urged: Doctor says marijuana legalization premature,'
Montreal Gazette, 26 February 1970.
26 'The Le Dain Report: A Detailed Analysis and Critique of the "Interim
Report" by F.W. Lundell, M.D., Assoc. Prof. Psychiatry, McGill University,
5 November 1970, NAC, RG 33/101, vol. 18, file 5906.
27 Canadian Student Affairs Association, *The Loyola Conference on Student Use
and Abuse of Drugs* (Montreal: 1968), 37.
28 Ibid., 38.
29 Letter to Gerald Le Dain from Conrad J. Schwarz, Consultant Psychiatrist,
University of British Columbia, 6 November 1969, NAC, RG 33/101, vol. 9,
file 498.
30 'A Critique of the Interim Report of the (Le Dain Commission)' by Conrad
J. Schwarz, 30 June 1970, NAC, RG 33/101, vol. 13, file 1536.
31 Letter to Dr R.B. Miller (Le Dain Commission), from Conrad J. Schwarz,
30 June 1971, NAC, RG 33/101, vol. 19, file Schwarz.
32 Submission by Lionel Solursh, the Toronto Western Hospital, 7 November
1969, NAC, RG 33/101, vol. 16, file 1735.
33 All submissions are to be found in NAC, RG 33/101. Brief by the Administrative Staff of Charlottetown Public Schools (vol. 17, file 2079); Brief by the
British Columbia Parent-Teacher Federation (vol. 10, file 982); Brief by the
Edmonton Public School Board, September 1969 (vol. 12, file 1166); Brief
by the London Board of Education, 22 May 1970 (vol. 13, file 1356); Brief by
the Ottawa Roman Catholic Separate School Board (vol. 14, file 1692); Brief
by the PEI Federation of Home and School Associations (vol. 15, file 1720);
Brief by the Protestant School Board of Greater Montreal (vol. 14, file 1680);
Brief by the Regina Board of Education (vol. 11, file 1114); Brief by the Sudbury Board of Education (vol. 12, file 1240); Brief by the Toronto School
Board (vol. 15, file 1721).

34 In 1971, the Catholic church did not comment on the marijuana issue, except to state that society had the right to put control mechanisms in place to regulate illegal drugs. However, it invited society, and in particular youth, to question their use of non-medical drugs. Épiscopat canadien, 'La drogue: Un document de travail sur l'usage non médical de la drogue,' *Information sur l'alcoolisme et les autres toxicomanies* 7:2 (March–April 1971), 25.

35 Brief to the (Le Dain Commission) by the Toronto Stake of the Church of Jesus Christ of Latter-Day Saints, NAC, RG 33/101, vol. 13, file 1510; and by the Wesleyan Methodist Church of America in Canada, Trenton, Ontario, 19 August 1970, ibid., vol. 16, file 1834.

36 All submissions are to be found in NAC, RG 33/101. Brief by the Charlottetown Inter-Faith Group and the Priests' Senate of the Diocese of Charlottetown (vol. 16, file 1728); Brief by the First United Church, Port Alberni (vol. 15, file 1706); Brief by the Salvation Army, February 1971 by Commissioner C.D. Wiseman, Leader of the Salvation Army in Canada (vol. 18, file 3074); Recommendation from Hamilton Conference of the United Church of Canada, 17–20 May 1971 (vol. 18, file 4653); Brief by the Board of Evangelical and Social Service of the United Church of Canada (vol. 13, file 1631); 'Marijuana: A Study and Recommendations by a Subcommittee of the Social Responsibility Committee of the Unitarian Church of Vancouver,' April 1968 (vol. 15, file 1707).

37 Lettre de Jean-Guy Cardinal, ministre de l'Éducation, à Gerald Le Dain, Président, 9 octobre 1969, NAC, RG 33/101, vol. 21, file Quebec Government; Rapport à la (Commission Le Dain) de l'(OPTAT), Novembre 1969, ibid., vol. 14, file 1676.

38 'Brief on a Suggested New Approach to the Increasing Problem of the Use and Abuse of Mood Changing Drugs' by the (NAFBC), First issue – February 1968, Second issue – August 1968, NAC, RG 33/101, vol. 10, file 969; NAFBC Presentation to the (Le Dain) Commission, 30 October 1969, ibid., vol. 16, file 1746.

39 The Ontario health minister expressed his satisfaction that the Le Dain Commission would call upon ARF. Letter from Thomas L. Wells to Gerald Le Dain, 7 October 1969, NAC, RG 33/101, vol. 21, file Ont. Government.

40 Addiction Research Foundation of Ontario, *Preliminary Brief to the Commission of Inquiry Into the Non-Medical Use of Drugs* (Toronto: ARF, 1969), 27.

41 All submissions are to be found in NAC, RG 33/101. 'A Brief to the (Le Dain Commission) on behalf of the Alberta Government' by Robert Clark, Minister of Education and Minister of Youth, 17 April 1970 (vol. 13, file 1519); Brief by the Alcoholism Foundation of Manitoba, December 1969

(vol. 14, file 1691); Brief by the New Brunswick Interdepartmental Committee on Drug Abuse, February 1970 (vol. 16, file 1725); Summary of Brief prepared by the Department of Public Welfare, Province of Nova Scotia, 29 January 1970 (vol. 14, file 1668); Brief by the Alcoholism and Drug Addiction Foundation of Newfoundland, 31 January 1970 (vol. 15, file 1695); Brief by the Saskatchewan Alcoholism Commission, Division of Education, 9 April 1970 (vol. 11, file 1111).

42 Although the Montreal Police Department submitted a brief, I was unable to find it at the National Archives of Canada.

43 The Non-Medical Use of Drugs: A Report to the (Le Dain Commission)' by the Vancouver City Police Department, October 1969, NAC, RG 33/101, vol. 15, file 1702.

44 Memorandum to the Deputy Commissioner OPS from the DCI, 20 August 1969, NAC, RG 18, vol. 4831, file GC 310-10 (1969) pt 1.

45 Outgoing Message to RCMP Divisions from J.A. Macauley, Insp. Asst. OIC CIB, 15 December 1969, NAC, RG 18, vol. 4831, file GC 310-10 (1970) pt 2.

46 Letter from J.R.R. Carriere, A/Comm'r, Director, Criminal Investigation, to various RCMP divisions, 23 September 1969, NAC, RG 18, vol. 4831, file GC 310-10 (1969) pt 1.

47 Royal Canadian Mounted Police, *Brief to the Committee of Inquiry Into the Non-Medical Use of Drugs*, 1969, 17–18; Memorandum to the Deputy Commissioner OPS from the DCI, 20 August 1969; Memorandum to the OIC CIB Attn: Insp. Macauley, 6 August 1969; From J.A. Macauley, Insp., Assistant Officer in Charge, Criminal Investigation Branch, to CO E Victoria, 26 August 1969; Letter from J.R.R. Carriere, A/Comm'r, Director, Criminal Investigation, to CO E Victoria, 2 September 1969, NAC, RG 18, vol. 4831, file GC 310-10 (1969) pt 1.

48 Second Brief Presented to the (Le Dain Commission), 11 March 1971, NAC, RG 33/101, vol. 19, file 7446.

49 RCMP, *Brief to the Committee of Inquiry*, 22.

50 Second Brief Presented to the (Le Dain Commission), 11 March 1971, NAC, RG 33/101, vol. 19, file 7446.

51 RCMP, *Brief to the Committee of Inquiry*, 27.

52 A letter to D.H. Christie from J.A. Macauley, Insp., Assistant Officer in Charge, Criminal Investigation Branch, 2 December 1968, NAC, RG33/101, vol. 9, file 309; Memorandum to Officer from the DCI, 26 August 1969, NAC, RG 18, vol. 4831, file GC 310-10 (1969) pt 1; Second Brief Presented to the (Le Dain Commission), 11 March 1971, NAC, RG 33/101, vol. 19, file 7446.

53 RCMP, *Brief to the Committee of Inquiry*, 16.

54 Ibid., 21–2.
55 Second Brief Presented to the (Le Dain Commission), NAC, RG 33/101, vol. 19, file 7446.
56 Brief from the Department of the Solicitor General, December 1969, PAO, RG 4-2, file 445.3.
57 Ibid.
58 Brief by the Saskatchewan University Students' Union, Regina Campus, 9 April 1970, Brief by Unnamed Fourth Year Student in the Education Department of the University of Saskatchewan, NAC, RG 33/101, vol. 11, file 1113.
59 Submission to the (Le Dain Commission), Law Student's Association, UBC, October 1969, NAC, RG 33/101, vol. 15, file 1710.
60 Brief by Rochdale College, 9 June 1970, NAC, RG 33/101, vol. 9, file 742.
61 Remarks submitted to the (Le Dain Commission), 8 November 1969, by John L. Aimers, National Director for Quebec Young Progressive Conservatives of Canada, NAC, RG 33/101, vol. 14, file 1685; Brief to the (Le Dain Commission) by the Canadian Student Liberals, 14 November 1969, ibid., vol. 16, file 1741; Brief to the (Le Dain Commission) by the Toronto and District Liberal Association, 29 October 1970, ibid., vol. 17, file 2497.
62 NAC, RG 33/101, vol. 18, file 3288, CEGEP de Trois-Rivières, 15 October 1970.
63 NAC, RG 33/101, vol. 14, file 1682, Dawson College, 7 November 1969.
64 Brief Prepared for the (Le Dain Commission), by the Council of the Students' Union, Drug Committee, Memorial University, 31 January 1970, NAC, RG 33/101, vol. 15, file 1694.
65 Brief by John F. Brady, Daniel R. Ross, Carl F. Grindstaff, and Edward F. Ryan, 22 May 1970, NAC, RG 33/101, vol. 13, file 1298.
66 Burnham, *Bad Habits*, 126.
67 *La Presse*, 4 June 1971, A2; Burnham, *Bad Habits*.
68 Gormely, *Drugs and the Canadian Scene*, 105.
69 Brief by the Young Lawyers Conference of the Alberta Section of the Canadian Bar Association, by Gilbert J. Clark and Brian C. Stevenson, 16 April 1970, NAC, RG 33/101, vol. 12, file 1173.
70 Brief by the British Columbia Civil Liberties Association, 30 October 1969, NAC, RG 33/101, vol. 15, file 1713.
71 Opposition to legalization (all submissions to be found in NAC, RG 33/101): besides the Vancouver District of the WCTU and the WCTU of BC, there were the B'nai B'rith Women of Canada, the Canadian Federation of Christian Reformed Ladies Societies (vol. 13, file 1522), the Edmonton North Presbyterian United Church Women (vol. 18, file 3572), the Elizabeth

242   Notes to pages 142–4

Fry Society of British Columbia, letter from Phyllis Haslam, Executive Director, the Elizabeth Fry Society, Toronto Branch, to Chair Gerald Le Dain, 27 October 1969 (vol. 15, file Elizabeth Fry Society), the Hamilton and District Council of Women (vol. 12, file 1275), the Hamilton Presbyterian United Church Women (vol. 17, file 3031), the Manitoba Women's Institute (vol. 19, file 6427), the Moose Jaw Council of Women (vol. 18, file 3184), Mouvement des femmes chrétiennes (vol. 17, file 2332), the Peel North District Woman's Institute (vol. 19, file 7468), the Provincial Council of Women of Ontario (vol. 12, file 1247), the Provincial Council of Women of Saskatchewan, the Saskatchewan Hospital Auxiliaries Association (vol. 19, file 7466), the St Patrick's Catholic Women's League (vol. 17, file 2383), the Saskatchewan Federation of Home and School Associations (vol. 10, file 878); the Swift Current Local Council of Women (vol. 11, file 1118), the University Women's Club of Mississauga (vol. 17, file 2371); the Woman's Christian Temperance Union of Manitoba (vol. 10, file 854).

72 Presentation to the (Le Dain Commission), Provincial Council of Women of Saskatchewan, 1970 (vol. 12, file 1200). The briefs by the B'nai B'rith Women of Canada (ibid., vol. 18, file 3186) and by the Swift Current Local Council of Women (ibid., vol. 11, file 1118) contained similar references.

73 The authors quoted an article by Jurate Kazickas, *Vancouver Sun*, 22 November 1969. Brief to the (Le Dain Commission), (WCTU) Vancouver District, NAC, RG 33/101, vol. 13, file 1590.

74 Ibid.

75 Letter to the General Secretary, CMA, from the Vancouver District, WCTU, 3 February 1971, NAC, RG 33/101, vol. 23, file BC Rehabilitation and Welfare Agencies.

76 Brief prepared for the (Le Dain Commission) by the Elizabeth Fry Society of British Columbia, NAC, RG 33/101, vol. 15, file Elizabeth Fry Society of BC.

77 The following groups opposed legalization but supported some form of liberalization of marijuana's legal status: the B'nai B'rith Women of Canada, the Elizabeth Fry Society of British Columbia, the Swift Current Local Council of Women, the Elizabeth Fry Society, Toronto Branch, the Provincial Council of Women of Ontario, the St Patrick's Catholic Women's League, the Saskatchewan Federation of Home and School Associations, the University Women's Club of Mississauga, the Woman's Christian Temperance Union of Manitoba.

78 Brief by the WCTU Vancouver District, 19 June 1972, NAC, RG 33/101, vol. 19, file Vancouver District WCTU.

79 Brief by the (WCTU of BC), NAC, RG 33/101, vol. 23, file BC Rehabilitation and Welfare Agencies. In her book on gambling, Suzanne Morton identified

the Woman's Christian Temperance Union as one of many groups opposed to the legalization of gambling. She argues that this organization feared for the welfare of families and children. Although Morton does not identify any specific groups among the WCTU movement that was very active on the gambling issue, the WCTU's views expressed on gambling were similar to the ones expressed by the WCTU of BC on illegal drug use. In *The Age of Light, Soap, and Water: Moral Reform in English Canada, 1885–1925*, Mariana Valverde underlines the WCTU's role in the anti-smoking movement. When it embarked on the issue of illegal drug use, the Vancouver chapter was pursuing another social issue.

80 Submission to the (Le Dain Commission) by the Victoria Voice of Women, NAC, RG 33/101, vol. 17, file 2114.

81 To Committee Investigation Non-Medical Use of Drugs, from Genevra Richards, Executive Director, 7 May 1970, NAC, RG 33/101, vol. 13, file 1521 Sudbury Young Women's Christian Association.

82 Brief by the National Council of Jewish Women of Canada, Vancouver, 20 November 1970, NAC, RG 33/101, vol. 9, file 248.

83 Brief by the Legalize Marijuana Committee, 16 October 1969, NAC, RG 33/101, volume 16, file 1739.

84 Besides the RCMP, the Vancouver City Police Department, some church groups, women's groups, some provinces, and health professionals already mentioned, the following groups opposed the legalization of marijuana: the Alcohol and Drug Concerns Inc. (NAC, RG 33/101, vol. 17, file 2058), the Alcohol-Drug Education Council of Vancouver (ibid., vol. 17, file 2420), Boy Scouts of Canada (Kingston) (ibid., vol. 11, file 1133), the Vancouver Board of Trade (ibid., vol. 17, file 2123).

85 Barbara M. Freeman, *The Satellite Sex: The Media and Women's Issues in English Canada, 1966–1971* (Waterloo, ON: Wilfrid Laurier University Press, 2001), 36.

86 Archibald, *The Addiction Research Foundation*, 100.

87 Commission of Inquiry into the Non-Medical Use of Drugs, *Interim Report* (Ottawa: Information Canada, 1970), 189, 537, 467.

88 Commission of Inquiry into the Non-Medical Use of Drugs, *Interim Report*.

89 Ibid., 537.

90 Memorandum to the Members of the Commission from Gerald Le Dain, Policy Re Cannabis, 7 January 1972, NAC, R 923, vol. 10, file 7.

91 Commission of Inquiry into the Non-Medical Use of Drugs, *Cannabis Report* (Ottawa: Information Canada, 1972), 268–72, 293, 303, 309, 315.

92 *Globe and Mail*, 20 June 1970.

93 *Le Devoir*, 22 June 1970, 4.

94 *La Presse*, 20 June 1970, 4.
95 *Toronto Star*, 18 May 1972, 6.
96 *Globe and Mail*, 18 May 1972, 6.
97 *La Presse*, 19 May 1972, A4; *Le Devoir*, 20 Mai 1972, 4.
98 Second Brief Presented to the (Le Dain Commission), 11 March 1971,
   NAC, RG 33/101, vol. 19, file 7446.
99 *Montreal Gazette*, 15 October 1971, 3; *House of Commons Debates*,
   13 March 1972, 790.
100 'An Evaluation of the Interim Report (Le Dain Commission)' by the
   NAFBC, August 1970, NAC, R 923, vol. 23, file BC Rehabilitation and Welfare; Letter to Dr K.C. Charron, Deputy Minister of Health, from H. David
   Archibald, Executive Director, 3 November 1970, CAMHA, ARF collection, box 63-22, file Provincial Government: Minister of Health, 1970 (2).
101 'Brief on the Need for a National Plan for the Control of Drug Abuse in the
   Interim Period,' prepared by H.F. Hoskin, September 1970, NAC, RG 33/
   101, vol. 10, file 832.
102 Commentaires sur le rapport de la Commission Le Dain (le traitement),
   sans date; Quelques notes et commentaires au sujet de la Commission Le
   Dain (rapport final) en vue de la préparation de documents à être remis au
   Premier ministre, sans date, ANQ-Q, E8, 84-05-001/4, file Commission Le
   Dain.
103 Lettre d'André Boudreau, directeur général, à Jacques Brunet, sous-ministre, ministère de la Santé, 24 juillet 1970; Quelques commentaires concernant le rapport provisoire de la (Commission Le Dain), sans date, ANQ-Q,
   E8, 84-05-001/4, file Commission Le Dain; Rapport Le Dain. L'usage des
   drogues à des fins non médicales. Position du ministère de la Santé, sans
   date (1970), ANQ-Q, E8, 1960-01-580/150, file Décembre 69 à Mars 70,
   Ministère de la santé (dossier général) Québec.
104 Le rapport de la Commission Le Dain et le Ministère de l'Éducation du
   Québec par Paul Clermont, consultant, et Robert Trempe, Directeur du
   Service des programmes, sans date (vraisemblablement rédigé après le
   dépôt du rapport préliminaire et celui sur le cannabis), ANQ-Q, E13, 1992-
   11-000/111, file Rapports divers toxicomanies, 72–7.
105 Author's translation: 'entraînera un développement rapide de son usage
   et conséquemment, des problèmes de santé et des problèmes sociaux
   extrêmement importants. Les coûts de l'assurance-santé seront certaine-
   ment augmentés.' 'Quelques notes sur le rapport de la Commission Le
   Dain sur le cannabis' par André Boudreau, directeur général de l'OPTAT,
   17 juillet 1972, ANQ-Q, E8, 84-05-001/4, file Commission Le Dain.
106 'Summary with Comments on the Interim Report of the (Le Dain Commis-

sion) by the (ARF),' 15 July 1970, NAC, RG 29, vol. 1281, file 55-10-2 pt 5.

107 'Proposed Comments of the Ontario Government Interim Report of the Le Dain Commission,' by Thomas L. Wells, Minister of Health, Memorandum to Cabinet, 5 November 1970, PAO, RG-10-6, box 163, file 1610.

108 Letters from Thomas Wells to John Munro, 23 July and 1 October 1970, letter from Munro to Wells, 3 November 1970, PAO, RG 10-1, file 2-544 Le Dain Commission report.

109 'Assessment of the Views of the (ARF) on the Le Dain Cannabis Report' by A.B. Morrison, Ph.D., Health Protection Branch (Federal Ministry), 28 July 1972, NAC, RG 29, box 1584 file 1018-7-7 vol. 1; Submission to Cabinet, The Le Dain Report on Cannabis, Report of the Interministerial Committee, June 1972, PAO, RG 4, series A-2, file 679.7.

110 *House of Commons Debates,* 19 June 1970, 8330–2.

5. A Small Step beyond the Status Quo

1 Letter from J.N. Crawford, Deputy Minister of National Health to the Minister of National Health, 15 July 1968, NAC, RG 29, vol. 1581, file C-1016-7-1A pt 1.

2 Memorandum from Acting Deputy Minister, J. L. Fry, to the Minister (National Health and Welfare), Subject: Clarifications Concerning Certain Applications for Funding Under the Innovative Services Contributions Program, NAC, RG 29, vol. 1582, file 1018-7-1 pt 6.

3 Cabinet Conclusions, 4 November 1966 and 6 April 1967, NAC, RG 2, vols. 6321 and 6323.

4 *Toronto Daily Star,* 19 April 1967, 5; *Globe and Mail,* 19 April 1967, 1.

5 Resolution adopted by the United Nations Economic and Social Council, 16 May 1967, NAC, RG 25, vol. 10488, file 45-9-1-1 pt 2.2; Resolution adopted by the United Nations Economic and Social Council, Plenary Meeting, 23 May 1968, NAC, RG 25, vol. 10487, file 45.9.1 pt 1.

6 The *Halifax Herald, Winnipeg Free Press, Globe and Mail, Toronto Daily Star* and *Vancouver Province* covered the Senate debate. The *Toronto Daily Star* expressed its dissatisfaction with the repressive approach adopted by the government. Entitled 'LSD Is More Than a Crime Problem,' its 21 April 1967 editorial argued that LSD had 'no addictive properties.' 'It would be foolish to treat the possession of LSD as a major felony and write off anyone found possessing or using it as a hopeless derelict, to be locked up for as long as possible.' Education was seen to be a better approach.

7 *Senate Debates,* 25 April 1967, 1829.

8 *Senate Standing Committee on Banking and Commerce*, 26 April 1967, 811.
9 *Senate Debates*, 19 April 1967, 1793.
10 Ibid., 20 April 1967, 1814.
11 Ibid., 19 April 1967, 1796.
12 Ibid., 1 November 1967, 339.
13 Ibid., 25 April 1967, 1825.
14 Ibid., 19 April 1967, 1797.
15 *Senate Debates*, 26 April 1967, 1845–1847.
16 'Some Senatorial Fantasies,' *Globe and Mail*, 1 May 1967, 6.
17 Memorandum for D.S. Thorson from N.M. Thurm, 5 May 1967, NAC, RG 13, accession 1997–97/416, box 13, file 213 000 7-1.
18 *Toronto Daily Star*, 21 August 1969, 1; 22 August 1969, 1.
19 *Standing Committee on Health, Welfare and Social Affairs, House of Commons*, 22 April 1969, 886–7.
20 Ibid., 913.
21 Lemieux, *L'étude des politiques publiques*, 31–4.
22 Memorandum to the Cabinet, 16 September 1968, appendix C, NAC, RG 29, vol. 1581, file 1018-7-1 pt 1.
23 Whitaker, *Drugs and the Law*, 100–1.
24 Erickson and Smart, 'Canada,' 112–13.
25 Memorandum, Narcotic Enforcement General, from R.C. Hammond, Chief, Division of Narcotic Control, Department of National Health and Welfare, 21 September 1966, NAC, RG 29, 1983–84/118 box 4, file K321-5-7; Department of Justice, 19 April 1967, Note re: Meeting Friday 21, 1967 Food and Drugs Act, NAC, RG 13, accession 1997-97/416, box 13, file 213000-7-1.
26 C.G. Farmilo, United Nations, 'Revised Draft Protocol on Psychotropic Substances and Its Relation to Federal Legislation of Drugs on Schedules F, G, J, H and N and Federal-Provincial Matters,' 6 November 1970, NAC, R923, vol. 23, file 1.
27 H. Wayne Morgan, *Drugs in America: A Social History, 1800–1980* (Syracuse, NY: Syracuse University Press, 1981), 149.
28 Letters from J.N. Crawford, Deputy Minister of National Health, to the Minister of National Health and Welfare, 22 July 1968 and 16 September 1968, NAC, RG 29, vol. 1581, file C-1016-7-1A pt 1; Speech by John Munro, Minister of National Health and Welfare to Canadian Pharmaceutical Association Annual Convention, 19 August 1968, CAMHA, ARF Collection, box 63-25, file John Munro; Memorandum to the Cabinet, 16 September 1968, NAC, RG 29, vol. 1581, file 1018-7-1 pt 1; Speech by John Munro at Loyola University Conference on Drugs: 'Student Use and Abuse,' Montreal, NAC, RG 29, access 1985-86/235, vol. 55, file 6025-M4-1/2 pt 1.

29 (Draft) Report of the Interdepartmental Committee on the Interim Report on the Non-Medical Use of Drugs submitted to the Minister of National Health and Welfare, November 1970, NAC, RG 29, vol. 1540, file 1003-1-1-2 pt 1.

30 Summary of Meeting of the Special Committee of Caucus on the Non-Medical Use of Drugs (15 October 1970), NAC, RG 29, box 1281, file 55-10-2, pt 5; Rationale for Recommending Transfer of Cannabis (Marijuana) from the Narcotic Control Act to the Food and Drugs Act, Dr Maurice LeClair, Deputy Minister of National Health, 19 October 1970, NAC, RG 29, vol. 1540, file 1003-1-1-2 pt 1; Position of the Department of National Health and Welfare on the Status of Cannabis (Marihuana), 7 April 1971, NAC, RG 29 box 1584 file 1018-7-7 vol. 1.

31 (Draft) Report of the Interdepartmental Committee on the Interim Report on the Non-Medical Use of Drugs, November 1970; Minutes of the First Meeting of the Interdepartmental Committee on the Interim Report on the Non-Medical Use of Drugs, 9 October 1970, NAC, RG 29, vol. 1540, file 1003-1-1-2 pt 1.

32 Letter from Allan J. MacEachen to Solicitor General L.T. Pennell, 11 April 1968, NAC, RG 29, vol. 1581, file 1018-7-1 pt 1.

33 Resolutions adopted by the United Nations Economic and Social Council, Plenary Meeting, 23 May 1968, NAC, RG 25, vol. 10487, file 45.9.1 pt 1.

34 Letter from R.E. Curran to V. Jusevic, Director, Division of Narcotic Drugs, United Nations Office at Geneva, 8 March 1968, NAC, RG 29, vol. 1645, file 75-4-5, pt 2.

35 Letter from R.E. Curran to J.N. Crawford, Deputy Minister of National Health, 26 February 1968, NAC, RG 25, vol. 10488, file 45.9.1.1 pt 3.

36 Canadian Student Affairs Association, *The Loyola Conference on Student Use and Abuse of Drugs*, 17–19.

37 *Ottawa Citizen*, 13 September 1971, 4.

38 Kelly, *The Royal Canadian Mounted Police*, 256.

39 Steve Hewitt, *Spying 101: The RCMP's Secret Activities at Canadian Universities, 1917–1997* (Toronto: University of Toronto Press, 2002), 102–18, 130–1. On the FBI, see James K. Davis, *Assault on the Left: The FBI and the Sixties Antiwar Movement* (Westport, CT: Praeger, 1997); and David Cunningham, *There's Something Happening Here: The New Left, the Klan, and FBI Counterintelligence* (Berkeley: University of California Press, 2004).

40 Gormely, *Drugs and the Canadian Scene*, 147; Commission of Inquiry into the Non-Medical Use of Drugs, *Cannabis Report*, 239–43.

41 Kelly and Kelly, *The Royal Canadian Mounted Police*.

42 'Summary of Measures to Control the Heroin Abuse Problem' by J.A. Hunter, January 1972, NAC, RG 29, vol. 1549, file 1006-5-1 pt 4.

43 Letter to D.H. Christie from J.A. Macauley, Insp., Assistant Officer in Charge, Criminal Investigation Branch, 2 December 1968, NAC, RG33/101, vol. 9, file 309.

44 Memorandum from G.L. Tomalty, Insp., Officer in Charge, Drug Enforcement Branch, 23 August 1974, NAC, RG 18, vol. 4832, file GC-310-10 pt 11; Excerpt from Position Paper by RCMP, NAC, RG 29, vol. 3468, file Outline of the Le Dain Commission Recommendation.

45 Memorandum to Solicitor General from E.A. Côté, Deputy Solicitor General, 1 June 1970, NAC, RG 18, vol. 4831, file GC 310-10 (1970), pt 3.

46 Letter to D.H. Christie from J.A. Macauley, Insp., Assistant Officer in Charge, Criminal Investigation Branch, 2 December 1968, NAC, RG33/101, vol. 9, file 309.

47 *House of Commons, Standing Committee on Justice and Legal Affairs*, 31 October 1968, 33; 7 November 1968.

48 Letter to D.H. Christie from J.A. Macauley, Insp., Assistant Officer in Charge, Criminal Investigation Branch, 2 December 1968, NAC, RG33/101, vol. 9, file 309.

49 'Lawless "beat" generation must be controlled says RCMP Commissioner,' *Ottawa Citizen*, 21 February 1968.

50 Letter to D.H. Christie from J.A. Macauley, Insp., Assistant Officer in Charge, Criminal Investigation Branch, 2 December 1968, NAC, RG33/101, vol. 9, file 309; Memorandum to Officer from the DCI, 26 August 1969; Report from the Calgary Drug Section, 24 October 1969, NAC, RG 18, vol. 4831, file GC 310-10 (1969) pt 1.

51 *House of Commons Debates*, 7 November 1968, 47.

52 Memorandum to the Deputy Comm's (OPS) from the DCI, subject: (Le Dain Commission), 20 October 1969, NAC, RG 18, vol. 4831, file GC 310-10 (1969) pt 1; Letter from J.R.R. Carriere, A/Comm's, Director, Criminal Investigation, to James J. Moore, Executive Secretary, Commission (Le Dain), 3 November 1969, NAC, RG 18, vol. 4831, file GC 310-10 (1970) pt 2; 'Comments by NH&W Working Party on Interim Report of the (Le Dain Commission),' no date, NAC, RG 29, vol. 1540, file 1003-1-1-2, pt 1.

53 International Criminal Police Organization (INTERPOL), 36th General Assembly Session, Kyoto, September 27th–October 4th, 1967, Resolution Narcotic Drugs, NAC, RG 33/101, vol. 16, file 1846.

54 Letter from J.R.R. Carrière, Deputy Commissioner (Criminal Operations), to the Under-Secretary of State for External Affairs, 4 October 1971, NAC, RG 25, vol. 10488, file 45.9.1 pt 3. Appendix D, ICPO-Interpol General Assembly Brussels – 1970, Second Brief Presented to the (Le Dain Commission by the RCMP), 11 March 1971, NAC, RG 33/101, vol. 19, file 7446.

55 Minutes of the Second Meeting of the Interdepartmental Committee on the Interim Report on the Non-Medical Use of Drugs (29 October 1970), NAC, RG 29, vol. 1540, file 1003-1-1-2 pt 1.

56 Memorandum for Interdepartmental Committee on the Le Dain Report from the Department of Justice, 15 October 1970, NAC, RG 29, vol. 1540, file 1003-1-1-2 vol. 2.

57 Jay Sinha, *The History and Development of the Leading International Drug Control Conventions* (Ottawa: Library of Parliament / Bibliothèque du parlement, 2001), 2.

58 Commission of Inquiry into the Non-Medical Use of Drugs, *Interim Report*, 372.

59 Letter from J. Dittert, Secretary of the Board, United Nations International Narcotics Control Board to R.C. Hammond, Chief, Division of Narcotic Control, Department of National Health and Welfare, 18 March 1970, NAC, RG 29, access 1983–84/151, vol. 10, file 322-9-11.

60 Memorandum to the Cabinet Committee on Social Policy and Cultural Affairs, Re: Cannabis, 10 March 1969, NAC, RG 29, vol. 1540, file 1003-1-12, vol. 1.

61 Report on Meeting of the World Health Organization, Expert Committee on Drug Dependence, October 1968,' by H. David Archibald, Executive Director, ARF Foundation, December 1968; World Health Organization Technical Report Series no. 407, WHO Expert Committee on Drug Dependence, 16th Report, Geneva, 1969, CAMHA, ARF Collection, box 23-71, file WHO Expert Committee on Drug Dependence.

62 McAllister, *Drug Diplomacy in the Twentieth Century*; Kettil Bruun, Lynn Pan, and Ingemar Rexed, *The Gentlemen's Club: International Control of Drugs and Alcohol* (Chicago: University of Chicago Press, 1975).

63 Ibid.

64 Letter from Robert Curran to J.N. Crawford, Deputy Minister of National Health, 26 February 1968; Letter from J.N. Crawford, Deputy Minister of National Health, to the Under-Secretary of State for External Affairs, 4 December 1968, NAC, RG 25, vol. 10488, file 45.9.1.1 pt 3.

65 Letter to H.B. Robinson, Minister, Canadian Embassy, Washington, DC, from External Affairs, 26 November 1962; To House of the High Commissioner for Canada, London, from the Under-Secretary of State for External Affairs, Subject: 1961 Single Convention on Narcotic Drugs and the 1953 Protocol, 4 January 1963, NAC, RG 25, vol. 4952, file 8-R-6-40 pt 6.

66 Jack L. Granatstein and Robert Bothwell, *Pirouette: Pierre Trudeau and Canadian Foreign Policy* (Toronto: University of Toronto Press, 1990), 12.

67 Prime Minister's Meeting with the President of the United States, Washing-

ton, 6 December 1971, NAC, RG 25, vol. 10489, file 45.9.1.1 pt 10.1; Visit of President Nixon to Canada, 13–15 April 1972, NAC, RG 25, vol. 10490, file 45.9.1.6 pt 3.

68 Summary of Meeting of the Special Committee of Caucus on the Non-Medical Use of Drugs (15 October 1970), NAC, RG 29, box 1281, file 55-10-2 pt 5.

69 Letters from J. Robarts, PAO, RG 3-26, box 124, files Alcoholism & Drug Addiction.

70 *Senate Standing Committee on Banking and Commerce*, 22 November 1967.

71 *Standing Senate Committee on Legal and Constitutional Affairs*, 11 March 1975; 25 March 1975.

72 Department of External Affairs, Submission to Interdepartmental Committee on Heroin Control, no date (1971), NAC, RG 25, vol. 10490, file 45.9.1.6 pt 1; Memorandum, Visit of President Nixon, 13–14 April 1972, Functional Cooperation among Police Forces on Narcotic Law Enforcement, NAC, RG 25, vol. 10488, file 45-9-1 pt 4.2.

73 Martin Booth, *Cannabis: A History* (London: Doubleday, 2003); Meier, *The Politics of Sin*.

74 Office of the White House Press Secretary, the White House, 'Highlights of Nixon Administration Actions in the Drug Field,' 17 June 1971, NAC, RG 25, vol. 10488, file 45.9.1 pt 3; US Department of Treasury News, Statement of Eugene T. Rossides, Assistant Secretary of the Treasury (Enforcement, Tariff and Trade Affairs, and Operations), 6 July 1972, NAC, RG 25, vol. 10488, file 45-9-1 pt 5.

75 Booth, *Cannabis*.

76 To the Under-Secretary of State for External Affairs from the Canadian Ambassador, Ankara, 9 July 1970, NAC, RG 25, vol. 10487, file 45-9-1 pt 2; Au Sous-Secrétaire d'État aux Affaires extérieures de l'Ambassade du Canada, Ankara, Gilles H. Duguay, Chargé d'affaires, 23 juillet 1971; Office of the White House Press Secretary, the White House, 'Highlights of Nixon Administration Actions in the Drug Field,' 17 June 1971, NAC, RG 25, vol. 10488, file 45.9.1 pt 3; Memorandum to Mr Thibault (UNS) from R.G. Seaborn (United Nations Economic and Social Affairs Division), 22 December 1971, NAC, RG 25, vol. 10490, file 45.9.1.1 pt 11.

77 To the Under-Secretary of State for External Affairs from Permanent Mission of Canada to the United Nations, New York University Reference: Geneva Telegram 215 of 5 February 1970, Subject: Economic and Social Council, 48th Session, Agenda Item 5: Narcotic Drugs, 20 April 1970, NAC, RG 25, vol. 10489, file 45.9.1.1 part 5; Memorandum to PDM from Harry Jay, Director General, Bureau of United Nations Affairs, Question of a Contri-

bution to the UN Fund for Drug Abuse, 4 March 1971, NAC, RG 25, vol. 10489, file 45.9.1.1 pt 8.1; Department of External Affairs. Submission to Interdepartmental Committee on Heroin Control, no date (1971), NAC, RG 25, vol. 10490, file 45.9.1.6 pt 1.

78 Cabinet Committee on Government Operations, Meeting of December 21st, 1970 (confirmed by Cabinet, 23 December 1970), NAC, RG 29, vol. 1549, file 1006-5-1 vol. 1.

79 News Release, Department of National Health and Welfare, 1 March 1971, 'National Health Minister Tables Psychotropic Drug Substances Document,' NAC, R 923, vol. 7, file 7-18.

80 'Report on the Conference to Adopt a Protocol on Psychotropic Substances, January 11–February 21, 1971, 13 April 1971,' by R.A. Chapman, Assistant Deputy Minister, Food and Drugs, Department of National Health and Welfare and J.D. McCarthy, Director, Legal Services, Department of National Health and Welfare, NAC, RG 29, access 1985–86/235, vol. 60, file 602.8-1-6.

81 To Mr Thibault UNS (Director of UN Economic and Social Affairs Division) from V. Edelstein, United Nations Economic and Social Affairs Division, Subject: Session of Edosoc – Narcotics Items: U.S.A. Views, 19 April 1972, NAC, RG 25, vol. 10490, file 45.9.1.6 pt 3; Notes of meeting re 25th Session of United Nations Commission on Narcotic Drugs, Geneva, 20 January– 9 February 1973, NAC, RG 25, vol. 10490, file 45-9-1-1 pt 13.2.

82 'Report of Tri-Partite Narcotics Control Talks – Canada–Mexico–United States, Washington, 12 October 1971,' by R.C. Smith, Legal Operations Division, Department of External Affairs, NAC, RG 25, vol. 10490, file 45.9.1.6 pt 1; Letter from D.M. Miller, Director, Legal Operations Division, 28 June 1972, NAC, RG 25, vol. 10490, file 45.9.1.6 pt 3; Memorandum for the Minister, 18 January 1972, Subject: Narcotics: December 21 Visit of the United States Ambassador, NAC, RG 25, vol. 10490, file 45.9.1.1 pt 11; Message to ISBAD, Ref: Yourtel 428, 6 April 1972, Subject: Narcotics: Request by USA Emb in Pak for cooperation, NAC, RG 25, vol. 10488, file 45-9-1 part 4.2.

83 To D.M. Miller from R.C. Smith, Subject: Narcotics Control – Tripartite Meetings – Canada–Mexico–United States, 24 September 1971; Note de service au Solliciteur général du solliciteur général adjoint, sujet: Réunion technique au sujet des stupéfiants tenue à Washington le 12 octobre 1971 et réunissant des représentants du Mexique, des Etats-Unis et du Canada, 13 octobre 1971, NAC, RG 25, vol. 10490, file 45.9.1.6 pt 1; Memorandum to the Cabinet, Mexican–U.S.–Canadian Ministerial Meeting on Drugs – Mexico City, 10 March 1972; TELEGRAM from Mexico, 27 March 1972, NAC, RG 25, vol. 10490, file 45.9.1.6 pt 2.

84 Letter from Allan J. MacEachen, Minister of National Health and Welfare, to Larry T. Pennell, Solicitor General, 11 April 1968, NAC, RG 29, vol. 1581, file 1018-7-1 pt 1.

85 Ibid.

86 Speech by John Munro, Minister of National Health and Welfare, to Canadian Pharmaceutical Association Annual Convention, 19 August 1968, CAMHA, ARF Collection, box 63-25, file John Munro.

87 *House of Commons Debates*, 19 September 1968, 202; 24 September 1968, 390.

88 Memorandum to the Cabinet Re: Marihuana Legislation and Studies by George J. McIlraith, 5 March 1969, NAC, RG 29, vol. 10487, file 45-9-1 pt 1.2; Memorandum to the Cabinet Committee on Social Policy and Cultural Affairs, Re: Cannabis, 10 March 1969, NAC, RG 29, vol. 1540, file 1003-1-12, vol. 1.

89 Cabinet Conclusions, 5 March 1969 and 20 March 1969, http://data2 .archives.ca/e/e034/e000834361.gif and /e000834389.gif.

90 'Munro Indicates Marijuana Laws Will Be Softened,' *Toronto Daily Star*, 31 October 1969, 1.

91 *Montreal Star*, 4 June 1970, 1; *Toronto Telegram*, 12 June 1970.

92 Further Memorandum to the Cabinet Re: Interim Report (Le Dain Commission), 15 June 1970, NAC, RG 29, vol. 1540, file 1003-1-1-2, pt 1.

93 Cabinet Conclusions, 18 June 1970, http://data2.archives.ca/e/e001/ e000002399.gif.

94 *House of Commons Debates*, 19 June 1970, 8329; 22 June 1970, 8395.

95 Letter to M.A. Crowe, Chairman, Interdepartmental Committee on the Non-Medical Use of Drugs, to John Munro, Minister of Health and Welfare, 3 December 1970, NAC, RG 29, volume 1540, file 1003-1-1-2 part 1.

96 Draft Report of the Interdepartmental Committee on the Interim Report on the Non-Medical Use of Drugs submitted to the Minister of National Health and Welfare, November 1970, NAC, RG 29, vol. 1540, file 1003-1-1-2 pt 1.

97 The Committee on Youth, set up by the Secretary of State, recommended the legalization of marijuana in 1971. The report created some waves in the media (*Ottawa Citizen*, 15 July 1971; *La Presse*, 27 August 1971).

98 Memorandum to the Cabinet, Program Related to the Status of Cannabis, 11 July 1972; Cabinet Conclusion, 14 July 1972, NAC, RG 29, vol. 1584, file 1018-7-7 vol. 1.

99 Statement on Government Policy respecting Cannabis, 14 July 1972; Statement by John Munro, Minister of Health and Welfare, 31 July 1972, NAC, RG 29, box 1584, file 1018-7-7, vol. 1.

100 *Toronto Star*, 2 August 1972, 6.

101 *Vancouver Sun*, 2 August 1972, 4.

102 *Winnipeg Free Press*, 2 August 1972, 19; *Halifax Chronicle-Herald*, 2 August 1972, 6.

103 *Montreal Gazette*, 2 August 1972, 2; *Ottawa Citizen*, 31 July 1972.

104 *Le Devoir*, 2 August 1972, 4; *La Presse*, 2 August 1972, A4.

105 *Globe and Mail*, 1 August 1972, 6.

106 *The Journal* (ARF), 1 November 1973, 9.

107 Ibid., 1 February 1973, 5; 1 February 1974, 1.

108 Meeting of the Interdepartmental Committee on the Le Dain Commission's Final Report, 28 June 1974, NAC, RG 18, vol. 4832, file GC-310-10 pt 11.

109 *The Journal* (ARF), 1 March 1973, 1.

110 Ibid., 1 March 1974, 2.

111 Ibid., 1 January 1975, 1.

112 Draft Briefing Paper on the Possessional Offence, 29 October 1974, NAC, RG 29, access 1985–86/235, box 57, file 6027-3-6 pt 4; Letter from Marc Lalonde to the members of the Senate Committee, NAC, MG 32 C-55, vol. 5, file Information kit on cannabis by the Minister of National Health and Welfare, 1975.

113 Ibid.

114 *Standing Senate Committee on Legal and Constitutional Affairs*, 4 February 1975, 6.

115 Ibid., 11 February 1975, 5.

116 Ibid.

117 *The Journal* (ARF), 1 March 1975, 1, 4.

118 *Standing Senate Committee on Legal and Constitutional Affairs*, 25 February 1975; 5 March 1975.

119 *The Journal* (ARF), 1 August 1975, 4.

120 *Standing Senate Committee on Legal and Constitutional Affairs*, 18 February 1975.

121 *Canadian Police Chief*, July 1975, 12.

122 *Standing Senate Committee on Legal and Constitutional Affairs*, 22 April 1975, 6.

123 Ibid., 12 February 1975, 18.

124 Proposed Cannabis Legislation Bill S-19, NAC, MG 32 C 55, vol. 5, file 5/4; Letter from Paul V. Fontana, Captain, Commander Special Investigations Division, Bureau of Police, Portland Oregon, to (RCMP), Narcotics Enforcement Division, Ottawa, 21 April 1975. A copy of the letter was sent to Senator Carl Goldenberg, who was the chair of the Senate Committee. NAC, MG 32 C-55, vol. 5, file Drugs Correspondence.

125 *Standing Senate Committee on Legal and Constitutional Affairs*, 18 February 1975.
126 Ibid., 5 March 1975; 18 March 1975.
127 *La Presse*, 28 November 1974, A12.
128 *Senate Debates*, 19 December 1974, 451.
129 Ibid., 5 December 1974, 361.
130 Ibid., Joan Neiman, 5 December 1974, 355; J. Harper Prowse, 12 December 1974, 384; Lorne Bonnell, 19 December 1974, 448; 11 June 1975, 1046; H. Carl Goldenberg, 27 May 1975, 970–1.
131 Ibid., 10 June 1975.
132 Ibid., 17 December 1974, 406; 4 June 1975, 1016; 10 June 1975, 1038.
133 Ibid., 5 December 1974, 359.
134 Ibid., 11 December 1974, 375.
135 Ibid., 17 December 1974, 405.
136 Ibid., 19 December 1974, 450.
137 Ibid., 19 December 1974, 450; 10 December 1974, 368; 17 December 1974, 403.
138 *Standing Senate Committee on Legal and Constitutional Affairs*, 27 May 1975, 5–9.
139 *The Journal* (ARF), 1 November 1975, 1.
140 Memorandum from A.B. Morrison, Assistant Deputy Minister, Health Protection Branch, to J. Lupien, Deputy Minister, National Health, 22 May 1975, NAC, RG 29, vol. 1582, file 1018-7-1 pt 6.
141 Memorandum from A. B. Morrison, Assistant Deputy Minister, Health Protection Branch to P. Woodstock, Principal Executive Officer to the Deputy Minister, National Health, 20 February 1975; Memorandum from T.R. McKim, Director, Bureau of Dangerous Drugs to Dr A.J. Liston, Acting Director General, Drugs Directorate, 16 April 1975, NAC, RG 29, box 1584, file 1018-7-7 vol. 2.
142 Commission of Inquiry into the Non-Medical Use of Drugs, *Cannabis Report*, 246.
143 Confidential Summary of Conviction and Habitual Drug User Statistics – 1972, NAC, RG 29, vol. 1581, file 1018-71 pt 2.
144 *Toronto Star*, 1 August 1972, 1, 4.
145 *Standing Senate Committee on Legal and Constitutional Affairs*, 29 April 1975.
146 Michael Bryan, 'Cannabis in Canada – A Decade of Indecision,' *Contemporary Drug Problems* 8:2 (1979), 175.
147 Letter from M.B. Dymond, Minister of Health, to John Munro, Minister of National Health & Welfare, 28 May 1969, NAC, RG 33/101, vol. 21, file Ont. Government; Memorandum to Commissioners and Staff, from C.G.

Farmilo, RE: Recommendations Federal-Provincial Drug Abuse Advisory Committee, 13 November 1970, NAC, R 923, vol. 10, file 5; Federal-Provincial Conference of Ministers of Health, 10 December 1970, NAC, RG 29, vol. 1290, file 5618-2-701 pt 2; Document prepared by the Department of National Health and Welfare, NAC, R 923, vol. 10, file 3; Memorandum to Dr A.B. Morrison, Assistant Deputy Minister, Health Protection Branch, from R.A. Draper, Director-General, Non-Medical Use of Drugs Directorate, 6 February 1976, NAC, RG 29 (Health), access 1985–86/235, box 57, file 6027-3-6, pt 5; Ninth Meeting of the Interdepartmental Committee on the Le Dain Commission Final Report, 10 September 1974, NAC, RG 29, access 95–96/224, box 53, file 6030-J4-1 vol. 2.

148 Treasury Board Submission on Organization, Organization of the Non-Medical Use of Drugs Directorate, 22 September 1972, NAC, RG 29, access 1985–86/235, vol. 44, file 6001-1-10 pt 1; Organizational Development Plan Non-Medical Use of Drugs Directorate (1973), no author, NAC, RG 29, box 3142, file 9000-5-6.

149 *Standing Senate Committee on Legal and Constitutional Affairs*, 12 February 1975, 7–10; Rapport de la vingt-troisième réunion du Comité interministériel sur les toxicomanies tenue le 28 février 1974, ANQ-Q, E8, 1984-05-001/3.

Conclusion

1 Burnham, *Bad Habits*.
2 Krista Foss, 'The Transformation of Mary Jane,' *Globe and Mail*, 24 November 1998, C10; Krista Foss, 'Chronically Ill Cheer Marijuana Trials,' *Globe and Mail*, 5 March 1999, A12.
3 Bruce Cheadle, 'Medicinal-Pot Terms Eased on Trial Eve,' *Globe and Mail*, 6 October 1999, A13.
4 'Ottawa doit changer sa loi sur la marijuana,' *Le Soleil*, 1 August 2000, A7. In December 2000 the Alberta Court of Queen's Bench ruled that the federal drug legislation was 'unconstitutional because it [did not] allow the medicinal use of' marijuana. 'Ailing Alberta Man Wins Right to Grow Pot,' *Globe and Mail*, 12 December 2000, A6.
5 Colin Freeze and Carolyn Abraham, 'Marijuana Regulation Draws Fire,' *Globe and Mail*, 31 July 2001, A1, A8.
6 André Picard and Carolyn Abraham, 'Ottawa Shelves Medicinal Pot' *Globe and Mail*, 20 August 2002, A1.
7 Dean Beeby, 'Health Canada Dope Stinks, Patients Say,' *Globe and Mail*, 16 September 2003, A11.

8 Editorials, *Globe and Mail*, 28 May 2003, A16; 14 July 2002, A14; 4 June 2001, A14; 20 August 2001, A12; 21 August 2001, A14; 22 August 2001, A14; 23 August 2001, A14; 7 September 2002, A20; 16 December 2002, A16.

9 *Globe and Mail*, 5 September 2002, A8.

10 Editorial, *Globe and Mail*, 4 June 2001, A14.

11 'Fantino Urges Decriminalizing of Marijuana,' *Globe and Mail*, 3 June 2000, A25.

12 According to the November 2004 Ipsos-Reid poll, 51% of Canadians supported decriminalization and 33% opposed it; *Globe and Mail*, 25 November 2004, A3. Of Canadians who answered the Leger Marketing survey 46.8% favored legalization and 47% opposed it. 'Canadians Evenly Split on Legalizing Pot,' *Globe and Mail*, 25 June 2001, A4.

13 'Pot Possession Doesn't Warrant Jail Term, Day Says,' *Globe and Mail*, 16 May 2000, A4.

14 Jane Taber, 'A Glimpse into Martin the Man,' *Globe and Mail*, 19 December 2003, A6.

15 'Marijuana Party Causes Buzz,' *Globe and Mail*, 2 December 2000, A2.

16 Senate Special Committee on Illegal Drugs, *Cannabis: Our Position for a Canadian Public Policy* (Ottawa, 2002), 614, 618.

17 Brian Laghi and Kim Lunman, 'Parliamentary Committee to Recommend New Pot Law,' *Globe and Mail*, 11 December 2002, A10; 'U.S. Fears Change in Marijuana Laws,' *Globe and Mail*, 13 December 2002, A9; House of Commons Special Committee on Non-Medical Use of Drugs, *Policy for the New Millennium: Working Together to Redefine Canada's Drug Strategy* (Ottawa, 2002).

18 House of Commons Special Committee, *New Millennium*, 131.

19 A study by the Addiction Research Foundation found that in 1999, 29% of students from grades 7 to 13 in Ontario had smoked cannabis once in their lives. The percentage was 13% in 1993. Editorial, *Globe and Mail*, 4 June 2001, A14. In July 2004, Statistics Canada released a survey revealing that between 1989 and 2002, 'the percentage of Canadians 15 and over who admitted using cannabis in the previous year almost doubled – from 6.5 per cent to 12.2 per cent'; *Globe and Mail*, 22 July 2004, A6. Senate Special Committee on Illegal Drugs, *Cannabis: Our Position for a Canadian Public Policy.*

20 For instance, it was estimated that there were more than 20,000 marijuana-growing operations in Vancouver and Lower Mainland British Columbia. The annual revenues were estimated at $30 billion. Editorial, 'O Cannabis,' *Globe and Mail*, 29 June 2002, A16. Editorial, *Globe and Mail*, 14 July 2002, A14; 20 August 2001, A12; 21 August 2001, A14; 22 August 2001, A14; 23 August 2001, A14.

21 'Ottawa's Marijuana Plans Get Pat from UN Agency,' *Globe and Mail*, 5 June 2003, A11; Janice Tibbetts, 'Liberals' Pot Bill Denounced. Even Caucus Opposes Plan,' *National Post*, 28 May 2003, A4; *Globe and Mail*, 27 May 2003, A1; 17 July 2002, A3; 10 December 2002, A1.

22 *Globe and Mail*, 20 August 2002, A1; 5 September 2002, A1.

23 Andrew Mitrovica, 'U.S. Targets Canada for Drug Blacklist,' *Globe and Mail*, 14 August 1999, A1.

24 Erin Anderssen, 'Would Softer Pot Law Stir Wrath of U.S.?' *Globe and Mail*, 13 July 2002, A5.

25 Kim Lunman, 'Senators Want Pot Legalized' *Globe and Mail*, 5 September 2002, A1.

26 Graeme Smith, 'Canada's Pot Policy Under Fire from U.S.,' *Globe and Mail*, 13 September 2002, A7.

27 Kim Lunman, 'U.S. Fears Change in Marijuana Laws' *Globe and Mail*, 13 December 2002, A9; 'Cellucci Repeats Warning over Decriminalizing Pot,' *Globe and Mail*, 3 May 2003, A4.

28 Canadian Press, 22 August 2003, quoted in Kyle Grayson, 'Chasing Dragons: Security, Identity, and Illicit Drugs in Canada,' Doctoral dissertation, Political Science, York University, 2004, p. 135.

29 *Globe and Mail*, 13 September 2003, A7; 'Chrétien Blasts His MPs for Meddling with Pot Bill,' *Globe and Mail*, 21 August 2003, A4; Tibbetts, 'Liberals' Pot Bill Denounced'; Kim Lunman, 'Ottawa Delays Introduction of Marijuana Legislation,' *Globe and Mail*, 15 May 2003, A7.

30 Kirk Makin, 'Pot Still Illegal, Top Court Rules,' *Globe and Mail*, 24 December 2003, A1.

Bibliography

Archival Sources

Canadian Association of Chiefs of Police
  CACP Board of Directors, Minutes
Centre for Addiction and Mental Health Archives
  Addiction Research Foundation Collection
City of Toronto Archives
  Series 10 and 40
National Archives of Canada
  John G. Diefenbaker Papers
  Carl Goldenberg Papers
  Gerald Le Dain Papers
  Grace MacInnis Papers
  Lester B. Pearson Papers
  Philip Bernard Rynard Papers
  Robert Stanfield Papers
  Canadian Psychiatric Association Records
  Commission of Inquiry into the Non-Medical Use of Drugs Records
  Department of External Affairs Records
  Department of Justice Records
  Department of National Health and Welfare Records
  Prime Minister Office Records. 1963–5
  Royal Canadian Mounted Police Records
National Archives of Quebec, Quebec City
  Ministère des Affaires intergouvernementales
  Ministère de l'Éducation
  Ministère de la Santé

Commission d'enquête sur la santé et le bien-être social (Castonguay-
Nepveu)
Prince Edward Island Public Archives and Records Office
   Attorney General Collection
Provincial Archives of Ontario
   Department of Education Records
   Department of Health Records
   Ministry of the Attorney General Records
   Office of the Premier – John Robarts
   Ontario Provincial Police Records
   John Robarts Papers
York University Archives
   Murray G. Ross Papers
   York Students Federation Papers

Primary Printed Sources

Newspapers

Calgary Herald
Le Devoir
The Excalibur. York University. 1968–74
Globe and Mail
Halifax Chronicle Herald
The McGill Daily. 1968–74
Montreal Gazette
Montreal Star
La Presse
The Province
Toronto Star
The Varsity. University of Toronto. 1964–74

Journals, Magazines, and Proceedings

Addiction Research Foundation of Ontario. *Addictions.* 1963–75
– *The Journal.* 1972–5
Canadian Bar Association Proceedings. 1967–75
Canadian Bar Journal. 1965–75
Canadian Bar Review. 1965–75
Canadian Medical Association Journal. 1965–75

Canadian Police Chief. The Official Magazine of the Canadian Association of Chiefs of Police. 65–75

Office de la prévention et du traitement de l'alcoolisme et des autres toxicomanies. *Information sur l'alcoolisme et les autres toxicomanies.* 1966–75
– *Toxicomanies.* 1968–75

Library of the Canadian Medical Association. Proceedings of General Council. 1969–75

Ontario Provincial Police Review. 1965–75

RCMP Gazette. A National Police Service. 1965–75

Legislative Debates

Assemblée législative / Assemblée nationale du Québec. 1964–75
House of Commons and Senate. 1964–75
Legislature of British Columbia. 1970–75
Legislature of Ontario. 1964–75

Primary Sources

Addiction Research Foundation of Ontario. *Preliminary Brief to the Commission of Inquiry Into the Non-Medical Use of Drugs.* Toronto: Addiction Research Foundation, 1969.

Archibald, H. David. *Alcohol and Drugs: Government Responsibility.* Melbourne, Australia: Third Leonard Ball Oration, Alcoholism Foundation of Victoria, 1970.
– *A National Response to the Non-Medical Use of Drugs in Canada.* San Antonio, TX: NAAAP 21st Annual Meeting, 1970.
– 'Where We Are At ... A Time of Assessment.' Presentation to Staff Conference, Geneva Park, 1971.
– 'Action communautaire face à l'alcool et aux drogues.' *Information sur l'alcoolisme et les autres toxicomanies* 7:2 (March–April 1971), 3–8.
– *Weighing the Alternatives.* Quebec City: Canadian Conference on Social Welfare, 1972.

Association des Chefs de Police et Pompiers de la Province de Québec. *Police-Jeunesse.* Montréal: Graph-O Pier Inc., 1970.

Boudreau, André. 'Les toxicomanies: Causes et prévention.' *Information sur l'alcoolisme et les autres toxicomanies* 5:6 (Janvier–February 1969), 3–6.
– 'Le médecin face à la drogue.' *Information sur l'alcoolisme et les autres toxicomanies* 7:1 (January–February 1971), 4–6.

Bougie, Marcel. 'Le phénomène de la drogue: Occasion de réfléchir et point de départ.' *Information sur l'alcoolisme et les autres toxicomanies* 4:3 (May–June 1968), 5–6.

– 'Méthodologie et principes de base de la prévention.' *Information sur l'alcoolisme et les autres toxicomanies* 5:5 (November–December 1968), 7–9.

Canadian Medical Association. *Interim Brief Submitted by the Canadian Medical Association to the Commission of Inquiry into the Non-Medical Use of Drugs.* Ottawa: Canadian Medical Association, 1969.

– *C.M.A. Reaction to Final Report of the LeDain Commission on the Non-Medical Use of Drugs.* Ottawa: Canadian Medical Association, 1974.

– *Brief of the Canadian Medical Association to the Senate Committee on Legal & Constitutional Affairs re Bill S19.* Ottawa: Canadian Medical Association, 1975.

Canadian Student Affairs Association. *The Loyola Conference on Student Use and Abuse of Drugs.* Montreal: 1968.

Commission des écoles catholiques de Montréal. *Trouver le Joint: Guide de l'éducateur sur l'usage non médical des drogues.* Montreal: Office des relations publiques de la CECM, 1973.

Commission of Inquiry into the Non-Medical Use of Drugs. *Interim Report.* Ottawa: Information Canada, 1970.

– *Cannabis Report.* Ottawa: Information Canada, 1972.

– *Final Report.* Ottawa: Information Canada, 1973.

Épiscopat canadien. 'La drogue: Un document de travail sur l'usage non médical de la drogue.' *Information sur l'alcoolisme et les autres toxicomanies* 7:2 (March–April 1971), 24–5.

Lois refondues du Québec. Chapitres M-26 à P-41. Quebec: Éditeur officiel, 1978.

Narcotic Addiction Foundation of British Columbia. *Annual Reports.* 1964–1973.

Royal Canadian Mounted Police. *Brief to the Committee of Inquiry into the Non-Medical Use of Drugs.* Ottawa: 1969.

'Santé et hygiène mentale.' *Information sur l'alcoolisme et les autres toxicomanies* 4:4 (July–August 1968), 3–4.

Senate Special Committee on Illegal Drugs. *Cannabis: Our Position for a Canadian Public Policy.* Ottawa: 2002

Spry, Robin. *Flowers on a One-Way Street.* National Film Board of Canada, 1967.

Torsney, Padd, and House of Commons Special Committee on Non-Medical Use of Drugs. *Policy for the New Millennium: Working Together to Redefine Canada's Drug Strategy.* Ottawa: Special Committee on Non-Medical Use of Drugs, 2002.

United Church of Canada, Board of Evangelism and Social Service, in Collaboration with the Addiction Research Foundation of Ontario, *Handbook for Parents about Drugs* (Toronto: ARF, 1970).

Unwin, J. Robertson. *Review and Position Paper Re Non-Medical Use of Drugs with Particular Reference to Youth*. Ottawa: CMA Council on Community Heath Care Special Committee on Drug Misuse, 1969.

Secondary Sources

Adams, Mary Louise. *The Trouble with Normal: Postwar Youth and the Making of Heterosexuality*. Toronto: University of Toronto Press, 1997.

Adelman, Howard. 'A Postcript: Reflections on Rochdale' and 'A Post Postscript: Roots of Rochdale.' In H. Adelman, *The Beds of Academe: A Study of the Relation of Student Residences and the University*, 187–98, 252–9. Toronto: Praxis Press, 1969.

Archibald, H. David. 'Perspective on Marihuana.' *Addictions* 15:2 (Summer 1968), 1–5.

– *The Addiction Research Foundation: A Voyage of Discovery*. Compiled and edited by Barbara Fulton. Toronto: Addiction Research Foundation, 1990.

Beauchesne, Line. *Les drogues: Les coûts cachés de la prohibition*. Montreal: Lanctôt Éditeur, 2003.

Bennett, John Sutton. *History of the Canadian Medical Association, 1954–94*. Ottawa: Canadian Medical Association / Association médicale canadienne, 1996.

Bergeron, Pierre, et France Gagnon. 'La prise en charge étatique de la santé au Québec: Émergence et transformations.' In Vincent Lemieux, Pierre Bergeron. Clermont Bégin, and Gérard Bélanger. *Le système de santé au Québec: Organisations, acteurs et enjeux*, 7–33. Quebec: Presses de l'Université Laval, 2003.

Berton, Pierre. *The Smug Minority*. Toronto: McClelland and Stewart, 1968.

Bilodeau, Léandre. *Drug Use among the Students in the Secondary Schools and Cegep's on Montreal Island in 1969 and 1971*. Quebec: Office for the Prevention and Treatment of Alcoholism and the Other Toxicomanias, 1971.

Blackwell, Judith C., and Patricia G. Erickson, eds. *Illicit Drugs in Canada: A Risky Business*. Scarborough: Nelson Canada, 1988.

Boase, Joan Price. *Shifting Sands: Government–Group Relationships in the Health Care Sector*. Montreal and Kingston: McGill-Queen's University Press, 1994.

Booth, Martin. *Cannabis: A History*. London: Doubleday, 2003.

Boyd, Neil. 'The Origins of Canadian Narcotics Legislation: The Process of Criminalization in Historical Context.' *Dalhousie Law Journal* 8:1 (January 1984), 102–36.

Brisson, Pierre. 'Développement du champ québécois des toxicomanies au XXe siècle.' In Pierre Brisson, ed., *L'usage des drogues et la toxicomanies*, vol. 3: 3–44. Montreal: Gaetan Morin Éditeur, 2000.

Bruun, Kettil, Lynn Pan, and Ingemar Rexed. *The Gentlemen's Club: International Control of Drugs and Alcohol.* Chicago: University of Chicago Press, 1975.

Bryan, Michael. 'Cannabis in Canada – A Decade of Indecision.' *Contemporary Drug Problems* 8:2 (1979), 169–92.

Burnham, John C. *Bad Habits: Drinking, Smoking, Taking Drugs, Gambling, Sexual Misbehavior, and Swearing in American History.* New York: New York University Press, 1993.

Carstairs, Catherine. 'Innocent Addicts, Dope Fiends and Nefarious Traffickers: Illegal Drug Use in 1920s English Canada.' *Journal of Canadian Studies* 33: 3 (Fall 1998), 145–62.

– 'Deporting "Ah Sin" to Save the White Race: Moral Panic, Racialization, and the Extension of Canadian Drug Laws in the 1920s.' *Canadian Bulletin of Medical History* 16:1 (1999), 65–88.

– *Jailed for Possession: Illegal Drug Use, Regulation, and Power in Canada, 1920–1961.* Toronto: University of Toronto Press, 2005.

Cohen, P.D.A. 'The Case of the Two Dutch Drug-Policy Commissions: An Exercise in Harm Reduction, 1968–1976.' in P.G. Erickson, D.M. Riley, Y.W. Cheung, and P. A. O'Hare, *Harm Reduction: A New Direction for Drug Policies and Programs*, 17–31. Toronto: University of Toronto Press, 1997.

Cohen, Stanley. *Folk Devils and Moral Panics: The Creation of the Mods and Rockers.* London: MacGibbon & Kee, 1972.

Comack, A. Elizabeth. 'The Origins of Canadian Drug Legislation: Labelling versus Class Analysis.' In Thomas Fleming, ed., *The New Criminologies in Canada: Crime, State and Control*, 65–85. Toronto: Oxford University Press, 1985.

Cook, Shirley J. 'Canadian Narcotics Legislation, 1908–1923: A Conflict Model Interpretation.' *Canadian Review of Sociology and Anthropology* 6:1 (1969), 36–46.

– *Variations in Response to Illegal Drug Use: A Comparative Study of Official Narcotic Drug Policies in Canada, Great Britain, and the United States from 1920 to 1970.* Toronto: Alcoholism and Drug Addiction Research Foundation, 1970.

Cooperstock, Ruth. 'Sex Differences in the Use of Mood-Modifying Drugs: An Explanatory Model.' In Paul C. Whitehead, Carl F. Grindstaff, and Craig L. Boydell, eds., *Alcohol and Other Drugs: Perspectives on Use, Abuse, Treatment, and Prevention*, 173–81. Toronto: Holt, Rinehart and Winston of Canada, 1973.

Courtis, Malcolm C., assisted by Inez Dussuyer. *Attitudes to Crime and the Police in Toronto: A Report on Some Survey Findings.* Toronto: Centre of Criminology, University of Toronto, 1970.

Courtwright, David T. *Forces of Habit: Drugs and the Making of the Modern World.* Cambridge, MA: Harvard University Press, 2001.

Crozier, Michel, and Erhard Friedberg. *L'acteur et le système: Les contraintes de l'action collective.* Paris: Seuil, 1977.

Cunningham, David. *There's Something Happening Here: The New Left, the Klan, and FBI Counterintelligence.* Berkeley: University of California Press, 2004.

Davis, James Kirkpatrick. *Assault on the Left: The FBI and the Sixties Antiwar Movement.* Westport, CT: Praeger, 1997.

Dion, G. 'Le rôle des intervenants du monde médical dans le contrôle des drogues au Canada au début du XXe siècle.' Montreal: École de criminologie, Université de Montréal, 1999.

Erickson, P.G., and R.G. Smart. 'Canada.' in Stanley Einstein, ed., *The Community's Response to Drug Use,* 91–129. New York: Pergamon Press, 1980.

Fejer, Dianne, and R.G. Smart. *Drug Use and Psychological Problems among Adolescents in a Semi-Rural Area of Ontario: Haldimand County.* Toronto: Addiction Research Foundation, 1971.

Fejer, Dianne. Reginald G. Smart, and Paul C. Whitehead. 'Changes in the Patterns of Drug Use in Two Canadian Cities: Toronto and Halifax.' In Paul C. Whitehead, Carl F. Grindstaff, and Craig L. Boydell, eds., *Alcohol and Other Drugs: Perspectives on Use, Abuse, Treatment, and Prevention* 156–64. Toronto: Holt, Rinehart and Winston of Canada, 1973.

Foucault, Michel. *The Order of Things: An Archaeology of the Human Sciences.* New York: Vintage Books, 1973.

Freeman, Barbara M. *The Satellite Sex: The Media and Women's Issues in English Canada, 1966–1971.* Waterloo, ON: Wilfrid Laurier University Press, 2001.

Gagnon, Robert. *Histoire de la Commission des écoles catholiques de Montréal. Le développement d'un réseau d'écoles publiques en milieu urbain.* Montreal: Boréal, 1996.

Gaumer, Benoît, Georges Desrosiers, and Othmar Keel. *Histoire du Service de santé de la ville de Montréal, 1865–1975.* Quebec: Les éditions de l'IQRC, 2002.

Giffen, P.J., S. Endicott, and S. Lambert. *Panic and Indifference: The Politics of Canada's Drug Laws.* Ottawa: Canadian Centre on Substance Abuse, 1991.

Giffen, J., and S. Lambert. 'What Happened on the Way to Law Reform?' In J.C. Blackwell and P.G. Erickson, eds., *Illicit Drugs in Canada: A Risky Business,* 345–69. Scarborough: Nelson Canada, 1988.

Goode, Erich, and Nachman Ben-Yehuda. *Moral Panics: The Social Construction of Deviance.* Oxford: Blackwell, 1994.

Gormely, Sheila. *Drugs and the Canadian Scene.* Toronto: Pagurian Press, 1970.

Granatstein, J.L., and Robert Bothwell. *Pirouette: Pierre Trudeau and Canadian Foreign Policy.* Toronto: University of Toronto Press, 1990.

Grayson, Kyle. 'Chasing Dragons: Security, Identity, and Illicit Drugs in Canada.' Doctoral dissertation, Political Science, York University, 2004.

Hay, Colin. 'Mobilization Through Interpellation: James Bulger, Juvenile Crime and the Construction of a Moral Panic.' *Social and Legal Studies* 4 (1995), 197–223.

Hall, Stuart, Chas Critcher, Tony Jefferson, John Clarke, and Brian Roberts. *Policing the Crisis. Mugging, the State, and Law and Order.* London: Macmillan, 1978.

Heron, Craig. *Booze: A Distilled History.* Toronto: Between the Lines, 2003.

Hewitt, Steve. *Spying 101: The RCMP's Secret Activities at Canadian Universities, 1917–1997.* Toronto: University of Toronto Press, 2002.

Higley, Dahn D. *O.P.P.: The History of the Ontario Provincial Police Force.* Toronto: Queen's Printer, 1984.

Howlett, Michael, and M. Ramesh. *Studying Public Policy: Policy Cycles and Policy Subsystems.* Toronto: Oxford University Press, 1995.

Hunt, Alan. *Governing Morals: A Social History of Moral Regulation.* Cambridge: Cambridge University Press, 1999.

Jenkins, Philip. *Synthetic Panics: The Symbolic Politics of Designer Drugs.* New York and London: New York University Press, 1999.

Jenkins, William I. *Policy Analysis: A Political and Organizational Perspective.* London: Martin Robertson, 1978.

Kelly, Nora, and William Kelly. *The Royal Canadian Mounted Police: A Century of History, 1873–1973.* Edmonton: Hurtig Publishers, 1973.

Kingdon, John W. *Agendas, Alternatives and Public Policies.* Boston: Little, Brown and Co., 1984; 2nd ed., New York: Harper Collins, 1995.

Kostash, Myrna. *Long Way From Home: The Story of the Sixties Generation in Canada.* Toronto: James Lorimer, 1980.

Laforest, Lucien. *La consommation de drogues chez les étudiants du secondaire et du collégial de l'île de Montréal.* Quebec: OPTAT, 1969.

Le Dain, Gerard. 'The Canadian Commission of Inquiry into Non-Medical Use of Drugs.' In Arnold S. Trebach and Kevin B. Zeese, eds., *The Great Issues of Drug Policy,* 1–5. Washington: Drug Policy Foundation, 1990.

Lemieux, Vincent. *Les cheminements de l'influence: Systèmes, stratégies et structures du politique.* Quebec: Les Presses de l'Université Laval, 1979.

– *L'étude des politiques publiques: Les acteurs et leur pouvoir.* 2nd ed. Quebec: Les Presses de l'Université Laval, 2002.

Light, Lois. 'They Jailed My Son for Smoking Marijuana.' *Chatelaine* 41:9 (September 1968), 38, 107–8, 110–11.

Malleck, Daniel J. ' "Its Baneful Influences Are Too Well Known": Debates over Drug Use in Canada, 1867–1908.' *Canadian Bulletin of Medical History* 14 (1997), 263–88.

Marquis, Greg. *Policing Canada's Century: A History of the Canadian Association of Chiefs of Police*. Toronto: University of Toronto Press, 1993.

– 'Uptight Little Island: The Junction '71 Affair.' *The Island Magazine* no. 52 Fall/Winter 2002, 10–14.

Marquis, Greg. 'Public Drunkenness and the Justice System: Canada, 1945–1980.' Unpublished paper. Canadian Historical Association Conference, Dalhousie University, May 2003.

Martin Goldfarb Consultants. *The Media and the People: A Report*. Report of the Special Senate Committee on Mass Media. Vol. 3. Ottawa, 1970.

Marwick, Arthur. *The Sixties: Cultural Revolution in Britain, France, Italy, and the United States, 1958–1974*. Oxford: Oxford University Press, 1998.

McAllister, William B. *Drug Diplomacy in the Twentieth Century: An International History*. London and New York : Routledge, 2000.

Meier, Kenneth J. *The Politics of Sin: Drugs, Alcohol and Public Policy*. Armonk, NY: M.E. Sharpe, 1994.

Mietkiewicz, Henry. *Dream Tower: The Life and Legacy of Rochdale College*. Toronto: McGraw-Hill Ryerson, 1988.

Miller, Timothy. *The Hippies and American Values*. Knoxville: University of Tennessee Press, 1991.

Monnier, Daniel. *Les étudiants du Québec et les drogues hallucinogènes*. Quebec: Direction générale de la planification, Ministère de l'Éducation, 1970.

Moore, Marie-France. *Contre-culture et culture politique au Québec: Une analyse de contenu de la revue Mainmise*. Montréal : Mémoire de maîtrise en science politique, Université du Québec à Montréal, 1975.

Morgan, H. Wayne. *Drugs in America: A Social History, 1800–1980*. Syracuse, NY: Syracuse University Press, 1981.

Morton, Suzanne. *At Odds: Gambling and Canadians, 1919–1969*. Toronto: University of Toronto Press, 2003.

Murray, Glenn F. 'Cocaine Use in the Era of Social Reform: The Natural History of a Social Problem in Canada, 1880–1911.' *Canadian Journal of Law and Society* 2 (1987), 29–43.

Musto, David F. *The American Disease: Origins of Narcotic Control*. 3rd ed. New York: Oxford University Press, 1999.

Owram, Doug. *Born at the Right Time: A History of the Baby Boom Generation*. Toronto: University of Toronto Press, 1996.

Palmer, Bryan D. *Working-Class Experience: Rethinking the History of Canadian Labour, 1800–1991*. 2nd ed. Toronto: McClelland and Stewart, 1992.

Parker, Graham E. 'High Sentences.' *Canadian Forum*, June 1969, 56.

Paulus, Ingeborg. *Psychedelic Drug Use in Vancouver: Notes on the New Drug Scene*. Vancouver: Narcotic Addiction Foundation of British Columbia, 1967.

Radouco-Thomas, Simone, André Villeneuve, Marcel Hudon, Claude Tanguay, Daniel Monnier, Claire Gendron, and Corneille Radouco-Thomas. 'Enquête sur l'usage des psychodysleptiques (hallucinogènes) dans les collèges et universités de la province de Québec. Partie II: Méthodologie et résultats préliminaires.' *Laval Médical* 40 (January 1969), 103–7.

Ricard, François. *The Lyric Generation: The Life and Times of the Baby Boomers*. Translated by Donald Winkler. Toronto: Stoddart Publishing Co., 1994.

Rosecrance, John. 'Compulsive Gambling and the Medicalization of Deviance.' *Social Problems* 32:3 (February 1985), 275–84.

Roszak, Theodore. *The Making of a Counter Culture: Reflections on the Technocratic Society and Its Youthful Opposition*. Garden City, NY: Doubleday, 1969.

Russell, John. *Survey of Drug Use in Selected British Columbia Schools*. Vancouver: Narcotic Addiction Foundation of British Columbia, 1970.

– *Drug Use among Vancouver Secondary Students*. Vancouver: Narcotic Addiction Foundation of British Columbia, 1971.

Russell, John S., and Marcus J. Hollander. *Drug Use among Vancouver Secondary School Students: 1970 and 1974*. Vancouver: Narcotic Addiction Foundation of British Columbia, 1974.

Sheridan, Alan. *Michel Foucault: The Will to Truth*. London: Tavistock Publications, 1980.

Sinha, Jay. *The History and Development of the Leading International Drug Control Conventions*. Ottawa: Library of Parliament / Bibliothèque du parlement, 2001.

Sloman, Larry. *Reefer Madness: The History of Marijuana in America*. Indianapolis: Bobbs-Merrill Co., 1979.

Smart, Reginald G., and Dianne Fejer. 'The Extent of Illicit Drug Use in Canada: A Review of Current Epidemiology.' In Craig Boydell, Carl F. Grindstaff, and Paul C. Whitehead, eds., *Critical Issues in Canadian Society*, 508–20. Toronto: Holt, Rinehart and Winston of Canada, 1971.

– *Changes in Drug Use in Toronto High School Students between 1972 and 1974*. Toronto: Addiction Research Foundation, 1974.

Smart, Reginald G., Dianne Fejer, and Eileen Alexander. *Drug Use among High School Students and Their Parents in Lincoln and Welland Counties*. Toronto: Addiction Research Foundation, 1970.

Smart, Reginald G., Dianne Fejer, and Jim White. *The Extent of Drug Use in Metropolitan Toronto Schools: A Study of Changes from 1968 to 1970*. Toronto: Addiction Research Foundation, 1970.

– *Drug Use Trends among Metropolitan Toronto Students: A Study of Changes from 1968 to 1972.* Toronto: Addiction Research Foundation, 1972.

Smart, Reginald G., and David Jackson. *The Yorkville Sub-Culture: A Study of the Life Styles and Interactions of Hippies and Non-Hippies.* Toronto: Addiction Research Foundation, 1969.

Smith, Bruce L.R., *The Advisers: Scientists in the Policy Process.* Washington: Brookings Institution, 1992.

Solomon, R., and M. Green. 'The First Century: The History of Non-Medical Opiate Use and Control Policies in Canada, 1870–1970.' In Judith C. Blackwell and Patricia G. Erickson, eds., *Illicit Drugs in Canada. A Risky Business,* 88–116. Scarborough: Nelson Canada, 1988.

Solomon, R., E. Single, and P. G. Erickson. 'Legal Considerations in Canadian Cannabis Policy.' In Blackwell and Erickson, eds., *Illicit Drugs in Canada,* 370–91.

Springhall, John. *Youth, Popular Culture and Moral Panics: Penny Gaffs to Gangsta-Rap, 1830–1996.* New York: St Martin's Press, 1998.

Tatalovich, Raymond. *The Politics of Abortion in the United States and Canada: A Comparative Study.* Armonk, NY: M.E. Sharpe, 1997.

Thompson, Kenneth. *Moral Panics.* London: Routledge, 1998.

Valverde, Mariana. *The Age of Light, Soap, and Water: Moral Reform in English Canada, 1885–1925.* Toronto: McClelland & Stewart, 1991.

Verzuh, Ron. *Underground Times: Canada's Flower-Child Revolutionaries.* Toronto: Deneau, 1989.

Weir, Richard A. 'Federalism, Interest Groups, and Parliamentary Government: The Canadian Medical Association.' *Journal of Commonwealth Political Studies* 11:2 (July 1973), 159–75.

Whitaker, Reginald. *Drugs & the Law: The Canadian Scene.* Toronto: Methuen, 1969.

Whitehead, Paul C. 'The Epidemiology of Drug Use in a Canadian City at Two Points in Time: Halifax, 1969–1970.' In Craig L. Boyell, Carl F. Grindstaff, Paul C. Whitehead. eds., *Critical Issues in Canadian Society,* 520–33. Toronto: Holt, Rinehart and Winston of Canada, 1971.

Whitehead, Paul C., Carl F. Grindstaff, and Craig L. Boydell, eds. *Alcohol and Other Drugs: Perspectives on Use, Abuse, Treatment, and Prevention.* Toronto: Holt, Rinehart and Winston of Canada, 1973.

Whitehead, Paul C., Reginald G. Smart, and Lucien Laforest. 'La consommation d'autres drogues chez les fumeurs de marjuana de l'Est du Canada.' *Toxicomanies* 3:1 (January–April 1970), 49–63.

Index